A TREE CALLED
MORALITY

A TREE CALLED
MORALITY

MICHAEL TSAPHAH

 iUniverse®

A TREE CALLED MORALITY

iUniverse books may be ordered through booksellers or by contacting:

iUniverse
1663 Liberty Drive
Bloomington, IN 47403
www.iuniverse.com
844-349-9409

ISBN: 978-1-6632-0129-4 (sc)
ISBN: 978-1-6632-0130-0 (e)

Print information available on the last page.

iUniverse rev. date: 08/24/2020

PREFACE

"There is a way which seems right unto a man and appears straight before him, but its end is the way of death." (Proverbs 14:12 AMP)

People see death all around them, and they refuse to acknowledge it all around us. Humankind numbed liberal conclusions about wickedness around us that have brought darkness to America. It was this same numbness that caused the Roman Empire to implode, and we in the United States are coming too near that same end.

In these times, the church has of mass division to raise in the body of Christ, and the clouded understanding of the difference between morality and righteousness. Allusions of confusion of what is right and evil in our society seems to keep changing. We see that the division is causing the rise of the spirit of the antichrist. This spirit will cause many to stumble, and this spirit will use religion as a cover, much like Adam and Eve did with the fig leaves. In the garden basilicas that are designed to worship God. We allow fear to grip us if we see the Holy Spirit walk in the estates of our churches.

We need to keep ourselves stayed upon Jesus Christ and not religious performances. This performance plays on the will by using man's emotions, morality, and natural affections to keep us in the spirit of bondage. Satan uses this fear to keep his people in a state of the fear of death, and in the roots of bitterness that will bring hard bondage by not trusting in the words of Christ. Christ Jesus knocks at the door of the church to wait for his people to ask him to come in.

So, many saints of God are bitter. They bound us up because there is no unity in the body to bring justice. There is none to proclaim what is righteous, so let me ask a question. What does right or wrong have to do with getting into heaven? Is being a right or good moral person all it takes to please God? So, when you look at your life through the lens of the Word of God. Do you measure up? Are we free, or do we have freedom in captivity?

This kind of broad-stroke painting about humanity's history toward morality has judged us always. Can we keep judging ourselves, others, and even God by right and wrong? This judgment only proves that we lack understanding. In history, ancient civilizations had created a moral code based on God's law of the Ten Commandments, although the Ten Commandments pre-dated between 1441 or 1440 BCE when God wrote them with his finger.

Man had a law written on his heart. The Ancient Sumerians had scripted rules of social order around 4500 BCE. After we left the Garden of Eden, all the ancient civilizations used a moral code based on right and wrong. Does God judge us on reasonings of right and wrong? Is there another law or principle that does judge us? Are we just following the long run of the morality of the traditions of men?

The doctrines of the devil's and the traditions of men have replaced the Word of God. And these traditions give Christians a false feeling of the Holy Spirit. So, the spiritualists try to provide the appearance to move in the lives of the Holy Spirit freak everyone out in the church. They stop the flow of the Holy Spirit in the church today.

Does religion used by man's natural emotions, sensual affections, and secret devilish doctrine of morality to keep us in the spirit of bondage? These fallen people have a fear of death, and the root of bitterness of hard slavery. We see this in the church today. We see it with no one being healed by the elders of the congregation, psychosocial community meetings, Alcoholics Anonymous, and Narcotic Anonymous have replaced prayer meetings. Testimony and Praise services have been replaced with Christian Concert. —

So, many saints of God are bitter, fearful, and bound by oppressing spirits. How do I know? My story is about my long forty-years walking in my soulish and carnal wilderness. The wilderness reminded me of when my adopted mother, Mildred Jones, would send me to my room to think about what I did to offend her.

So, God, the Father, sent me to my room in the streets of homelessness? He marked me like Cain, who was a vagabond; I had received, as when I got stabbed. I roamed for many years from place to place. In and out of homelessness, and I never got as high as Corporal (E-4) in the military. I was an alcoholic and brute.

Leaving the Marine Corps with my separation pay, I tried to start a business in graphic arts, but it, like many of my endeavors, would never succeed. I decided to become a Private Investigator, but that foolish decision cost me ended up homelessness and an unsuccessful career in another career in my life. I got stabbed while as Private Investigator, and I die on the operating table and stood before God the Father. And he judged me of the iniquities of my soul. Like myself, many are looking for other religious experiences to fill the void. We changed the splendor of the everlasting God into an image made by men resemblance to a bent image of deities. Much like my many endeavors, they all burned upon the altar of God.

I searched all of my teen years and young adulthood through many religious beliefs being empty. Only for God, the Father, to remind me. I asked Jesus Christ into my spirit as a child at twelve.

Yet, I had no person willing to disciple me for sixteen years. Like the bamboo nut tree, the root system grew in the ground for seven years. The Word of God broke slowly through the ground from the view of civilization as the Spirit of God told me to read the Gospel of John several times. Until seven years later, I came back to Christianity briefly, trying to be a good father to my first two children.

The second time I rededicated my life was eight years later, and I got filled with the Holy Spirit. My soul was still wild and unlawful. I had rebelled in the Call of God when I was seventeen. I've served in the Marine Corps in various Military Occupational Specialties as an infantry. Then after being injured in the spine right before the Desert Storm invasion, I was given an honorable discharge for medical reasons. God allowed the Corps to teach me discipline. Because I didn't give God the glory, he seared my heart until I cried out!

I left the Marine Corps with only $26,000. I decided to move back to Portsmouth, Virginia. And I work as a security officer and private investigator while working for Burk Security on a case about stolen videotapes. On December 12, 1990, a friend of my sister stabled, and although the Emergency Surgeon worked on me. I slipped out of consciousness, and God judged my soul. When I went to heaven, for my sins and iniquities, they're in heaven, and I cried out to God the Father! However, I was still wondering in my soul and fleshly wilderness.

Many people would try to bring healing to my body, but they would fail. And that's when I realized. The clairvoyant spiritualist invaded Christ church, and the more they did, their magic shows, the more confusion rose in the church. False prophets and teachers of men and women oppressed with the spirit of whoredom created magician of lust in materialism.

God also gave them up to uncleanness. These actions bring dishonor to their bodies and the Church of God. As the works of the flesh kill off people. We see an overflow of lust, covetousness, idolatry, and charismatic witchcraft. This is the fruit that came from the tree amid the garden. Many liberal imam's, rabbinical, protestant, and Catholic scholars teach that God was the embodiment of both good and evil using Isaiah 47:7; Lamentations 3:38; Quran (Suras) chapter An-Nisa'4:78. But they take these texts out of context.

The tree in the garden's mist of our soul is the worshiping of Satan. The Antichrist with Satan to influence people to worship him. One day, the Son of Perdition will have a man in worship of him through witchcraft and spiritualism. The false prophet will use witchcraft, and spiritualism bring nations to worship Satan.

These religious orders of Satanism, paganism, and Wiccan are growing in popularity. These religious group's goal is to become gods and goddesses. These three religious movements will one day merge with Antichrists principles or standards in coming closer to Satan.

One will follow and reverence more doctrines of devils continuously for the next generations to come. In my opinion, I rationalized all humanity can only see the world altered by the unrepentant soul through our reprobate personality.

When I thought about my reprobate personality of my soul, God took me on a forty-year quest, going from mountaintop to mountaintop. *"Make haste, my beloved. And be thou like a roe or a young hart upon the mountains of spices."(Song of Solomon 8:14 KJV)* I define the soul as the mind, will, and emotional state of the person. Our soul must cry out to God and yearn for his presents more than our daily bread.

The study of the soul can sometimes help humanity. My soul deliverance came poetically through the Veterans Affairs Hospital here in Reno, Nevada taught me valuable concepts. First, I needed to stop acting out of my personality, child-like behaviors. Second, I needed to be present in life.

Third, the soul's redemption of the mind, will, and emotions needs to learn steps through the divine nature of God found in Second Peter chapter one verses four through eight, which, when the soul learns these steps, brings deliverance from repetitive past actions. The souls can become delivered from a reprobate soul. However, God used both psychosocial therapy and the church to liberate me. Many times, I felt like a lab-rat. Unless Christ does it himself through the Holy Spirit, and the fire of the Holy Spirit through fasting will deliver the body, soul, and the spirit of man.

Satan used the personality of the woman in the garden. He experimented on Eve like a psychological cadaver by watching her spirit and soul. He didn't ask God for permission to tempt the woman like Job.[8] The man and woman were ignorant of the power of Satan.

He had studied man, and he challenged Eve understanding. When he deceives her on thinking, the knowledge she had was wrong. Satan did this by controlling her mind, will, and emotional state, which he did by giving her post-hypnotic suggestions.

The deception of the serpent to fool man, who walked on four legs, used devices of allusion, which Satan is the master of suggestion. Metaphorically, his legs were what Satan used to deceive others. Satan's legs of delusion are the vision of worldliness through covetousness, which is the lust of the eyes, working to get God's approval through the lust of the flesh, and boasting in your accomplishments through those works of the flesh brings the pride of life.

Satan tempted Eve using the powers suggestion through the lust of the eyes, the lust of the flesh, and the pride of life. The reason Prince of Darkness spoke to the emotional man (female), rather than to the personality of the logical man (male). So, I will define these problems dealing with judging God and in this book with several points.

First, the book purpose gives everyone an understanding of being right or wrong. Second, I will endeavor to provide the true meaning of righteousness? Third, how can you define morality? Fourth, what do traditional values mean? Fifth, what is the noticeable or academic belief about the spiritual and the natural laws, and who created them?

I must first warn the potential reader before they start. This book is not politically correct. And this book may offend those who are not in a mature relationship with Christ Jesus. Otherwise, the person may not see things in a spiritually inclined viewpoint. In this book, we will explore many characteristics of the true meaning of morality and righteousness.

The beginning of the origin of right and wrong came from outside of God. Do many of the religious doctrines in our church today fall short? And are these dogmas line up with the doctrines of Christ? Does the serpent's lies seduce us? We will see. Therefore, I hope this book enlightens you and your friends and family. Most of all, may the grace of the Lord Jesus Christ be with you. I hope God, the Father, shows you the truth that will make you free. Enjoy this Michael Tsaphah for "The Chronicle."

CHAPTER 1
IS IT I'M RIGHT OR HIS RIGHTEOUSNESS?

A white 1969 Ford Thunder Bird rolled down interstate 264 toward the Norfolk Tunnel. It was nine seventy, and I was with my sister Alicia and mom Mildred Lavern Jones. Trying to run some errands before five o'clock. My dad Raymond Jones Jr was getting off work soon from Channel Furniture. We were going to Norfolk from where we lived in Portsmouth, Virginia. The summer days in Tidewater felt muggy and unbearable. And the breeze that cools my sweaty brow. We passed many people in the downtown Norfolk area of and East Brambleton Avenue and Granby Street area. I saw a man in the downtown area of Norfolk. He was dressed shabbily, and his clothes were dirty.

"Why is that man dressed like that?" I asked.

"He's a hobo,"

"What that?" I asked.

"A bum," Alicia shouted.

"Remember, I told you not to be a starving artist," She said.

"Yes, mama," I replied.

"That's what I'm talking about," She said.

I sunk in the back seat humiliated I felt I met my destiny, and I felt sick in my heart… *Not me, I don't want to meet those types of people.* I thought to myself, like it was a disease. Thirty-three years passed, and my children were taken. My second wife divorced me, and I was in Orlando, Florida, back in the hole again. This time when I was homeless, I wasn't doing ministry with my best friend, Marcus.

I was by myself dirty, addict to alcohol, and alone. I would panhandle or work at labor pools to get enough money to pay my child support and try to live on the rest for food and cigarettes. I could understand why I was a vagabond, and then I met some Christian psychologists that God sent to help me. They gave me a place to live, and they started digging around in my soul.

I stopped drinking and attended Alcoholics Anonymous. I even enrolled in Film School at Florida Metropolitan University. But when I got in a fight with a meth-addict who accused me of stealing. I was kicked out of the program and went back to drinking. I didn't need counseling.

I need deliverance from the spirit of bondage that was oppressing me. How did I realize what was wrong with me? When I took a film and video course at Florida town Metropolitan University, I learned in film school. One of my classes was screenwriting. In screenwriting, we learned about building great character based on the seven personality traits of the *"Seven Dwarfs."*

There was Bashful, and he is reticent. The Doc he's a cognition, the puppet master Dopey was sagacious. The character Happy was an optimistic, also known as a sanguine. That definition means optimism—the annoying one Sleepy, who was phlegmatic, and the apathetic acts out as a calm head person. The dwarf Sneezy, who is the melancholic this means he always sad. The dwarf called Grumpy acts like a personality trait of a choleric, which is the angry one ready to charge up toward the battle of life.

My mother and sister were all choleric person. As a baby, I acted like a melancholic in my personality, but I grew to become like the choleric. My dad's personality trait operated like a reticent. I got into an argument no matter what the subject. I always had to fight. I would always say in my heart, "It's my right to defend myself."

When I fought in the military, I would get arrested. The point was simple. I was wrong, and I broke the law. *"Dearly beloved, avenge not yourselves, but rather give place unto wrath: for it is written, Vengeance is mine; I will repay, saith the Lord." (Romans 12:19 KJV)*

It these personalities that Satan pulls on, and it is the downfall of every psychologist that doesn't go deeper into the spirit of man. I found out this fact from going through a SPIRITUAL HEALING PRAYER CLASS sponsored by John and Elaine. God told me that the seed of what you biological and adoptive parents did and said must be rooted out, but before this could happen, righteous seeds must be in place.

The Christian psychologist never dealt with my grieved spirit, and I need deliverance through the prepared ground by much prayer and fasting. I didn't need to know that my parents didn't have the right to do what they did; because they were fallen people and couldn't help it.

A person may say that the police must limit their uses of excessive uses of force, and people must bring justice by the protection to armed citizens. But we see when a crowd or mob is in rule. What is it when a group of people attack another defenseless group of people? It's called terrorism. Our protection by constitutional rights gave us our protection. We don't need police enforcement. That's what the second amendment enforces. Yet, the mob rule of militias in the past violated the rights of others because of racism.

Are their violations of civil rights done against others? Yes, there have seen these in our history massacres of Wounded Knee, Brownsville, Sweet Auburn, Rosewood proved we only wrong is right when you are in power. Look at the Jim Crow Laws of the Reconstruction Era.

It doesn't matter if it is a pro-life demonstrator throws blood on a client of an abortion clinic or demonstrators blowing up abortion clinics. Whether the pro-choice demonstrator's riot with coat hangers waving. It is unrighteous. Jesus never show protest signs against the Sanhedrin, the Roman Empire, or the Herodians. Jesus of Nazareth just loved them and healed the people he in countered. Christ Jesus spoke the truth of the other's sinful nature. Jesus spoke to the hypocrite's iniquities and exposed their true nature.

History has proven that America has violated many people's civil rights based on race, faiths, and sexual orientation. What is the difference between violating someone's civil rights and the country protecting the common defense against aggression? A person never moves in foolish behavior when acting in wisdom. Their deeds in understanding should give others the clear paths to understand God. When seeing pastoral influence, others to walk in faith and love give people the example of righteousness.

Century after century, many scholars in the past seventy-eight years are watering down the word to mean what it says. This out-side the-box thought causes the growth of Skeptics who wish to destroy the influence of God in our country. At the beginning of our countries birth we the people, starting with the Puritans, formed the Mayflower Compact, and the founding fathers wrote the Declaration of Independence and the Constitution. They set a foundation that should govern themselves in God's laws. These guys were godly fathers. How did we change from this nation under The Almighty? Now the Pagan daily tries to remove the acknowledgment of God from the public view.

Now I'd like to make this second point, which a personal lifestyle or choice of sexual preference isn't a right, but this preference is just that: it is a choice! Do we need individual amendments to define someone's decisions or reasons? The answer is no! Knowing your rights will never change the world. We don't have freedom of choice, but we have the freedom to work for what humanity chooses.

What makes the freedom of religion understandable? Does this freedom of religion mean to suppress other's rights to exercise what they believe? Does the freedom of religion mean to control others belief behind an iron wall of no personal expression of how they see and worship God? Can we trust and allow the Holy Spirit to draw them?

The Bill of rights gives our media the express right to print or report to the people to expose the evil in our government through written press. Nevermore does the freedom of the media means to have the liberty of vulgar expression that violates children and women by objectifying them as objects of pleasure. We have the privilege of lawful assembling, and not the freedom to pillage and riot at will. The rights to bear and own rifles and pistols for an American to protect ourselves and our property doesn't mean to wage warlike terrorism on innocent people.

"We hold these truths to be self-evident that all men are created equal. And are endowed by our Creator with certain inalienable rights, and among these rights are the rights to life, liberty, and pursuit of happiness." [1] xii

---

Now, if our Creator with artistic purpose created us with certain absolute rights, when we have liberals that say there are no absolutes. Who are we going to believe? The concept *"right"* has many definitions. What is the true meaning? Something for my readers to think about while you sit drinking that cold or hot beverage. I'm not trying to throw rocks at any liberal atheist, or agnostic, while I stand in a glass house of the church on this issue of rights. It is a choice being a liberal or conservative, not a right.

I'm not a conservative, nor am I religious, but a moderate, and a believer. As a Republican and Democrat, I never vote according to my party affiliation, which I have middle of the rode affiliation. I never vote on what my party beliefs, nor do I allow others to influence me through pressure or extortion.

Now concerning the subject of right and wrong, here's my third point in the form of an example. Let's say you have just spent a year studying to near madness for your exam. Besides, I have rewarded your work with a 100%. Only to find out the person who never showed up to class. The day the exam started, she got a copy of the test from the dean of students, for doing some special favor for him in his office behind closed doors. Please tell me down in your soul. Would you hire her in your company?

Being very honest with yourself, you would judge that person as untrustworthy. And you may go out for drinks and even sleep with the person, but trust them with doing your taxes or give them a position in your company? The answer would be no!

Because you know that you passed with that 100% by your efforts, and not on the fact of how good you were in bed, now tell me if that action was right? I said this example to ask this next question again. Where does the word "right" come from in a definition?

The word "right" comes from the Hebrew word MISH-PAT [(מִשְׁפָּט)] including a specific right, or benefit toward any statutory or customary entitlements.[2] The word rights in the Hebrew defines a person of impressive style action done. And in the Greek

---

[1] (Jefferson, 1776 [Public Domain])
[2] (Strong, 1890 [Public Domain]) H4941

orthōs *pronounced or-thoce`* [(ὀρθῶς)] means an object becomes straight or level.[3] Right in the Greek also refers accuracy of time. And this measurable substance of time and space is now both in the past, present and future. But according to the dictionary, the word right means.

Rights bring entitlements to certain kinds of treatment, based on one's status, which in the modern Western tradition is a person's natural rights, in which each person is born with certain rights as a human being. Other gained rights because of contract or ownership.

Now the total definition of *"right"* then means to be of good moral character; to make correct decisions, which will both help anybody and the common good of humanity. Then further define the word "moral" means classified in both character and actions.

In the Hebrew, the concept described *TAW-HORE* (טָהֹור) as a person or objected to make pure.[4] The purification of the person or object must wash the object or set fire to have physical, chemical, ceremonial purity. In the sense of the same Hebrew word, morals can bring moral logic is understood as pure or the thought is pure.

In the Greek, the word is eleutheria *(pronounced el-yoo-ther-ee-ah[1]* (ἐλευθρία) meaning to have freedom.[5] The freedom given to a person brought legitimate or removed licentious morals from the shamed person through a ceremonial action. These freedoms gave liberty to the person. The freedom, purity, or moral behavior never changed. But what if the right of yesterday is no longer the right thing of today? Is the wrong in the world today's social order changing? What if the wrong of today is now the right thing to do?

"Woe unto them that all say evil equal to good, and good equal to evil; that put darkness for light and light for darkness; that put bitter for sweet, and sweet for bitter!" (Isaiah 5:20 KJV)

What if the correct decision we measure isn't by good and evil, but by what we can get away with in society? Now consider this as an example. Let's say that a political official is in an election, and they favor him to win regardless, so to ensure that he will win. The Presidential Candidate comes to several areas where the opposing candidate is winning in the area and taking the county.

Being the winning candidate calls the governor of that state. And the runner tells him to close the specific areas where fifty to a hundred people will be voting. This

---

[3] (Strong, 1890 [Public Domain]) G3723
[4] (Strong, 1890 [Public Domain]) H2889
[5] (Strong, 1890 [Public Domain]) G1657

candidate doesn't care that those people have been in the standing heat for hours, waiting to exercise the freedom to vote.

Many people have fought and died to get us the rights that take for granted. Americans can't allow the government to remove civil rights for the sake of personal security. The attack on 9/11 can't excuse everything by violating other's liberties. Neither can humanity hide behind our government.

As Thomas Paine said, *"Government, even in its greatest state, is but a necessary evil..."*[6] So, the United States of American government has become the solver to the country's problems of personal responsibility. The question of right and wrong has been with us since our fall in the Garden of Eden.

These right and wrong decisions have caused humankind to leave from God's truth. The bitten tree of the knowledge of good and evil gave human beings the fruit of morality. This morality is how civilization measures right and wrong.

This type of morality is something to think. I read a story in a newspaper as an example. A woman got so angry at her husband after he gloated his rights when he rapes her while she slept. She cut off a piece of his body in protest.

Is the desire of the right decision more important than another, right? Is it being used in this example wrong? In the garden, human beings were given the right to cultivate the garden. But did God give mankind the right to dangerously wreak havoc on the environment to make it unlivable?

Then humankind decides without asking God. Who is the owner of us all? Could these actions be wrong according to the Bible? When people say to others, *"I want it right now!"* Is this right-now-decision based on the righteousness of God, or are they selfish rights?

The theory is that God must honor our rights even when they dishonor his scriptures. God doesn't care about our freedoms when they are in direct violation of his righteousness. Humanity has divorced the wife of justice, and we have married the whore of being right. What is the measuring stick that we use when we are trying to act, right? Does being correct all the time please God? If being right doesn't please God. What pleases him?

Let us see what truly pleases God according to His-story, which the story I'm referring to is the Bible. *"But first and most importantly seek (aim at, strive after) His kingdom and His righteousness [His way of doing and being right–the attitude and character of God], and all these things will be given to you also."* (Matthew 6:33 AMP)

---

[6] (Paine, Thomas, *"Common Sense"* 1776 [Public Domain])

CHAPTER 2
THE TRUE MEANING OF RIGHTEOUSNESS

The definition of the word's morals, rights, and righteousness gave use the understanding that we have a moral code on the inside of us. In this chapter, we look closer at the word righteousness. The word righteousness forms godly two principles (laws). I learn these principles when the Holy Spirit leads me to the Apostle Paul's Epistle of first Thessalonians chapter five, verse eight of the King James Authorized Version. The scripture reads, *"... putting on the breastplate of faith and love."(1 Thessalonians 5:8 KJV)*

We need to know the difference between being always right and walking in the righteousness of God, the Father. The foundation of laws of righteousness devotes themselves to seeking his will. Being righteous isn't just talking the language of mental permission of being in like God's creature. The demonic realm does this by intellectually asserting that God is who he is in the universe.[19] But your actions end to use in gross error, and you're legalistic against others, not giving them the grace God the Father gave you through Christ Jesus.

When we act in faith and love toward God and man. These two actions make two laws: the laws of faith and the royal law of love. The principle of faith, according to the King James Authorized Version in the epistle of Romans chapter three, twenty-seven verse reads: *"Then what becomes of our boasting? It is excluded. By what kind of law? By a law of works? No, but by the law of faith."(Romans 3:27 ESV)*

The law of faith states that faith always happens in the present, and faith is in eternity at the same time. The ingredient of faith moves God to act on your behalf. It will be the proof by how you put total trust or your hope in what God said in his word.

God's must be trusted, and if God isn't trusted through his word. The evolution of faith won't work. Besides, this evidence and hope, the agreement from you towards God's word, and agreement from Christ Jesus and another person are like-minded in the Spirit of faith. This trust and agreement in knowing that God will reward everyone that seeks him first. If this law doesn't operate totally, then you don't have faith, but you are afraid. And you are working in the spirit of fear.

The element of love operates by the royal law of love explained in the King James Version of the Epistle of James, chapter two verse eight, which reads: *"If, however, you are [really] fulfilling the royal law according to the Scripture, 'YOU SHALL LOVE YOUR NEIGHBOR AS YOURSELF' [that is, if you have an unselfish concern for others and do things for their benefit]" you are doing well." (James 2:8 [Leviticus 19:18] AMP)*

This law will discuss more in-depth in a later chapter, because this will show you the reader. How far we have departed from the truth of God's word.

The combination of these two principles (laws) gives you God's absolute righteousness, and they make up the policies kingdom of God. God based kingdom on who he is right now! The entire realm of heaven and the whole universe operates under the law of faith and love, along with abiding under the several other principles that we discuss later on in this book. We must learn how to operate in righteousness, and we must define the true meaning of the word.

Paul the Apostle wrote in King James Authorized Version in the letter to the Romans, chapter fourteen verse seventeen, that the sovereignty of God isn't meat or drink, which in layman's terms means. God's kingdom doesn't include the possession of material things of the sensual world, nor by what we try to get for ourselves. Then, we must learn to maintain what God has given us both spiritually and naturally. God uses what we call gold and other precious metals and gems to build his kingdom. He doesn't care to indulge the worldly views of mammon or in its values, nor does he lust to get more.

The Kingdom of God drives itself on righteousness, peace, and joy, in which these fruitful spiritual attributes emanate from the find presence of the Holy Spirit. Those attributes of the kingdom of God are the character of the Spirit of God. God wants humanity to search after him with the same intensity, as a soldier attacks after the enemy.

I warn you of this intense nature of going after righteousness. If the person goes after his virtue in a legalistic fashion. The person doing these principles of faith and love leads to a delusion of grandeur. The word faith turns to a philosophical viewpoint. The love of God turns to a lust for power that controls others. These attributes lead to the error of self-righteousness.

You could end up working into a doctrine of devils and form a heresy that can make you misread the below passage of the gospel of Luke chapter sixteen verses sixteen and seventeen. Like many denominations have done with many scriptures. Better yet, I will let you read the same passage in the Amplified Bible.

"The law and the writings of the Prophets were proclaimed until John the Baptist. Since then, the proclamation of the gospel of the kingdom of

God goes forth to the world, and everyone tries forcefully to go into it.
Yet it is easier for heaven and earth to pass away than for a single stroke
of the letter of the law to fail and become void." (Luke 16:16-17 AMP)

Now God isn't telling the believer that their work in the kingdom of God is worthless. Is God telling the believer to be quiet being righteous? Jesus is saying for the believer to strive toward the narrow and straightway of the kingdom. Jesus spoke, *"But he that entered in by the door is the shepherd of the sheep." (John 10:2 ESV)*

The only ones that come in the Kings gate are the sheep and the valid owner of the sheep. The Chief Shepherd, Jesus Christ, the savior of humanity. Yet if he that climbed up the other way the same is a thief and a robber.

Now going back to the previous chapter when we talked in the story and used the word *"right now,"* that would mean owning something you have bought, and you have taken ownership of the item you purchased.

That is the only reason we may demand to have something *"right now."* So, where we, the believers, or sinners get off saying we have rights. How does one buy righteousness? What is the interest rate percentage, or the suggested retail price for a two-piece faith and love dinner? How much stock of pure joy could a person purchase at 100 shares?

This kind of thought to the average person may not make sense, but it makes as much sense as someone trying to become right, or them buying their way in front of a holy God. The Bible reads, *"He that in these thing serves Christ is acceptable to God." (Romans 14:18 ESV)*

I am reminded of one time in my life when I was in college my first year, and I walked to class. The bright, crisp winter morning, the morning air made me skip to my first class. As I passed by the main auditorium, I noticed that the college was having an event with the alumni.

They were buying items, and I saw a woman behind the counter. She sold the merchandise and products of the prestigious university. I was ready to pass the procession of people. When I saw in the corner of my eye, the woman who sold the merchandise. She jumped on the counter, and she opened her legs to have sex with one of the male customers. In my rage, I turned only to see the alumni of the prestigious college going on with their next purchases of items.

So, I turned again, ready to call my doctor when I saw the same people engaged in the same activity over and over again. Only to turn around seeing nothing but people buying and selling, and they even waved at me. I thought to myself, *"Does anybody have any Prozac?"*

I will talk more later in orientation to this crazy vision and its meaning later on in the book. My point in saying this statement is that what we added up only by what we see right through oneself. Now seeing what is righteous, you need more than what you see, or your righteousness will become self-righteousness.

God purifies our works by the fire of faith and love. And if our actions turn out to as the kingdom's principles of righteousness. Then the Holy Spirit will speak the wisdom that is pure as gold, and our works become eternal. Now we see that the worship of the Holy Ghost is always righteousness.

Also, these two principles are the key to keeping us from destruction, and these principles are the door by which the shepherd comes into us. Therefore righteousness, according to the Bible, proves to be both faith and love.

Now, can you tell me how we become the right witness without these two elements? Being right and not righteous is the burden of proof that when a person thinks naturally! Furthermore, the belief that we only judge by being right or wrong is leading me to my next question. Is thinking in the realm of right and wrong crazy to God, or is this thinking human nature? Let's find out.

CHAPTER 3
IS IT ALL NATURAL, OR YOUR NATURE?

How many of us have gone down to the local supermarket? Grabbed our shopping cart, then off we went down the first center aisle, and then go to the frozen food section? We go get the ice cream of choice, which the ice cream reads *"ALL NATURAL"* on the package. How about this, for example? You and your partner of the opposite sex take a walk in the woods, and you notice a quaint little spot where you both can be alone. Both of you stay a little past dark. So, you do not want to interrupt the mood.

You start to build a fire from the dried branches that have fallen to the ground. Suddenly, both of you hear the crackling of limbs, and the rustling of leaves through the forest. Someone comcs from the dark who resembles Paul Bunyan, but he's just a little smaller.

The warmth of the fire goes down. While Paul Bunyan starts babbling about the wildlife in the forest, both you and your and date think that the squirrels running in the trees aren't the only thing crazy. The place he's been in the wild. Mostly he talks to you about respecting the trees, and everything is vital to nature. Because according to him the forest is our friend. Then he begins to cross-examine you as if he's an undercover forest ranger for Smoky the Bear.

Now some would call him a "nature lover" as he tries to explain to you that, *"Using those dead branches for your fire is illegal. Because it messes up the forest environmental system."* However, to you, he's a nut, and both of you leave the area to avoid slapping him into the fire.

Now let me ask you some particularly important questions. While you were in this personal presence, were you loving nature? I mean, these kinds of people have the nickname *"NATURE LOVER,"* right?

Does everything that states that it is *"ALL NATURAL"* or that has to do with nature mean it necessarily is wholesome or tasty? The wildlife of this kind has proven at times to be dangerous. Besides, the laws of nature and natural production prove many times harmful if not prescribed by a doctor.

This fact, brings up another question of what do these words nature and natural mean? Where did they originate to find their way into our now liberal society of today? I must warn the reader about this section of the book, in which this section of the origin of the word will be very sluggish and dull. So, please put up with me while I explain some especially important devices that Satan uses.

Institutions of both secular along with Christian institution, use the words nature and natural indiscriminately. The Philosophers Greece and Roman coined the phrase about the natural laws and the laws of nature. We will learn how these doctrines have crept into the Body of Christ.

Plato's Republic and the Iroquois Confederations gave the natural laws we trust that bring certain people in the class society. Although many may think that this knowledge is necessary for the success of our lives, we will find out that these areas of collective expertise are not all from God. Our pursuit of happiness with experience, liberty has its foundation in these philosophers. But these words of natural and nature definitions come from earthly, sensual, and even demonic sources.

First, let us do some needed background work on were the words "natural" and "nature" come from in scholarly characterizations. The terms have their sources from Greek and Latin origins. Likely when we define these words accurately, we see their exact origin and their intent.

How do you embrace who I am in my state of existence? Will I embrace an action of straight forward, or do I act out artificially? These bring me to understand the word *"NATURE"* definition as to relate to that, which substance is not fake. These solid, liquid, or gas objects in nature, came and were created from the ninety chemical elements of the periodic chart. The word nature also means lifelike, or candid (unworldly), nor the object from nature is having any sophistication or artless.

Now the word *"NATURAL"* definition to the sophistication or artless in the substance that the original chemical compound necessary foundation. The permanent characteristic of something derived from a "Natural" material with human or animal essence, in which the being can serve as a standard for evaluating conduct and civil laws.[31] The words can also be from, as I said before.

Thus, the *"NATURAL LAW"* considers an ideal to which humanity aspired or a general fact of the way human beings and animals will usually act. The word changes the consideration fundamentals become unchanging and universally applicable also to mean that natural isn't likely to be changed or evolved, but the object is constant. The words, *"NATURE,"* and *"NATURAL"* then rise from ambiguous definitions. We must examine their interpretation in the Latin and Greek words. This concept started the movement of naturalism or the creation of natural laws. Besides, we can define the meaning of the natural law.

In about the words *"NATURE"* and *"NATURAL,"* I can rethink all the truth about the definition of birth, the realism movement in art and literature that described these words. I was a Commercial and Fine Artist, and I study the forms of nature. I experimented with using natural raw materials to achieve my goal of a rustic look.

This particular definition comes from the philosophical study of the *"NATURAL LAW,"* which this thinking went in the Stoic period in Greek, and these philosophers of Ancient Greece and Rome believe that the Natural Law was motivated by fate, divination, and universe of gods.[7] These thoughts become the basis of the words *"NATURAL LAW"* derive from the word *"NATURE,"* and the mere definition suggests that I believe these laws or body of laws to be binding upon human actions apart from or with rules established by human authority.

What is Stoicism, and what is the meaning of logic? How did all of this become a part of modern society and Christian theology? To understand these theories that became facts, and to learn more about the thousands of different *"OCRARY,"* *"ISMS,"* and *"OLOGIES"* that planned the numeral sects of opinions and ideologies in the modern church and society today. We must go back to 580 BC, so we can do a study on some men that lived on the Ionian coast of Ancient Greece.

In the city of Miletus vi, they revered an Asia Minor Babylonian astronomer named Thales by later scientists and philosophers, as one of the seven wise men of the world. We considered Thales, the father of classical philosophy. He was also interested in astronomical physics, meteorological phenomena, and his scientific investigations led him to speculate that all things came from natural wonders.

Now speed through time to a man who studied Thales works. His name was Socrates, born in 469 B.C. The Athens native maintained a philosophical dialogue with his students until Athens condemned Socrates to death when they made him drink poison 399 B.C.

Unlike the otherwise men of Greece, the pessimist Socrates refused to receive payment for his teaching. He believed and accepted the awareness of a human need for more knowledge. Socrates left no writings as a record of his thoughts.

In the dialogues of Socrates, he taught that every person has full knowledge of the ultimate truth contained within the soul. The fundamental doctrine that these wise men of Greece, Socrates, Plato, and Aristotle started at the school of the Pythagorean, held to certain Babylonian mysteries. vii These believers were similar regarding the Orphic secrets.

The Orphic myths rose from the classical Greek religion and mystic cults that back the Sumerian kingdom. The Orphism mysteries believed to be from the writings of the legendary poet and musician Orpheus.

---

[7] (Kirby, 2020) Wikipedia, the free encyclopedia: **Chrysippus of Soli** philosophy of fate

Fragmentary poetic passages, including the inscription on gold tablets found in the graves of Orphic followers from the 6th Century B.C. In the tablets, was the belief of purging one sins in moral and ritual purification from evil. The Orphism foundation came from cosmogony the centered on the myth of the God Dionysus Zagreus, the son of Zeus and Persephone.

The jealous Titans murdered Dionysus and dismembered and cannibalized the young god. The Titans decision was based on Zeus' wished to make his son ruler of the universe. The goddess wisdom Athena rescued Dionysus's heart. She brought it to Zeus, who shallowed it, and he gave birth to a new Dionysus. Zeus then punished the Titans by destroying them with his lightning, and from their ashes, he created the human race.

The Titans, according to Ancient Cuneiform from Sumer, Chaldean, Egyptian, and Greek mythology is also known as the Watcher's, gods, angels, or the sons of God. The Titans were from a family of god-like giant deities that numbered into forty-three. The Watchers were seventeen, which they had mated with the daughter of men, and created a race of giants.[8]

As a result, according to the Orphic religion, humans had a duel nature. The earthly body was the heritage of the earth-born Titans. Dionysus soul mixed with the ashes of the Titans made Humans duo in our origin.

However, our Lord Christ Jesus, who was a historical figure, did bodily ascend from the dead. Dionysus was a mythical legend that never existed. The belief in gods rising from the dead in myth is nothing new, because the Egyptian Aton's, which this cult worshipped the sun god, for this reason, the Egyptians used the symbol of the Aton as we see it below.

Figure 1

The symbol not only was a symbol of life, but the Aton was a symbol of death. Because whoever wore this mark on them. It became a mark of death by the temple priest of the Egyptian people. The Egyptian cult believed in monotheism, and their leader came into enormous influence with Pharaoh Akhenaton. Who, through this cult, he became the living God of the Aton's?

---

[8] (Draper, 1882) 1 Enoch 1:7; 7:2; 8:1-3; 10:6; 14:1; Genesis 6:1-4 AMP

As history would have it, the same thing would happen to the believers in the Egyptian cult that the believers to prove their loyalty to their leaders, Akhenaton. His followers were all killed, and they murdered the Pharaoh. They put their remains in his tomb. The priest that died him and his followers stated that they were sacred.

Now, in today's social order, Akhenaton is making their living gods. Although they have no shrines to consider them heroes. They were monotheists, but the claiming of being a god wasn't enough. Their god status was giving them the privilege of molesting innocent children and murdering their parents to prove their divine deity. Unlike Jesus Christ, who gave his life by choice. Because he was the prophesied Messiah of the Old Testament.

The infamous preacher of Guyana massacres, his followers, and the leader of a religious group raided in Texas murdered and molested their followers. Both men claimed to be Christ. Each false-Christ foolishly died by his hand. Today society never considered these children-molesting murderous gods as holy men of our day; however, their actions count as evil men.

The more we educated ourselves to learn about good and evil. The more we remain the same in this revolving door of life. Instead of mankind growing and evolving into a kinder and gentler nation. We are retrogressing into demonic monsters, like the walking dead.

We are straying back into a more original form of a Cro-Magnon ape-like evolutionary zombie that this evolved human tries to outsmart history. We keep missing the point! You can't outsmart history; it will repeat itself.

I can prove this statement with these modern-day Akhenaton, which they give their followers a fantasy-land belief in Utopia. Then when their leaders' plan fails, they make them drink poison-laced Kool-Aid believing in a rapture to escape their sin, or they have a shootout with the authorities. These dull-of-hearing deacons from hell have morality.

According to the great wise men who were the leaders of the Pythagoreans, they believed they were only following their fate, and the gods gave which. Besides, if they gave their generation wisdom to enrich their souls. Then they will eventually reach the state of Utopia.

The theory of Utopia is an ideally perfect place, especially in its social, political, and moral aspects. The belief of Utopian society has its roots in the garden of Eden, but the theory is impractical, illogical, and we can never reach it can never. In this idealistic scheme, that is the carrot on the stick belief our leaders give our followers for social and political reform.

The Pythagoreans wise men, they founded this belief in a perfect society. Plato believed in Utopia and immortality of the soul, which this eternal life for the soul came in the form of ghosts. Their school was the first to consider the earth was a globe revolving with the other planets moving around the sun. Although we can find these truths in the book of Job chapter nine verse seven and Solomon wisdom in the book of Ecclesiastes chapter one verses one through eighteen both in the New American Standard Bible. Not one of these philosophers in all their logical dialogue will recognize the Almighty God as the creator of these phenomena.

They explained the harmonious orchestration of the effects as that of the body in a single, all-encompassing theme of reality, moving in agreement with an infinite world. Meaning these natural phenomena just happened. The Pythagoreans thought these disassociated the heavenly bodies from one another, which these actions of nature were an accident, and even the creation of man's soul is the carrier of the body, but we have no spirit.

These beliefs sowed seeds that grew into the spiritualist movement founded in the 18th and19th century. They believed that man was a soul rather than a spiritual being, and these men of this school of the Pythagoreans, they were the father of modern Darwinism, and they were the first scientist of their time. Is this where morality and the natural law mated, and these beliefs bore their offspring of metaphysics and Wicca?

Aristotle began his return to Athens to be the founder of the Lyceum. The Lyceum was a school, much like Plato's Academy, remained for centuries. Becoming one of the learning centers of Greece. In 399, they quoted BC Socrates as saying, *"Bad men live that they may eat and drink. Whereas good men eat and drink that they may live."*[9]

vii Many of the Socrates protégés ate and drank their belief to live, charging many to attend their schools. The men at the Lyceum lectured the power of life to seek truth for a price. Even though it cost Socrates his life, many of his students all enjoyed his wisdom.

The great philosopher Aristotle defined the basic concept and principles of many of the theoretical sciences, such as logic, biology, physics, metaphysics, and psychology came from these men. They based these sciences on logic. Aristotle developed the theory of deductive reason, represented the uses of logical arguments, to sum up, the conclusion. Aristotle brought the scientific method to come up with a solution to a problem by the uses of this scientific.

Aristotle found the view of logic or *"logos"* creates a base for in many of the religious sects of Buddhism, Judaism, Islamic theology, and in many Catholic dogma of the Middle Ages. And these beliefs of logic appear in most Christian denominational institutions as a view of nature consistent with their religious beliefs. Aristotle and Aquinas both designed and held that all things in life, including many human beings, evolved toward a specific goal or ends.

---

[9] (Qoutes.net Editioral, (470-399 BC)) Socrates quotes about good and bad men actions

That's where the word *"logos"* (λόγος) comes from the wood fire. In Greek, it means the name of reason, or to bring to the sum or conclusion of a ratio.[10] In the ancient and especially in the medieval philosophies and theologies taught that all the theories of divine reasoning come from logic. I thought the belief about logos that acts of faith came from the power of the "logos," and this power was the ordering principle of the universe.[11]

In the 6th-century B.C., Greek philosopher Heraclitus, one founder of Stoicism, [viii,] which he founded in Athens about 319 B.C. by Zeno of Citium, developed out of the earlier movement of Cynics. They rejected social institutions and material values, and they believed that they achieve freedom and tranquility.

Only these Stoics believed in becoming insensitive to material comfort and external fortune. Some early Franciscan monks adopted this Stoic belief by taking vows of poverty, which they came from the previous movement in the Cynics.

Heraclitus believes that one could dedicate oneself to a life of reason and virtue. Many Buddhist monks hold to these same beliefs. Keeping a somewhat materialistic conception of nature. They followed Heraclitus in believing the empowerment of logos, the primary substance in the fire, and the realm's worship of logos.[12]

Heraclitus followers identified with the energy behind logos, laws of nature and physics, reason, and the providence found throughout life. The pseudoscience of metaphysics studied the word of logos and to understand the power of this force. Power humanity governed its world by an army of fire like logos. A divine authority of power that produces the order and pattern discernible in the flux of nature. Does this mean that these men believed in the God of Abraham, Isaac, and Jacob?

The bringing back of the word "logos" came by the Word of Faith movement, which the Charismatic movement was between 1951 to 1984 A.D. They stated that the translation of the word logos in the Biblical sense. This divine power comes from the Divine expression of God at the word translated by John's gospel that reads: *"In the beginning [before all time] was the Word [Christ] [Εv αρχη ην ο λογος και ο λογος])..."* *(John 1:1 AMP [and the Greek Translation]).* The transfer of logos power makes you a little god, this truth Kenneth Copeland said, *"'Adam was 'not a little like God... not almost like God...' and He has told believers that 'You don't have a God in you. You are one.'"*

This reasoning was the same strategy that Satan used to plant that if Eve ate the fruit of the knowledge of good and evil, then she would become as gods. Unlike other doctrines that theorized the belief that all forces manifesting in the universe are the

---

[10] (Strong, 1890 [Public Domain]) G3056
[11] (Wikipedia Foundation, 2006) Word of Faith and Kenneth Copeland
[12] (Strong, 1890 [Public Domain]) G3056

gods. These things (the elements of earth, fire, and wind) are deities deserve our worship, which this belief is the basis of the theology called pantheism.

This doctrinal belief that all living things evolve or form into gods. The view called pantheism, its actions. We dissolve into deities derive from an erroneous spirit. The force of logos in everything was the fruit that came from the tree of these philosophers.

The spirit of whoredom acts different in its function. The polytheism worships in the idolatry of over many gods, that belief is only manifest on the outside. The spirit of error works from the inside, and pantheism uses the erroneous belief that everything or person becomes a god.

This doctrine or philosophy is naturalism, and the idea that everything is worthy of our respect/worship seems good to the hearer. Because it will use natural thinking and powerful words of wisdom. Making the person think they are gods. These words never point to the Divine expression of God, but this belief brings many of these doctrines belief they can climb up these gods tree if they do enough good. We make this naturalistic belief of principles or laws. So, the root comes from the natural laws that derive from Stoicism, Aristotle, and the Roman Empire's laws.

Every empire and civilization understood who God was as a creator, but they never glorified him. Instead, these empires and civilizations turned God into idols of humanlike, animals, and reptiles. And because they did worship God sincerely, she turned them over to their desirer. (Romans 1:21-24 ISV paraphrased)

Now we will study the word *"natural," "nature," and "carnal."* So, the first word-study is natural are two words. The first is phusikos (υσικός) *pronounced foo-see-kos`* "physical," the meaning is inherent. Then there is the second-word psuchikos (ψυχικός) *pronounced psoo-khee-kos'* sensitive that is, animate, which is the higher or renovated nature; and on the other form, which is the lower or bestial nature.[13]

Then there is the word similar in Hebrew word nᵉshâmâh pronounced *nᵊsh-aw-maw* (נְשָׁמָה) defined as an angry wind coming from the word's intellect, soul, sensitive, and to animals or some becoming animated like a spirit.[14] The words definition of both nature and sexual in the same Hebrew word. We use the word in a context in Genesis, chapter two, verse seven. When God mated man by using his breath to make Adam a living soul.[15] In the same distinction, the Greek word *psuchikos,* which this word is meaning to have a higher or renovated nature.

---

[13] (Strong, 1890 [Public Domain]) G5446; G5591
[14] (Strong, 1890 [Public Domain]) H5397
[15] Genesis 2:25 AMP

The Greek word *pneumatikōs* (πνευματικῶς) *pronounced pnyoo-mat-ik-oce'* is an adverb meaning non-physically, that is to be divinely, celestial creature. Being in the likeness in spiritual form. Now the word carnal comes from the Greek word: *sarkikos* (σαρκικός) pronounced sar-kee-kos' about flesh, that extends a bodily dimension, which the subject is temporal, or the being is an animal.[16]

Being unregenerate or acting out to be fleshly. This word comes from the Greek word sarx (σάρξ), and this combination of meat, skin, or flesh.[17] This word carnal both uses the five senses touch, sight, hearing, smell, and taste, which these five senses opposed to the soul or spirit, which these realms become invisible.

The word definitions for nature means of the Greek show the simplistic definition of a person having a kindred life force. How the human nature action causes us to judge or discern others? These definitions give the faculties of passion of the human being. We see the operating sense of being carnally minded or, as the description says, fleshly.

The next time you see the word *"ALL NATURAL,"* the name means *"ALL CARNAL."* In conclusion, we express the term to say these points. It means everything natural to mean just what defined as being carnal or even fleshly. The purpose of this kind of thinking is to feel good about being simple, and we only design this thinking is only to tempt the person has to keep our physical nature.

Everything from nature keeps tempting society to be like we were in the garden of Eden. While Adam and his new wife walked on the earth in the garden. They both were nude and not embarrassed. [55] This judgment shames the person's physical nature of the human lacks something in their inward being. Keeping the in mind. This temptation to want more truth beyond what God already gave is true, in essence. We lack something in the spirit realm.

Now everything carnal is to keep the spiritual man's self-image above the Spirit of God. I hope by saying all that about the words carnal, natural, and nature. It didn't stop you from taking that next bite of your good old "ALL NATURAL" ice cream. Put, if we can ever realize the full existence of the words we see in our world. Besides, the importance we place on something that tries to make us feel wholesome or good.

These feelings only entreat to the human soul to act out emotionally. The emotion's actions compel the person to react or respond based on how the child's upbringing We see now how the personality drives the soul that defines our feelings in the soul. Then the mind, which in this section of the soul operates your five senses. Our minds power to reason gives us the strength to think *Cogito ergo sum* [I think therefore I am]. [18]

---

[16] (Strong, 1890 [Public Domain]) G4561
[17] (Strong, 1890 [Public Domain]) G4561
[18] (Descartes, 1637) p.24

It also houses the seven personality traits, which we will discuss later) and the will (which keeps human beings in a stubborn persistence state drive to live. Also, this part of the soul that keeps us in realities of motivations, whether being a pessimist, realist, moderate, or optimistic). Then are you only dealing with the soul of humankind? Do we judge everything, or everyone based on their outward appearance?

The conception of the natural laws is a philosophy asserting that certain rights, which these rights enlighten the virtue of humankind nature. This law is capable of rising nature to judge good and evil. These laws first gave use the limitation to recognize our sinful nature by God a supreme source by the Ten Commandments and the Levitical and Sabbatical laws.[19]

The other natural laws we will discuss later these laws. It gave the natural laws. So, very humanity can understand the universal thinking of right and wrong through human motives. As determined by nature, it implies the law of nature to be universal. All early philosophers of Greece and Roman established the Natural laws dealing with nature.

Then you will always think in a natural state of mind. Natural law can only then enforce carnal thinking and Judges thoughts by nature. [iii] These natural laws will govern humanistic, sensual thinking. Natural laws keep the use of unregenerate, and these laws of nature are temporary.

The natural laws can serve those of a sexual nature, and it is stating that the person operating in these laws of nature will always do the carnal laws or the actions of carnal knowledge, which this knowledge is an out-of-date or legal synonym for sexual intercourse.[61] This carnal or natural law can never make you spiritual. Pau the Apostle knew as a Pharisees he was sensual. But the Ten Commandments were created by the Lord God, which the Ten Commandments made them spiritual. [20]

As man—if we are born again—we must operate under the better which the law that will guide us to know the divine nature of Christ. (spiritual laws of Christ) These laws framed all that we see and know today.[21] Then why do we, as Gods people, try to obey the natural law, which these laws judge the sexual and sensual nature of human beings? That way, they call it *"NATURAL LAW?"* But why do we think we can keep the natural laws? The answer is simple.

"But I fear, lest by any means, as the serpent beguiled Eve through his grasp, so we should corrupt your minds from the simplicity that is in Christ. For if he that cometh preacheth another Jesus, whom we have

---

[19] Romans 7:12-14 ESV paraphrased
[20] Romans 7:14 KJV paraphrased
[21] Colossians 1:16 NASB paraphrased

not preached, or if ye receive another spirit, which ye have not received, or another gospel, which ye have not accepted, ye might well bear with him." —2 Corinthians 11:3, 4 KJV

In my opinion, the purpose of the design of the natural law made humans to look at themselves in a mirror of the Ten Commandments. Humankind thinks in a sinful nature only views our world as the scripture reads, we *"... see through a glass (mirror) darkly."— 1 Corinthians 13:12 KJV paraphrased* Satan tricked man like the proverb of the monkey with his hand in the jar. He was holding in his hand a banana in the jar.

And the hunter just picks up the monkey, because the monkey would let go of the banana. We become beguiled by wanting to be gods. We are in bondage. So, we must accept we can only be children of God because the word *"BEGUILED"* means to trick someone. Up till now, we, the body of Christ, are much like Eve. We have allowed God's people to trick us by reaching for the shiny banana of the God's gospel. Allowing the world way of doing what is natural to trick us. Therefore, it makes me ask. How were we as Christians beguiled? Besides, operating in natural laws, much like the sects of Israel.

The Pharisees and the Sadducees in 29 A.D. were both run by the Roman government to keep the Stoicism form of the natural laws. They incorporated 486 different laws of the Levitical and Sabbatical principals and the Liberal traditions of the Elders. So, we also are being run when we have faith-based incorporated and filing our 501c to be an organization. I said in a park in Georgia, *"The Church rises as a philandering organization, rather than a breathing, moving, and living organism of Christ."* We are just a snap from being a government-run, lukewarm state church. Those fingers of Satan might have already snapped.

Stop the world from dictating how the body of Christ should think, without the fear of legal action. Stop keeping the tax-free bracket form speaking the truth. We are nothing more than a sleepy church beguiled by the soul's nature! We would rather watch it on the sideline of the stadium. Being entertained by Christian television and rock concerts than going out as a body armed with the sword of the word to win the lost.

Some people in the church allow Satan to deceive by using our free will to listen and do evangelism like the world recruits someone for the military or get a job. Instead of working in the fruit of the spirit and praying by discerning them by the Holy Spirit. We only use entertainment or even self-help seminars to change the outward appearance and not save the soul. The fruit of the Spirit works to change a person and not the works of the flesh.[22]

---

[22] Galatians 5:23, 24 ESV paraphrased

We can never force us can never to do anything outside of our will (that is violating the word of God) Because the makeup of the soul is the mind, will, and emotion. Our *"FREE WILL"* given by God allows users to choose what path we operate in these spiritual principles he framed for humankind. And we should rebel when the natural law is putting us back in bondage. We should do what God's given us to do. We should line up with the Word of God. *"And whatever sins good may provoke themselves too. By their exercised and afflictions, God uses them."* [23]

The soul's beguiled nature outside of the word of God, and we can't trust to make a moral decision, so can humankind make up its mind to do what is ethical. I read in the book of Acts about the ordination of the Apostle Matthias and see if anyone took Judas Iscariot's place as the treasurer, however, God Almighty choose Paul as the twelfth apostle, and not Matthias.

They beguiled even the eleven Apostles into carnality by drawing lots. They did this method to select Matthias before they received the Holy Spirit. My definition of beguiling means deception by defrauding to a person of deliverance, and then to cheapen that price of salvation to make it worthless.

Satan did that to Eve, asking her, *"Did God actually say?" (Genesis 3:1 ESV paraphrased)*

That is what the serpent in the garden said to Eve, using that indirect speech of his doctrine and philosophy, which this pantheistic view used to defraud the woman (soul) of her being in a holistic state of safety, health, and prosperity. This spiritual, holistic thinking is true salvation.

This form of pantheism act was a direct form of rebellion. Because Eve's imagination was in a state that being a god wasn't in her reach, nor her action thorough, her being unfaithful discussion put doubt in her mind (unsound thinking). This thinking gave her the emotional state of fear.[24] Eve believed that she needed more than what God would offers.

This discussion of being a god, which thinking they need more power, brought man into fear and bondage. Satan was asking, *"Is what God said to believe? Is it so terrible to be like God?"* When humankind measured what God did as an unimportant act of doing what God did as a sense of duty? This thinking is judging the ethics of what God did as not good enough. Then we put ourselves as God's judge.[25]

We define morality as a sense of responsibility. Through a person move oneself to follow a natural law or moral code. Whether morality is religious, governmental, or our self-rules, which these morals will judge all people, place, or things based on that moral code. What is the name of that moral code?

---

[23] (Henry, 1662-1714 [Public Domain]) Bondage
[24] Roman 14:23 KJV paraphrased
[25] Job 40:1 AMP paraphrased

CHAPTER 4
ARE WE SAINTS OR AIN'TS
(THE TRUE DOCTRINE OF CHRISTIANITY)

As man—if we become born again—we must operate under the better law, which the law that will guide us to know the divine nature (spiritual laws of Christ) of Christ. These laws framed all that we see and know today. Then why do we, as Gods people, try to obey the natural law, which these laws judge the sexual and sensual nature of human beings? That's why they are called *"NATURAL LAW?"*

When we operate under natural laws. We create thousands of different *"OCRARY,"* *"ISMS,"* and *"OLOGIES"* that planned the numeral sects of opinions and ideologies in the modern church and society today. The natural never allow a human being to be complete. These laws create people that think that there many ways to get to God.

These *"ISMS,"* *"OCRARY,"* and *"OLOGIES"* now become objects we worship. Instead of allowing God through the Holy Spirit to give divine revelation, we have accepted these self-proclaimed prophets to speak. Are these the new prophet of Ba'al that speak?

When people think that there are many ways to get to God, the form their moral code. A moral code definition means a position taken by a philosophy that governs religious, government, or self-rule. Besides, these morality issues cause a person to judge all things, including God, by this moral code.

They create a new form of a different *"OCRARY,"* *"ISMS,"* and *"OLOGIES."* It did not differ from when Jesus Christ was throwing the money changers out of the Temple in Jerusalem.[75] It was just like when the Children of Israel were told to dispel all of the Canaanite people and not serve their gods and goddess.

"See to it that no one enslaves you through philosophy and empty deceit according to human tradition, according to the basic principles of the world, and not according to the Messiah." —Colossians 2:8 ISV

The word philosophy and tradition definition means precept or principle no long study the Mosaic law and the turning from sin and iniquities. Plus, these principles come from dangerous studies into the nature and classes of angels instead of the study of the divine nature of Christ. This type of study of the nature of angels leads to the mythology of the Titians, who was the fallen angel of the book of Genesis before the flood.[26]

When I was a little boy. I was visited by these Watchers that told me many strange things. They tried to get me to believe in some type of spiritism knowledge that doesn't come from God's divine word. I heard and had visions of things that were to come. I one time had a dream about the crucifixions, and I stood amongst a myriad of angels only to watched in hopeless anguish, Christ Jesus. People believed that our manifested destiny in becoming a country. Both Israel and America had similar effects.

We left the spirit of bondage Monarchies of Europe. We invaded this land and removed the Native Americans who worshiped pantheistic gods and goddesses. We had to drive them out of this land, or we could try to bring them to Christ Jesus. So, did the Israeli come from the bondage of Egypt and Israel rises to the great power for eighty years.

Becoming a trade outpost and a major city-state, Israel controlled the city called Tadmur during the time of the Kings of Israel, but as they declined to worship God Almighty. After King Solomon's reign, the Priest of Levites began erecting a temple to the Sun and fertility god (or Ba´al).

The worship of Ba´al came in many forms. One form of Ba´al came as the lord of the covenant called by the Shechemites Baal-Beritha because he required the people to make blood-covenant sacrifices humans by cutting themselves, killing an animal, or money. Then there is the deity Beelzebub (the lord of the flies), and he was the god of the Philistines. He was the mover of all things dealing with false prophecy, false miracles, and false worship.

The Israelites learned the unlawful worship of Ba´al from the agricultural Canaanite tribe.[78] Except for the offering of fruits and the firstborn of cattle. The Canaanite shrines were little more than temples of prostitution, which these temples altars with places of worship to had altars the symbol of the Canaanite female goddess named Ashtoreth.

Also, in the groves was the obelisk symbolized a sacred pillar of an erected male organ. Many times, the obelisk was behind the altars. These shrines the Almighty God of Israel hated, so much he poured out his wrath on them. In today's society, we give great offerings to the new agricultural god, another shrine. What is this new god that the Lord God will bring to its knees?

---

[26] (Draper 1882 [Public Domain]) Section II Chapter 6:2

We are constantly at the mercy of these nations, and we are building great shrines called gas stations. Being willing to sacrifice our firstborn to Moloch and Baʹal to the tunes of millions if not billions to make sure these new agricultural gods to protect the priest of Baʹal and Moloch. So, they can favor our country with plenty of gasoline. But Moloch sacrifices the unborn as well, and the battle between pro-choice or pro-life splits the country much like slavery did when the answer is simple on how the Lord God feels about life.

"I call heaven and earth to testify against you today! I've set life and death before you today: both blessings and curses. Choose life, that it may be well with you—you and your children." —Deuteronomy 30:19 KJV

Now out of respect to another man's religious belief or rights. God is both pro-choice set the word in the Hebrew is nathan (*pronounced naw-than'* [נָתַן]) mean to give or set before[27] your [reality] choices life and death, blessing and curse trust the system of Baʹal and Moloch worship, or you can change your life in Christ Jesus. Some say Jesus of Nazareth isn't the Son of God. Because Jesus never said he was the Son of God.

Then why did Caiaphas the High Priest say Jesus sinned blasphemy? If Jesus isn't the Son of God (they engrave this statement on the front of the (*"Allah had no sons"* [لم يكن لله ابن])[28] How is it he has fulfilled all of Old Testament law and Prophesies? Therefore, God Almighty will put to shame all those who mock his Son, Christ Jesus. Christ Jesus' maternal great, great, great, grandfather King Solomon built the nation of Israel, but like us, they did remove all the polytheistic worship.

The Israelites learned the unlawful worship of Baʹal from the agricultural Canaanite tribe. Except for the offering of fruits and the firstborn of cattle. The Canaanite shrines were little more than temples of prostitution, which these temples altars with places of worship to had altars the symbol of the Canaanite female goddess named Ashtoreth.

Also, in the groves was the obelisk symbolized a sacred pillar of an erected male organ. Many times, the obelisk was behind the altars. These shrines were objects of the Almighty God's wrath. Today, we give great offerings to the new agricultural god, another shrine. What is this new god that the Lord God will bring to its knees?

Becoming a trade outpost and a major city-state, Israel controlled Tadmur during the time of King of Israel, but as they declined to worship God Almighty. After King Solomon's reign, the Priest of Levites began erecting temple the Sun and fertility god (or Baʹal). The deity Baʹal is the name of the god of nature.

---

[27] (Strong, Strong Exhaustive Concordance, 1890) H5414
[28] (Wikipedia Foundation, 2018) Islam

The lord of the covenant called by the Shechemites Baal-Beritha; because, he required the people to make blood-covenant sacrifices human through cutting, animal, or money. Then there is the deity Beelzebub (the lord of the flies), and he was the god of the Philistines.

We are constantly at the mercy of these nations, and we were building great shrines called gas stations. We fought in several wars about oil. Being willing to sacrifice our firstborn to Moloch and Ba´al to the tunes of millions if not billions to make sure these new agricultural gods to protect the priest of Ba´al and Moloch.

Now let me continue, God commanded Israel to destroy these forms of worship by purging the land of Canaan. If Israel had done this, there would be no Palestinians, nor any other nation on the present-day Middle Eastern countries today. The word of God refers that these forms of worship lead to the spirit of whoredom. However, the dislodged shrines King Hezekiah completely in the 7th century B.C. Yet, something still left the people who worshipped Baal and Moloch still in the land. God Almighty wanted them, and their religion destroyed was for the simple fact the offerings of food, and the other rites were acts of whoredom.

The Roman Empire in the 1st century AD was finally sacked. The destruction of the city of Tadmur city, and brought under Roman rule, but the spirit was still there waiting. *"My people seek advice from their wooden idols, and their rod declares to them. The spirit of whoredom has led them astray. And they fornicated from under their God."— Hosea 4:12 KJV*

A Roman ally, Dianthus, regained the region of Tadmur. Palmyra was the new name of the old trade route, in which the city attracted the entire world to the oasis in the Syrian Desert. When Roman lost possession of King Shapur I with his reign between 241 B.C. through 72 A.D. in the Neo-Persian Empire. Upon the assassination of Odaenathus, his widow Zenobia succeeded him.

The Roman Emperor Aurelian, who invaded the city, ended Queen Zenobia's ambition to further expand Palmyra's influence in Asia Minor, and Egypt once again raped the city. Subsequently, the conquest of Palmyra was by the Rashidun Caliphate after its 634 A.D. He sends the Muslim general Khalid ibn al-Walid to destroy the city to ruin; because of its immoral and sexual acts in the temple prostitutes, both male and female.[29]

Now, what does this history lesson of Tadmur fall to Ba´al worship have to do with the subject of Christianity and the doctrines of Christ? Simple, look at the similarities between King Solomon building the trade city of Tadmur. And the historical building of how the United States of America rose to power from a Christian nation to now

---

[29] (Wikipedia Foundation, 2018) The Roman Empire 27 BC — May 29, 1453

coming one of the two legs of Babylon the Great. Both the city of Tadmur and the United States of America (formally the British Colonies) came from a king to fortify trade and keep military dominance against Spain and France.

Our Tadmur was the Vietnam War and the death of President Kennedy, who tried to avoid our involvement in the Far East. He knew we couldn't win. I believe President Kennedy removal put us in a state of warmongering. And to keep the industries of America working on war surplus. Those powers knew our government would fall for that peaceful need, and because President Kennedy wouldn't play ball, they killed him for it.

Both have seen their share of conflict from the Revolutionary War to the Islamic Jihad of September 11, 2001. We could see even our invasion or overthrow of another Civil War that could split America into five City-States. That would make America the Five-Toes-Romanic-Clay-Iron-Foot of the left, which the prophet Daniel saw in a vision. We have accepted the opinion of being right or wrong. Good is now evil, and evil is now good.

Hints in prophesy that we are the iron-and-clay mixture that makes our government much like the prophecy by Daniel. So, God the Father opens the seal of Mayhem and chaos to get the people on earth to repent, and to shake up the church to become the body of Christ. Remember Christ Jesus holds the keys to death and hell, not Satan.

In my opinion, I believe, the plans soon to come from a combined coalition effort by Iran (the New Persian Confederacy of Afghanistan, Pakistan, Iraq, and Lebanon), Ethiopia, and Libya back by the People Republic of China confederacy (Vietnam and North Korea). Kind of like a Red Dawn scenario of the New Persian Confederacy to slip cross Southern Border of the United States of America.[90]

The revolt weakens the United States of America, and when the Persian Confederacy attacks the United States of America, they attack Israel too. These actions of the New Persian Confederation cause the Third World War by the launch of nuclear missiles after Iran destroys New York City and Los Angeles. And we in the United States will require its citizens to pledge allegiance to our state to rally our militia and army to fight.

I will prove that American's new religion and the tradition that if some don't bow to this deity must die. It was the same religious ideology that caused Germany to fall, which their new religion became "nationalism." This definition of the word "nationalism" is anyone nation that uses patriotic feelings, principles, or efforts to be a separatist away from the common good against God's principles. The definition of a people withdraws from another countries government to form their own country. They become secessionist.

The definition of a country becoming divided up become a partitionist. An isolationist, on the other hand, keep his political views to himself, not wanting to get involved. The involvement sectarianism embraces religious ideology, patriotic ideology, or social ideology. Anyone wants to guess what will be our weakness will be? "Patriotism!"

I am not saying that saluting the flag or serving your country is wrong, but when the average white male and female feels that he or she is the only true American in the United States. This person ideology is operating dangerously close to the quality other than one of being patriotic with the rise of not becoming one of the "isms" or ideology. Adolf Hitler used the seed of *"NATIONALISM"* to rally the people to believe in another ideology tree called *"Aryanism!"*

I will tell you two stories. The truth, and not someone's tradition, is leading and guiding our faith. These stories and the rest of this book will prove whether faith or fear is what this country is following. The traditions of humanities religion are what we may be trusting.

Therefore, I will tell you the first story in which this story comes from the King James Version, and I reworded the story, but you can read it in **first Kings chapter eighteen verses seventeen through chapter nineteen verses twenty-eight.** The second one is, let's say, a parable of a friend of mine whom I hold dear in my heart.

Our first story was about Elijah, the Tishbite, when he met King Ahab of the Southern Kingdom of Israel. He was supporting the four hundred and fifty prophets of Ba′al. Elijah commanded that King Ahab and his prophets of Ba′al to show up at Mount Carmel. The word Carmel spelled Kar-mel′ (**[לְמִרְכַ]**) means a fruitful or plentiful place. And this is where Elijah chooses to meet the King and the false prophets of Ba′al. There was to be a showdown with Elijah on one side, and King Ahab and the four hundred and fifty false prophets of Ba′al on the other side. And the people of Israel met on Mount Carmel in the middle.

Now you can read the word of God to make sure I don't miss the mark. The story begins with Elijah asking three groups. The King, the prophets of Ba′al, and the entire nation of Israel, which they were all there with him.

"How long will you waver between two opinions? If the LORD is God, follow him. But if Ba′al, then follow him!" When the children of Israel refused to answer, Elijah continued by saying, 'Even I am a prophet of the Lord God, am the only one that remains, but look at the prophets of Ba′al, four hundred and fifty men.'

Then, with a bony finger pointing at them, he continued, 'Give us two bulls; and let them choose one ox for themselves, and cut it in pieces, and lay it on wood, and put no fire under it, and I will do the same to other oxen. And we call on the name of our god's or God, and the one that answers by fire. Let him be God.'

The four hundred and fifty prophets Ba'al received a bull, and they killed and cut it up in pieces, and they called on Ba`al from morning to noon, saying 'O' Ba'al hear us!' There was no answer, not even a roar of thunder or lightning from the sky, so Elijah mocked them, saying, 'Cry louder, maybe he or she pursues something. Maybe he walks on a journey, or on an adventure that caused him to sleep and must needs you to awake them?'

Now the prophets of Ba`al did something funny, which their action would be comical if it wasn't so bloody. The four hundred and fifty false prophets leaped on the altar, while they cut themselves until blood gushed out of their veins. When midday was past, and the priest of Ba`al started prophesying until the time of Israel's evening sacrifice. Do these actions of the false prophets sound familiar? Notice the truth of Elijah's joking that there was neither voice, or answer, nor sign from heaven.

Elijah called the people over to him, and as he prepares the altar of the Lord God Almighty, and with twelve stones that symbolized the twelve sons of Israel. Elijah made the men dig a trench around the altar. Then he commanded some men to fill four barrels of water. He killed and cut up the bull, and he lays it on the wood and the altar.

*After the men had filled the four barrels of water. Elijah told the men to take the water and pour it on the sacrifice and the altar three times. Elijah ordered the altar to saturate the already wet animal. The sacrifice was so wet that the water-filled the trench. Once this was done, Elijah said once and only once, 'LORD God of Abraham, Isaac, and of Israel, let it be known this day that thou **art** God in Israel, and **that** I **am** thy servant, and **that** I have done all these things at thy word. (God told Elijah while he prayed beforehand) Hear me, O LORD, hear me, that this people may know that thou **art** the LORD God, and **that** thou hast turned their heart back again.'"*

After Elijah prayed, fire, of course, came down. I hate to say it okay, I'm lying, but in this generation of the libertine, anti-conservative, pagan worshipping speckled owl-loving, tree-hugging, democratically equal-rights persons of the twenty-first century.

They would say that Elijah violated their civil rights of freedom of expression, worship, and choice. They would call Elijah a mass murder. However, that's just what Elijah did to all four hundred and fifty false prophets of Ba`al. He killed every one of them, and not one of them escaped.

Now I would like to tell you my story in the titled story *"THE COVENANT"* …First, thanks to my twenty-nine students. All of you instructed me as a teacher as I taught you; you taught me so much already. Your humility gives me hope for my life. The Word of our Lord said, *"And they have overcome (conquered) him by means of the blood of the Lamb and by the utterance of their testimony, for they did not love and cling to life even when faced with death [holding their lives cheap till they had to die for their witnessing]." (Revelation 12:11AMPC)*

So, I need to show transparency in everything I share. You know somethings about me, but I have tried to be open to my plight. The Roman Catholic Church of Saint Michael's christen me at fourteen months under the name Michael Raymond Jones, for most of my childhood in the Jones family since my adoption I was a very soft-spoken and removed child with my sister Alicia Ramona. My adopted father, Raymond Edward Jones Jr, was in the Air Force and knew my biological father, Tech Sergeant Bruce David Johnson.

Every morning I woke up to depression and some form of psychosis. So, because of this storm, I received salvation at 12 years old through the 700 Club broadcast on January 12, 1975, but didn't have anyone to disciple me and help me seek God's will in my life. I became in battered through the bullying of a neighborhood boy. I was one of ten light-skinned children in the Cavalier Manor area of the seaport town of Portsmouth, Virginia, during the sixties and seventies.

I fought everything and everyone that came at me. My mother, the late Mildred Jones, had her problems with my dad and sister. So, she just ignored my struggles, and I was raised the best she could do. I finished high school, and God told me to leave my mother and go to Tulsa to learn about my calling, but I ran from that calling like Jonah.

The Leviathan of the United States Marine Corps swallowed me, and they taught me things I regret in learning some things. I heard the voice of the Lord say while I was in Bootcamp that *"When he calls me again, I would answer him."* The Lord told me through many prophetic people that I was running from my calling while I was in the Marines. However, I just kept running.

After I was released with a Medical Discharge under honorable conditions, for both PTSD and five disk injuries in my back and neck, which I got in the Marine Corps. Married four times with five natural children and five step-children, I had my turn to be a normal parent, but to me, normal is a dial setting on a washing machine.

I drank to mask the pain of my clinical depression, psychosis, and PTSD. Once when I worked as a security officer and Private Investigator for Burk Security as a *"Skip-Tracker."* While I worked for them on a case, I was stabbed on December 12, 1990. Meanwhile, I was dying on the floor in my apartment in front of my three-year-old daughter Phalisha, I asked her to bring me the phone, and as she brought me the phone. I called the ambulance, and I went to the Hospital. As the blood-filled my lungs, I slowly slipped into death while on the operating table.

As the surgeon operated on me, suddenly, I opened my eyes to a different place. I was sitting on a golden seat with two books beside me in the enormous room. The massive place wasn't filled with clouds or mist, so it wasn't a dream-like colorless environment. I saw colors of different lights and things I never seen before.

A large celestial being was behind me with a lighted sword in his sheath, but it never spoke to me, and I did speak to it. As I sat their quietly, I watch a strange sight as the makings of a trial took place. On the floor in front of me, a dirty naked man knelt on the golden floor.

I saw ahead in the center of the room a large chair with its back to me, and the massive chair was surrounded by lights of wondrous colors, and a beautiful being in the light was sitting in the chair. The lights beamed in power and force while an awesome being sat from behind the chair.

As I looked to his left, I saw a dark presence in the form of a shadowy figure. His shadowy essence had the appearance of being dressed in a pin-striped suit that had a blackened tie, shirt, and other items I cast in darkness. The golden stripes woven into the black shadowed cloak, and the darkness ran down to the floor, covering his feet.

The shadowed terrestrial had red-eyes, well-groomed hair, but the mouth was murky, and the teeth were corruptly jagged and yellowed, which made the shadowy figure look eerier and shady. The shadow spoke to me, and about the naked man in foul language in the courtroom. However, he would speak to the Light behind the chair with reverential words of respect.

Then I saw to my right, a man who was dressed in a white robe that went down to his feet. And the man was wearing a coat of many colors. The coat he wore had on top a pure golden breastplate. On his head was a domed crown with a signet that read, *"Holiness to the Lord,"* and he had on the breastplate twelve colored stones on the front, and the breastplate had shoulder-pads with precious stones with a sash around his waist of pure gold that read, *"King of kings and Lord of lords."*

Light and the feeling of power, love, and hope surrounded this man, and he had an aroma of peace and kindness coming from him that had the essence like myrrh, frankincense, and aloes that filled the air. Right in front of me was the naked man who was weeping. It seemed he was being judged for some grievous sins.

As I watched the naked and never weeping once did, he looked up. I was sitting on the bench that was made of pure stone of clear gold, which the two books sat on both sides of me. The lord of Darkness, who was the shadowy figure, grabbed the first book and opened it.

Like a prosecuting attorney, the shadowy being read the naked and weeping man's sins from the time he was born until he was a young adult. The Shadow lawyer never even stops in his accusation before the Great Judge. And the Dark lord of the court reached over and picked up the other book.

When he opened the second book, a sea of blood came out of the book. Suddenly, I was covered in the blood that came from the book. All at once, I was transported from the seat where I sat, and I found myself being the one that was judging. The Dark lord came against me while ignoring the blood covering me. The verity of his accusation came at me like a pit-bull charging at a mail carrier.

The devilish prosecuting attorney threw the book behind him laughing he yelled, *"He's mine, he's mine he belongs to me, He's mine."* After stating that his graveness victory was final. He waited for the Great Judges verdict.

Meanwhile, I felt guilty of my sinful iniquities, and I began to sob as I knelt in a curled ball. As I looked over at the other man dressed in the Levitical high priest clothing. The man never spoke a word in defense of the guilty that the Dark lord spoke against me. My guilt was undoubtedly real and proven. The priest just smiled at me, and he moved toward the Great Judges chair, while positioning himself between the Great Judge and me. As he spoke, the room was quiet with reverent silence.

The High Priest turned the chair slightly and showed the Great Judge a hole about the size of a railroad spike in his left wrist, and he said with authority, *"Father look."* He shows the Judge the other hole saying, *"Father look."* Each time the High Priest showed a different wound. One in his side, both of his feet, and finally his head. He would say, *"Father look."*

Each time he showed the Judge one of the predominant scars or wounds on his body, he would repeat the phrase, *"Father Look."* After all this, the High Priest turned the chair fully around, pointing at the guilty man, I was covered in someone's blood. He said, *"Father, look."* The Great Judge's chair turned as the holy light of God filled the room, He was ready to pronounce the verdict to the accused.

As these words echoed in eternity. The Great Judge roared this phrase three times, *"I saw you as a babe bathed in your own blood, and I commanded you to live."* Upon the third time of the voice's proclamation. I was thrust into another part of a temple-like-room.

The curtain-like walls were held in glowing lights from a seven-branched lamp. There was an altar of incense in front of me, and a table with fine bread and wine to my right. Behind me was a large Brazen Altar that wasn't burning, and large wash-bowel. Each object was of fine gold, and then suddenly, from behind the curtain, the High Priest came out from behind the altar of incense.

The warrior of our salvation walked through the curtain towards me. In fear, I fell to my face, and while the high priest changed out of his garments. I trembled as I felt a gentle touch to my face, it was the master lifting me to my feet. The soft words of the master spoke to me not to be afraid. Then in one moment, the High Priest said, *"Do you know the reason why you were delivered?"* I said, *"I don't know."* The Lord replied, *"It was because of my blood."* Unexpectedly, as I was still looking around at all the beauty.

The High Priest lifted the lid of the altar of incense, and a scroll rose from the coals that were amid the popping kernel of glowing embers rose. The manuscript opened up with foreign words, unreadable to the common man of English. I tried several times to read the bright words as they burned into my soul, only looking at my master would my soul of my eyes receive comfort. It felt like seeing a thousand pictures all at once. It burned in my soul who Jesus Christ was in the Word. He was the Living Word Divine Expression of God.

Several times I looked back and forth from the scroll and the Lord when I looked at the scroll after several times it vanishes from my sight. Then the High Priest spoke to me, saying, *"Michael, who is like God?"* I said, *"You are the only one like God, my Lord."* Then the High Priest said with the sound like the voice of a waterfall, *"Michael, my word is in you. Go, tell my people that they have forgotten me, and have forgotten my covenant."*

These words I heard would cause me to begin my journeys to do my master's commission. As I talked with the Lord Jesus Christ for the three days, I was unconscious in the Intensives Care Unit at Maryview Hospital in Portsmouth, Virginia.

During that time, the Lord answered all questions about my life and the lineages of my mother, Carol April Cuff, and my father, Bruce David Johnson. He let me know that I was still in a spiritual wilderness, and I was in this wilderness for 40 years. Since the time I rebelled from my calling on June 5th, 1981. Christ Jesus told me that in my travels across America, he would teach me using twenty-nine students. I was to bring them to salvation, baptize them, and disciple them.

I would learn from each failure. I was told that each student must stay with me for three years, and if they left, and it was my fault. The Holy Spirit would reevaluate my method and failure of teaching, and I would get a new student. At the end of the 40 years, that will end June 5th, 2021, and I needed to seek the Lords will for me by going to the mountains of where I was born to pray and fast.

I awoke from the vision in the hospital and recovered for six months at my adopted mom's home. Then I left Portsmouth, Virginia, and moved back to Jacksonville, North Carolina. I rededicated myself into the faith for the second time, and I was baptized in both water and the Holy Spirit on April 15, 1991, at Living Water Fellowship. A Marine Gunnery Sergeant named Michael Rosewood disciple me using four books of the Bible (The Gospel of John, the book of Leviticus chapters 1-7, and the Epistle of Hebrews, and the Epistle of James) and the study was called: *"THE BLOOD OF THE LAMB SERIES."*

In the scriptures, John the Baptist said, *"I indeed baptize you in (with) water because of repentance [that is, because you changed your minds for the better, heartily amending your ways, with abhorrence of your past sins]. But He Who is coming after me is mightier than I, whose sandals I am not worthy or fit to take off or carry; He will baptize you with the Holy Spirit and with fire." (Matthew 3:11 AMP)*

This is how I receive life and true power (authority) from God. When I received the Holy Spirit. I got a characteristic of the Spirit of God. Mine was the Spirit of Wisdom and Understanding. And I work in the spiritual gift of a word of knowledge and word of wisdom.

This wilderness is the fire from the Holy Spirit, and his fire is the pruning and purging device God uses to make me pure and righteous in Christ Jesus. I still have depression over this, but after we placed another piece of the puzzle in on how I failed with the men, twenty-eight men and one woman I taught.

I took on a 29th student against God's design, and he turned out to be a Judas, betrayed me trying to accuse me of kidnapping him to the police, but they later put him in jail for the same thing he accused me of being a crime. He and the person that got him saved were the only students that finished the three-year discipleship program. However, you see where that result led me too. I became very bitter behind this, and for two-year, I took another lap around the mountain.

I don't think of myself as an anointed hero to save the day. And neither do I believe I am an apostle, prophet, evangelist, nor pastor. I am just a teacher; that's all, in a nutshell, nothing more and nothing less. A sidekick to Jesus Christ, the real hero in this greater picture of who the body of Christ needs to repent to in the world.

But I have a few things against you: you have some there who hold the teaching of Balaam, who taught Balak to put a stumbling block before the sons of Israel so that they might eat food sacrificed to idols and practice sexual immorality.—Revelation 2:14 KJV

We have left our first love, running away from our master's voice. We have listened to the voice of Jezebel while we ate the sacrifices of Ba'al. Allowing those who participate in the mass to receive forgiveness.

Let's start with how we have eaten from the table of the sacrifices of Ba'al. Why do I say we ate from this table? Because Jesus told us in the book of Revelation when it described the Pergamos. This church was us even if it showed us in a different light. Once the Church Era of the Laodiceans dissolve into the Ecumenical State Church. They will all need to embrace the doctrines of Pergamos and Thyatira.

One of the many questionable doctrines like embracement of philosophy, ideology, turning the communion element into the body, and blood sacrifice by transubstantiation. Is this true doctrine of Christ based on the epistle of Hebrews chapter six, verses one and two?

The Epistle of the Hebrew doctrine of Christ refers to the principle of repentance from dead works. When we repent from dead deeds. We embrace God's exchange in righteousness from our iniquities. The Lord supper reminds us of the exchange. The Lord's supper reminds of his death, resurrection, and ascension, we take the unleavened bread and wine for remembrance of what Christ Jesus did on the cross.

The doctrine of transubstantiation has a priest of the Catholic church do a prayer over the elements of Eucharist and the wine.[30] The either pray in Latin or English. The purpose must be done before given to their parishioner to receive the elements. The parishioner must also do confession to admit their sins and iniquities to the priest. The priest comes into perform the Mass ceremony, and that this ceremony is what the Mass is all about while being performed before God. It sounds like it of God, but which God?

They do the transference of these elements when the priest says these words in Latin: *"Quam oblationem tu, Deus, debemus orare. Benedictam, adscriptam, ratam, omnia, munus. Haec dona spiritualia acceptum. Ita, acceptabilemque facere digneris, ut nobis Corpus et Sanguis fiat dilectissimi Filii tui, Domini nostri Iesu Christi, amen."* These Latin words translate in this prayer, *"You, God, we pray. Bless and approve all function. These spiritual gifts are accepted. In this way, and acceptable, that it may become for us the Body and Blood of Thy most beloved Son, Thy Son, our Lord Jesus Christ, Amen."* As the priest holds the eucharist and the wine before a sunburst symbol called the ostensorium. Now the person in the church may think these actions are innocent.

They view this action by Catholic dogma as a continual sacrifice of Christ Jesus. Our Catholic brother uses this scripture to mean. We must take part in the Mass of our Lord. But is this what Christ had in mind when he instituted the sacrament of

---

[30] I learned this as an altar-boy at Holy Angels Roman Catholic Church, in Portsmouth, Virginia

Communion? We must take the rite of the Lord's Supper seriously. Read this, and I hope a Spirit of Understanding and Wisdom must act in under God's Holy Spirit.

Whoever eats my flesh and drinks my blood has eternal life, and I will raise him to life on the last day because my flesh is real food, and my blood is real drink. —John 6:53 KJV

When the priest raises the Eucharist and the wine toward the ostensorium. He brings down the Lord Jesus Christ being brought down from heaven to become the suffering savior as the priest acted might be considered as heresy. Do these actions by God's people show the worship of Ba'al? All who do this is eating a sacrifice to an idol. He never intended for us to make the Lord's Supper an idol, but it was intended for this sacrament to remind us of what he did on the cross.

Then there is the prayer and worship of the Virgin Mary. Is praying to Mary idolatry? Can we pray to her? Does the Bible say to pray and hold worship services toward dead saints? *"...A charmer or a medium or a necromancer or one who inquires of the dead."— Deuteronomy 18:11 KJV.* What is a necromancer? Is this type of prayer to Mary and other saints the inquiring of the dead? Does this worship of Mary bring a person to receive false vision (familiar spirits) from her? Is this form of worship what Revelation chapter two verse twenty?

A necromancer is one who speaks to the dead or uses spells to raise the dead through tetrodotoxin that the elements make up from plants and animals. Once the person rises from the dead. The voodoo priest, necromancer, witch, or wizard uses the person or spirits power as a weapon.

When I would further act toward praying to Mary. Calling her the Queen of Heaven. Does this make her the same Queen of Heaven talked about in the prophetic book of Jeremiah, chapter seven and verse eighteen? Who was the Queen of heaven?

In the Old Testament, the term Queen of Heaven was the goddess of Inanna, Anat, Isis, Astarte, or Hera. Besides this Jezebel worship and made the institution of worshiping both Ba'al and Astarte law in the Northern kingdom of Israel, and have heard the voice of that false prophetess, Jezebel. The real Mary mother of Jesus of Nazareth needed salvation and the infilling of the Holy Spirit like everyone else.

The hierarchy instituted into the Catholic Church, although being a member of the body of Christ, they still believe in Christ Jesus. I created the dogma to pray to Mary. Yes, she is considered blessed among all women, according to the Angel Gabriel. But she was never to be used as an object of worship or to pray to her. The word of God states there's only one meditator between God and man, and the meditator is Christ

Jesus, the savior, and Lord of all mankind. But what have the churches stated in their dogma?

In the First Vatican Council. In 1854, Pope Pius IX, with the support of the overwhelming majority of Roman Catholic Bishops. The Pope consulted these bishops between 1850 through 1853. He proclaimed the dogma of the Immaculate Conception, which had been a traditional belief among the faithful for centuries. I was taught in my catechism class that the Virgin Mary is the meditator for us before the Lord Jesus Christ. Because while she was carrying the Lord, she was without sin, and when she was taken up to heaven.

Here are some of her titles given in 1587 by Pope Sixtus V called the Litany of Loreto, entitling the Mary many titles. Mary was never called by the Apostle. However, Pope Sixtus 5th gave her the many titles as Queen of the Angels, Queen of Patriarchs, Queen of Prophets, Queen of Apostles, Queen of Martyrs, Queen of Confessors, Queen of Virgins, Queen of All Saints, Queen of Families. Mary, the mother of Jesus Christ, received the title of the Queen conceived without original sin, Queen assumed into Heaven, Queen of the Most Holy Rosary, and the Queen of Peace. These papal edicts made Mary more than just the mother of God but gave her a voice to as our intercessor to God the Father. This is heretical and against the bible doctrine of Christ.

Doing all of this, we have accepted the doctrine of the Nicolaitans. This definition is clear to mean: In the Greek: [Νικόαος] The name itself means *"victorious over people"* or *"victory of the people,"* but it is a name that a person gave at birth. The origin of this doctrine came from one deacon of the Jerusalem church named Nicolas, a convert to Christianity and proselyte of Judaism lived in Antioch. Formed a heresy about of internal sinning brought more grace.

This doctrine believed that the bishops were king and have the authority to rule over the church masses. Besides, they believed that sinfulness would bring you closer to God and to evoke. The person must deluge in drunkenness and sex outside of marriage. Instead of serving the people as Christ told his disciples to serve while before the people. Some of the Catholic priests, not all, would dominate their parishioners, making some priests use confession as a tool to fornicate with their young boys and girls. I see many Roman, and American Catholic priests work the fruit of the Spirit, and they love God's people.

Now, does this mean that the Catholic Church isn't a part of the body of Christ, no! It would be like saying the Sadducees and the Pharisees weren't Jews. They were a part of the tree of Israel, and this tree wasn't bearing fruit anymore. And it took God to cut the tree down. The Apostle Paul warned the church that we should beware because if God didn't spare the Natural branch of Israel, then he won't spare the church. If it goes prostitute oneself thinking after the world's system.

The nature of sin in humanity is to do whatever I want for selfish reasons. But these sins have consequences, and that consequence is death. Just like not abiding by the laws of the country. By not obeying the new religion of the American ideology of Neo-patriotism hiding under the smoke and mirror of Neo-nationalism.

And if we don't bow to the new whelms of the doctrine of the new leader's religion and belief, he will put you to death. Don't agree with this new president's way of doing things. Call the president a traitor or a terrorist, and you have spoken blasphemies to the new god of the country. Speak against any institution that is wronging humankind, and it will brand you a traitor or a terrorist. Don't obey your governor in a crisis of war, feminine, or pestilence, and you are an enemy of the state. You can practice your rights if you obey the state.

Not putting up flags or saying the Pledge of Allegiance will label you an enemy of the state. Please understand, I love my country. And I wouldn't too happy if someone I caught you burning any American flag that didn't touch the ground, and taking a knee isn't disrespectful. Because to take a knee to mean to me you are in prayer. However, I see something wrong with a lying president and a war that lost its true meaning about why we fought 9/11. You can fill in the blank about why we went over to Iraq for the second time. Because I have given up trying to even understand why we were over there!

Do we see any scary similarities in the New Roman Empire's appointed preachers and rabbinical minister of the New Testament that were appointed by the Roman Empire? The new religious leaders that call themselves untouchable, unapproachable, and unreachable Christian leaders. Did Jesus teach an untouchable, unapproachable, and unreachable gospel?

Now, if some of you are called yourselves Christians, the word means one who is professing the belief in Christianity, or we command them to believe in the teachings of Jesus Christ. Then we shouldn't have two, seven, four hundred and fifty, or even four hundred and eighty-five unapproachable, unreachable, and mostly not-teachable Christian opinions about the doctrines of Christ. Because he's the boss, right?

These doctrines are nothing more than the traditions of men. They have nothing to do with Christ and what he did for mankind. Now to those who are the modern-day Church of Balaam (lying spirit), and the prophetess Jezebel (the spirit of whoredoms) who think that they can hide using the traditions of man.

Meaning like Adam and Eve did in the garden after the fall. When they covered themselves with the fig leaves of the theology of the church of Christ. Being moral and trying to keep the separation of church and state. This action will be your fate.

In Revelation, Christ promised that if the Church Era of Thyatira judgment of the Great Tribulation, and the children of this church will die. It will come in the form of a whirlwind that the judgment will comb you out like the very lice that you are. As you are hiding in the back of some cave somewhere, you must make your decision of what opinion you are under, and I can only ask this question for now! *"How long will you conform between two opinions?"* — *1 King 18:21 NIV paraphrased.*

These traditions have allowed the church to become lukewarm, if not dead. I tell you this. Before he comes back, the Church of Philadelphian will arise again; because with these traditions, we can't operate.

We have been in the crippled state of powerlessness for so long these world and country keep mocking and laughing at us. Only weaken the church of God by making us void of operating in the same power that Christ operated in while he walked the earth.

The power he had touched mankind life more than any four hundred and eighty-five opinions have ever done. My next question to my readers is the tradition that has crept into the church today?

Now, before we end this chapter. I want you to read the article that has been paraphrased by myself, which came from the article named *"A Closer Look at the Rapture,"* by Bill Britton. [iv] I will explain this section and my personal belief, and I will tell what I think, much like what Paul said, *"But to the rest speak I, not the Lord..."* *(1 Corinthians 7:12 KJV)* And he also said, *"... all things are lawful unto me, but all things are not expedient: all things are lawful for me, but I will not be brought under the power of any." (1 Corinthians 6:12 KJV)*

There were two very moral people, and even though they never killed or molested anyone's children, nor attempted to bring down any government system. Their doctrinal tradition may bring many into a false sense of utopia. The two soulish prostitutes I am referring to were Edward Irving and Margaret MacDonald.

Perhaps you have heard of the Irvingite movement? No, well neither have many until now. These are the parents of the charismatic movement known as the Catholic Apostolic Church. Don't feel bad if you haven't heard of this denominational church, because this is a news flash to me. If you want more information about the Irvingite movement you can go to the Wikipedia article on the rapture and the Irvingite movement.

According to the article, it describes Edward Irving as a controversial teacher who had churches in Scotland and England in the early eighteen hundredths The Reverend Edward Irving was excommunicated by the London Presbyterian Church, and he was condemned and deposed from ministry in 1833. The Church of Scotland judgment was for teaching concerning Irving's thesis of the *"sinfulness of Christ humanity."*

Irving also taught about a "rapture of the Church," which he said came from a clairvoyant Scottish woman named Margaret MacDonald, who gave the message. The young Miss MacDonald was reported to have gone into a trance. She described a vision in which she saw the saints of God leaving the earth at the return of the Lord before the tribulation.

Miss MacDonald's trance-like vision took place in the Spring of 1830, while she was living in the Port of Glasgow, Scotland. Her revelation was recorded in a book written by R.N. Norton and printed in 1861. Bill Britton replied that he had a copy of the original article, although it is nearly impossible to obtain any copies.

Mr. Britton said emphatically that before the time of the Irvingite church. None of the Apostles ever preached the doctrine of the "escape rapture" doctrine. According to Britton said, "I believe the Church will go victoriously through the tribulation." In my opinion that would make sense, seeing that Jesus Christ didn't escape from his tribulation on the cross.

Moreover, in the book of Revelation when the fifth was open, and the saint was slain under the altar of God, they asked a question saying, *"How long, O Lord, holy and true, dost thou not judge and avenge our blood on them that dwell on the earth?"* Notice what the answered that was given to John the Apostle, *"And white robes were given unto every one of them; and it was said unto them, that they should rest yet for a little season, until their fellow-servants also and their brethren, that should be killed as they were, should be fulfilled."*

Maybe the Christian historians lied, or maybe the "Swoon Theory" really is true? You know the lie that Jesus didn't die on the cross, and that Judas Iscariot was the real one that got what was coming to him, and the answer to that is, no!

Maybe God the Father knew Jesus couldn't take it, so God let him rapture or faint, and they took a live Christ off the cross. Thus, he didn't feel the real pain of the crucifixion. Yeah, right, and if that were true, I would be the first to hold a public Bible burning, not! I saw those nail holes in person, big railroad spikes in his wrist and feet! The hole in his side was about the size of my sword from the lance. The lance pierced his lower lung as the fluid came from his side.

"But one soldier with a spear pierced his side and forthwith came there out blood and water. And he that saw it bare record, and his record is true: and he knoweth that he saith true, that ye might believe." John the Apostle also replied later in one of his epistles, "This is he that came by water and blood, even Jesus Christ; not by water only, but by water and blood. And it is the Spirit that beareth witness because the Spirit is truth."(John 19:33; 1 John 5:6 KJV)

This is an agnostic doctrine in the Gospel of Thomas and other Gnostic scriptures, and even Islam believes these heresies. Because the priest that taught the Prophet Mohammed gave him the same information.

Now, this part is for those of you who aren't religious and couldn't care less about whether or not we Christians leave. I know some confused religious fool would go somewhere to let the rest of the world have a little fun, they may say.

Well, to tell you the truth, why not a theory to "escape in the rapture?" Remember that person that came on the first day of the exams and got an A+, and all she did was give herself to the Dean of Student and her professor to give them something special?

Everybody else did it the old fashion way. Read took notes and studied. To earn their grade. Do you think this woman that cheated her way through getting an A+? Could she pass a real test as an entrance examination for a board?

The answer to that question is no. The same would be for the other five Church Eras of the world church known as the goats. These denominations sin and rob their flocks by not deal with their sins and iniquities, and they believe they will just dissolve into nothing or God will take them away from his children.

What I mean, acting in spiritual idolatry with the world system. And because God loved them, they get to go to heaven and escape in the rapture. While only suffering a spanking in the Judgment Seat of Christ. It is just like the doctrine of once saved always saved.

The blessed Hope, according to the Bible, is supposed to be a comforting factor. It brings comfort to those who are dead in Christ. Meaning my saved relatives and friends that went on to the grave are awaiting the return of Jesus Christ. We will both join him in the air. The dead in Christ first, and then the living. To go into the wedding feast of the Lamb of God.

Now my friends look at it from this standpoint. Christ and all the first-century saints suffered death without the honor and courage for their faith. Nobody took their life because they molested children, or stockpiled weapons of mass destruction, or drank arsenic-laced Kool-Aid ™. Because they thought their world would end.

When Christ Jesus comes back, will he see a church of faith or one of fear? The doctrinal combination belief of our religious system and phrases to get people their Biblical history goes through periods. These doctrinal combination theories state-certain events might happen in different Biblical arrangements.

According to the Apostles and the prophets, these doctrinal combination theories are never stated outright. However, this doctrine came from the Catholic Apostolic Church and Miss MacDonald's trance-like vision, which took place in the spring of 1830.

While she was living in Port Glasgow, Scotland, and notice no other Christian theologian, writer, or Church Father wrote about this in history *"escape in the rapture"* from the 5th to the 19th century. They recorded her revelation in a book written by R.N. Norton and printed in London in 1861.

As Christ said, the traditions of men make the Word of God of no effect, because it puts a false hope in something that Christ Jesus didn't say. *"Hope deferred makes the heart sick."—Proverbs 13:12 ESV.* Now, we in the Western Hemisphere have become the new era of Christianity, and we have adopted the theory of the "escape rapture." Because those ignorant fishermen and common people back then weren't educated, and we are more blest to have our college degrees.

I am a man of the sword, and I believe if you come from me. I will fight to my last breath, because I have doubts about defending my rights to exist. I no martyr, I am a soldier. Moreover, I have shocking news—this isn't for anyone not confessing Christ as savior and Lord—read this statement and say what you want, but we are living in that age. The book of Revelation, chapter six, verses nine through eleven of the Modern King James Version reads:

"And When He opened the fifth seal, I saw under the altar the souls of those who had been slain for the Word of God, and for the testimony, which they held. And they cried with a loud voice, saying. Until when, Master, holy and pure, do You not judge and avenge our blood on those who dwell on the earth? And white robes were given to each one of them. And it was said to them that they should rest yet for a little time, until both their fellow servants and their brothers (those about to be killed as they were) should have their number made complete."— Revelation 6:9-11 MKJV

Some in my profession may say that this is metaphorical language and doesn't apply but say what you want. If you are claiming Christ as your #1 religion, when the manure hits the fan, and it will, we will see if you are in the back of some cave crying your eyes red or your redeemer. Or, will you be bowing down to whatever statue, robotic idol, or microchip implanted that is set before you?

I know what I'll be doing, and there is no shame here, I will be like the kid in the Bible running to the hills living off the land. Even if I have to run in my bathrobe, showing my naked butt towards the hills. Jesus Christ even said make sure your flight isn't on the Sabbath, or that it's not during the Winter, nor that your wife isn't nursing a child. Minister William Britton concluded that there is no recorded of the *"escape rapture"* theory being ever preached before 1830. This was the time of the Church Era of Philadelphia (1790-1906).

However, on April 30, 1831, a Mrs. J.B. Cardale joined Reverend Irving's church, and she gave her revelation in a home prayer meeting, echoing Miss Margaret MacDonald's revelation of a pre-tribulation rapture. *"It was from this supposed revelation,"* said Britton then continued, *"The modern doctrine and phraseology arose."*

In Bill Britton's opinion, this doctrine didn't come from scripture, but this vision came from false pretenders of those who claimed they are of the Spirit of God. This point brings me to a study I had one day while I was in Burger King in Orlando, Florida. I was in the book of Proverbs, which is the study that even the Fonz's of the TV show *Happy Days* needs to study.

That's why I sometimes call this coarse the school of cool. *"He that hath knowledge spareth his word: and a man of understanding is of an excellent (this word translates as cool) spirit."* ——*Proverbs 17:27 KJV)* Meaning, simply, be quick to listen, slow to speak, and slow to wrath, furthermore, prove all vision by the doctrine of Christ, and try every spirit by the Word of God.

Paul used the word "content" in the book of: *"Not that I speak in respect of want: for I have learned, in whatsoever state I am, in addition to that to be content."*— *Philippians 4:11 ASV.* In this scripture, if I'm reading clearly, the Lord is that Spirit of God that is guiding Paul [not in the perfect state], but into the great state of contentment. Then God left him there to deal with his state of mind with his thinking until he got used to that state of being satisfied. *"And he (Jesus Christ) said to me, 'My grace is sufficient for you, for my power is perfected in weakness.' Therefore, I will rather gladly boast in my weakness, that the power of Christ may overshadow me." (2 Corinthians 12:9 KJV)*

Remember this, my beloved, that this isn't including a newly born Christian. Your life must mature in stages of growth that only God the Father has predestined. That's what I've learned when defining God as *"I AM."* When we humans say the word I am. They think it means a common personal pronoun, but it's deeper than that. The word *"I AM"* really means that God is the *"Great I AM"* [who has always existed] who is backing you, holding you, and keeping you in whatever state you are in.

When you know that then, and only then are you mature enough to grow to the next level. You see, life on this old earth is never perfect. Peter, James, and John had to learn that lesson on the Mount of Transfiguration (Mount Hermon*). "He tends ashes. A deceived mind has led him astray. It cannot be his life, nor can he say, "There's a lie in my right hand."— Isaiah 44:20 ISV*

They wanted to build some tabernacles to always remember that special occasion when they met Moses and Elijah. Because to try to remember the past of what God did is the failure in tradition. Nevertheless, Jesus taught them he was building an eternal tabernacle. It was the simple fact that Jesus was the fulfillment of what these two men stood for on Mount Hermon. The law given by Moses and the prophets who learned their precepts by Elijah, and it was also what God said about Christ Jesus in the cloud of witnesses. *"This is my beloved son, hear him!" — Luke 9:35 KJV*

Knowing this friend, I was foolish enough to try to make a tradition, even the vision God gave me by Jesus Christ. My foolish thinking, I could become a rich man from his gift of the gospel. I have received only one of my royalties [one check of $1.78] that all. Maybe this is the grief caused by the failure I have tried through becoming a famous author. I am a disabled veteran, and I get an income to live comfortably, so God is blocking me from becoming a best seller for his gospel.

I have recovered from drinking and smoking cigarettes, and I had the feeling of being potty trained. A faded memory that I long forgot. I mean, Jesus Christ is telling you that you will remind his children that we have forgotten him and his covenant. The question is never when, but how, because to tell the entire Body of Christ a message, this big can cause you to fall into some big traps.

The Christian believer goes through the same stages of growth. This spiritual growth becomes evident in our walk. The Bible states a righteous man's walk is ordered by the Lord. The Apostle Peter showed these steps. When he talked about how to receive the divine nature. And to receive the divine nature. You must accept the divine word and the divine expression of both who is in the person of Christ Jesus. Accept no imitation!

We learn how to accept our salvation and that God made us holy. This acceptance of grace in Christ completed work in salvation brings us the Spirit of faith. We use the power of faith to add virtue to your faith. Then we move in moral excellence instead of iniquity. The Holy Spirit adds knowledge. Because you have proven that you reverently fear the Lord.

Once your knowledge brings understanding and made full take that knowledge, add to it temperance. As the fire of the Holy Spirit makes you in actions of temperance. God shows you how to add patience in all things. The Holy Spirit teaches your soul patience by the thing you suffer through prayer. You learn patience by allowing the peace of God to calm you. Once you allow peace to move your action instead of fear. Then the Holy Spirit will add the fruit of godliness.

You move in godliness more and more day by day, so the Holy Spirit gives you opportunities to act in brotherly kindness. When we don't boast in our actions of brotherly kindness. We story in heavenly treasure charity that can never be destroyed.

"'For if these things, be in you and abound, they make you that ye shall neither be barren nor unfruitful in the knowledge of our Lord Jesus

Christ.' For if ye do these things, ye shall never fall. That's why the word reads: 'Pride goeth before destruction, and a haughty spirit before a fall.' Then there is this passage: 'Sanctify them through thy truth: thy word is truth.'"— 2 Peter 1:8; Proverbs 16:18; John 17:17 KJV

Normal People never fail; they just fall and never get up. This Edward Irving's fall was when he found that most of England didn't accept this teaching and the doctrine of the pre-tribulation rapture. Still, this prophecy was taught at prophetic meetings at the power's courthouse in Ireland, and this theory was taught to the Plymouth Brethren Organizer John Darby.

Reverend Irving's views influenced Darby, C.H. Mackintosh, and C. I. Scofield, the noted Bible scholar, gave interpreted with the new theory. When charts of the dispensationalism were produced. Therefore, a young Scottish girl originated the theory of the rapture doctrine." Did she say something else, and it was taken out of context, so that the educated few could profit from this revelation. Furthermore, was this the fall of men like Irving, Darby, Mackintosh, and Scofield?

These men have bought and sold this information to the war-weary few thinking and the many denominations wanting to escape from judgment. Time has repeated itself with the televangelist that sells everything from the "wood splitters" from the cross to the oil of Mary Magdalene, who anointed the feet of Jesus'. All you do is send that $29.99 offering for the ministry. It's the "Moneychanger's" in the temple all over again.

They fall with the beautiful women who are nothing but temple prostitutes trying to pose themselves as the innocent Mary Magdalene, with her special gift for the man of God. I got news for those temple whores. They'll be met by the many wives of these men of God after this book is published.

I was only selling this book to friends, and not one dime ever came back to me in my pocket. I will pay my taxes on any royalties over $5,000.00, but never told me to sell his gospel for a price. I will get a greater reward in heaven from every word in this book. I have repented from my error.

I have nothing to hide, because as it is written: *"For it is written in the Law of Moses, 'You shall not muzzle an Ox while oi is Do not muzzle the oxen that treading the Grain.'"— 1 Corinthians 9:9 [Deuteronomy 25:4] AMPC+* I have worked on this book ever since 1989, and I have work on it steady with sorrow, pain, four divorces, failed health, and homeless to finish this word from the Lord. However, God doesn't want me to sell it ever! Even before I had my encounter with the Lord.

Furthermore, do you think I care if some young Iscariot punk can tell me I should give this work away to feed the poor, the answer is no! It will cost my readers in all the novels I produce from these Biblical studies. Some may ask, then why are these traditions of the rapture and other doctrines so bad? If it doesn't affect me, why do you have a problem with these traditions and doctrines of these people?

In a true perspective, this is what I am saying. *"But the one who endures and bears up[under suffering] to the end will be saved." (Matthew 24:13 AMP)* To answer this important question in the last section of this chapter, I will call the passion. A story, whether fictional or non-fictional, is never great if the hero or heroine escapes before the end of the story.

THE PASSION

If I could personally describe how tradition affect a human being's relationship with God Almighty. I guess it would be by these two examples. The first one, please get a picture if you will, as I did the first time I went to church.

This is what I saw the first time I went into a Catholic Mass. Now a mass is a ceremony of one witness, and partaking in the Lord's Supper sacramental rite is believed to be of the very presence of God through our Lord Christ Jesus.

First, the two altar boys carrying long hook-like objects that have a bell on one end, and a flint-like lighter that lights the candles on the altar before the procession ever starts. After the candles are lit, we all rise to organ or guitar music.

Second, the procession started with the same two altar boys. A third person carries a golden cross with a robed priest swinging a Thurible swayed back and forth on a three chained brass ball. The Thurible held charcoal briquettes scented with frankincense that smoke came out of it. The fragrance was pungent, to say the least, and made me dizzy at times.

The purpose of the Thurible was to purify the church from evil spirits. When the first robbed monk passed, there was another altar boy or girl three-feet behind him carrying a large wooden-and brass framed book with a white leather pages, and the inscription read "THE HOLY BIBLE."

Fourth, there was another priest dressed in cope with a golden chasuble trim of the robe (purple for Advent, white and gold for Easter, green for Sunday after Pentecost, or traditionally: The Sunday after Trinity). The laced trimmed robe had on one side was a fancy quarto-foil with a folded hood called amice that had a papal symbol of the Roman Catholic Church. It looked like an X with P down the center of the symbol.

Fifth, after this man, passed other men dressed in suits with purple sashes. Sometimes the other men were seven, and other times they had twelve. Those were the deacons of the church. I didn't know the purpose of this procession. The procession moves forward, other items that would be a part of the Mass.

The chalice of the communion wine we drank was put in the Box under the cross at the altar, but the bowel with the Eucharist that was brought in as well. The bowel of the Eucharist held all cookie-like-wafers in the container. The Eucharist held the symbol of a French crucifix. On the side of the Cup had a raised symbol of the Cup and the Eucharist with a sunbeam

The Mass symbolized purpose as the body and blood of Jesus Christ. When the members go to confession. The Mass intended purpose to protect the member from receiving a curse because of unconfessed sins. The sacrament of Communion was always meant to keep the person to remember the death and burial of Our risen Lord.

In these contents of the cup of the host of the bread was the symbol of a curse for not items of, and if you went to confession on Saturday, that gave you the right to partake. The mood was often mysterious, often emotional, mythical, and breathtaking with the spectacle.

However, it was nothing like what I was reminded of when I was sitting and talking to a friend in the Orlando Historic Center Park, and I was talking with a man about my near-death experience when I had been stabbed some many years later.

You read about the experience in the parable, for lack of a better word, of the Covenant. That was me, if you didn't already know. It is this fact I am trying to describe everything I saw in that rendition.

Because my vocabulary isn't extensive enough to explain everything, I felt that day while I was in the presence, so I would tell just you the reader to go look at it again. Now you know that it's me in the story.

What I can say is this particular thing of the why doctrine and how the traditions of men are so minutely ingrained and the hatred I feel for religions that try to change what God did, so entirely in Christ Jesus' death, burial, and resurrection. To try to put his finished work into a tradition is foolish and wicked! The very fact of these turns of events and how I feel can sometimes bring me to either tears or into a blind rage.

The movie done by Mel Gibson, entitled *"The Passion of Christ."* Although it is a work of Hollywood shows a very graphic rendition of what Jesus Christ must have gone through on the day of his death. Imagine seeing that firsthand, not seeing it that day on a movie screen, or seeing that day of the crucifix like many of did witness.

Now imagine a day in which you meet the real man and see the real scars that His scars weren't makeup props that could be taken off and never applied again. Every scared bruised healed, the hairs of his beard that was ripped out by the angry mob. The wrists of his body with the holes, the punctured gash in his side. Right down to the tears of his flesh in his forehead where the crown of thorns made those eternal scars forever.

You looked into his eyes of eternity, whose only desire is to love you, and only you. As Christ begins to stare at you, you melt from the compassion he has in his eyes for you! Looking back at that, I sometimes think about what I saw that day of his compassion was shown to me. Because the tears are welling up in my eyes, and I must now take a break before I ruin my laptop. That's the Passion! Nothing neither in religion, or for that matter on earth can, nor any other place can remove those very vivid pictures in my mind.

I must be reminded every day for all eternity of what Christ did for me. As I look back in that one very moment in time, that day wasn't just done for mankind to try to make some mundane ritual of doctrinal tradition out of putting God in a box. Moreover, Christ did the compassion for me! That is *"The Passion."*

Christ did the compassion for me, if for none other, so please don't think that I am trying to fool you into getting you to buy into some false ministry that God never called me to be partaker off, then put some false corporate religious title on my corporate paper to get you thinking religious about me and give me money.

Remember the crazy vision of the alumnus of the prestigious college engaged in while I was at the college. Each time the alumnus was buying and selling with the next purchase of items. Was an act of worship, or was it divine by the spirit of whoredom, drove the alumnus? These are nothing but practicing church harlotry, better known as covetousness, which is idolatry!

My point in saying this is that what right in only seen through oneself, but seeing into what is righteous, you need more than what you just see, or it will become self-righteousness. God wasn't fooled, and I repented of the corporation of Menorah Outreach Ministries, INC.

Because I turned the work of God into another tradition of men. God isn't worth selling out his word. I am not saying the oxen should be muzzled. Nevertheless, ministers should never try to become the next millionaire at the pockets of the middle-class Christians, not taking them along to being productive.

This is what humankind has done to every movement of God for the past six thousand years, and we will continue until Christ return. Remember the brass serpent of Moses, even the Holy Grail, and the cross of Christ, we have tried to make them all tradition or doctrines of man.

"This is not the wisdom coming down from above, but is earthly, sensual, and devilish." (James 3:15 MKJV) Even the second coming: Christ himself doesn't even know the very hour he is coming back, so why would anyone know the date of the rapture?

CHAPTER 5
WHY NOT THE RAPTURE?

Now back to the theory of the *"escape rapture."* The only way we can prove that the "escape rapture" theory is true or false is to look and at it by three concerns and their results. On the spreading of the gospel, and judgment of the world system according to the facts that are present in history.

First fact: Paul the Apostle gave understanding about the blessed hope, also known as the first resurrection. The first resurrection based on what scripture is supposed to do. **Point one**—*"All scripture is given by inspiration of God, and is profitable for doctrine, for reproof, for correction, for instruction in righteousness: That the man of God may be perfect, thoroughly furnished unto all good works." (2 Timothy 3: 16, 17 KJV)*

This mean's the doctrine of the resurrections came from what Christ Jesus taught. In Norton's book on page fifteen, he mentions about the Catholic Apostolic Church, and how Darby, Scofield, along with Clarence Larkin and his charts began to teach the new theory.

In the nineteen hundredths, it reached its peak in popularity in both the Western and Eastern Hemisphere. Several divisions came about after the teaching of this theory, which these are broken down into multiple beliefs views of eschatological timing. I have come up with this chart to see how many times people have predicted Christ return. What should the doctrine of the resurrection do as far as the promotion of good works?

> ➤ **First: Pre-tribulationialist and Pre-millennialism** views: The Holy Spirit will no longer be on the earth. The Third Jewish Temple will be built with the antichrist giving Israel a seven-year covenant to have peace. Those left behind will suffer by either taking the mark of the Beast or become martyred for their faith. This theory is held by noted men.
>   - ❖ Pentecostal preacher Jimmy Swaggart. He is the founder of the Jimmy Swaggart Bible College & Seminary.

❖ Professor Emeritus Dwight J. Pentecost, who taught at Dallas Theological Seminary.

❖ Hal Lindsey wrote his book, *"The Later Great Planet Earth,"* in this book gave further details of the theory of dispensationalism.

❖ Tim LaHaye and Jerry B. Jenkins wrote the sixteen-novel series "Left Behind" that gave a colorful look at the Tribulation period.

❖ Doctor J. Vernon McGee, who taught the "Thru the Bible" broadcast.

❖ The prophetic teacher Perry Stone of the TBN show called *"Manifest."*

❖ Also, other pre-tribulationialist and pre-millennialism views like Chuck Smith, Jack Van Impe, Chuck Missler, Grant Jeffrey, Thomas Ice, David Jeremiah, John F. MacArthur, and John Hagee.

➢ **Second: Partial Pre-Tribulation and Pre-millennialism**: The Holy Spirit stays on earth for only three and half years during the Antichrist reign, and the Church falls into darkness, to become the Church of the Harlot. But an underground church becomes the body of Christ, and the groups will escape throughout the three and half period. We will escape the Bowel Judgments. Israel is saved by the 144,000 Israelis men.

❖ George. H. Lang - Author and Scholar of the Plymouth Brethren.

❖ Robert Chapman - pastor-scholar of the Plymouth Brethren

❖ G. H. Pember – pastor-scholar of the Plymouth Brethren

❖ Robert Govett – independent minister of the Church of England

❖ D. M. Panton – pastor of Surrey Chapel England

❖ Watchman Nee – author, Biblical scholar, and Church planter

❖ Ira E. David – a preacher of a church in Woodford, Illinois

❖ J. A. Seiss – author and lecture of a three-volume commentary on Revelations

❖ Hudson Taylor – Leader of the British Protestant Christian Church

❖ Anthony Norris Groves – English Protestant missionary of the Plymouth Brethren.

❖ Rev. John Wilkinson - Presbytery Church of England

❖ G. Campbell Morgan – Doctor of Divinity with the Plymouth Brethren.

❖ Otto Stockmayer Plymouth Brethren preacher

❖ Rev. J. W. (Chip) White, Jr. - Pastor of Courtland Baptist, Queen City, Texas.

➢ Third: Post-tribulationialist and Pre-millennialism: The Church goes through the entire time with Israel, 144,000, the Two witnesses, and the Holy Spirit show's it power and Jesus Christ Returns. This doctrinal view includes Pat

Robertson, Walter R. Martin, John Piper, George E. Ladd, Robert H. Gundry, and Douglas Moo.

> **Fourth: Amillennialism:** They believe they are the triumph church and are in the Millennial age right now! The Amillennialists believe that as the Global Church grows in power, and the world acceptance of the globe universal church. The Amillennialist's viewpoint held by the Roman Catholic, Eastern Orthodox, and Anglican churches, as well as mainline Protestant bodies, such as Lutherans, Methodists, Presbyterians, and many Reformed congregations. [31]

Point two— Now, my question is those who have an ear to hear. If the Rapture is true, then, is this event an escape from the death and destruction of the Church that we are trying to avoid? Is it a triumphal exit of the resurrection through that God has planned and will prove the Church is in Christ?

"And I heard a loud voice saying in heaven. Now is come salvation, and strength, and the kingdom of our God, and the power of his Christ: for the accuser of our brethren is cast down, which accused them before our God day and night. And they overcame him by the blood of the Lamb, and by the word of their testimony; and they loved not their lives unto the death. Therefore rejoice, ye heavens, and ye that dwell in them. Woe to the inhibitors of the earth and the sea! for the devil is come down unto you, having great wrath, because he knoweth that he hath but a short time." (Revelation 12:10-12 KJV)

Was this theory taught by Christ Jesus in the "Doctrine of Christ"? We need to look carefully at the scriptures to see what he said. First, let's look at the "Doctrine of Christ: This is what Christ Jesus taught his disciples, and the Apostles taught others, including Paul. The Doctrines of Christ comes from the King James Version from the epistle of Hebrews the sixth chapter, verses one and two, which this reads:

---

*"Therefore leaving the principles of the doctrine of Christ, let us go on unto perfection; not laying again the foundation of **repentance from dead works,** and **faith toward God,** of the **doctrine of baptisms,** and of **laying on of hands,** and of **resurrection of the dead,** and **eternal judgment**." (Hebrews 6:1, 2)*

Nowhere is there a mention of the taking away, but the word resurrection is mentioned. Now, the Greek word for **resurrection** is ἀνάστασις [pronounced *an-as'-tas-is*] *meaning to* be *standing up* again, that is, (literally) a *resurrection* from death by individual, general or [by implication (its author)], or to get up *recovery* of spiritual truth to be raised to life again, or rise from the dead, that should rise to life, by rising again. An **Epistle of First Thessalonians chapter four, verses thirteen through seventeen that reads in the King James Version:**

---

*"But I would not have you to be ignorant, brethren, concerning them which are asleep, that ye sorrow not, even as others which have no hope. For if we believe that Jesus died and rose again, even so, them also which sleep in Jesus will God bring with him. For this we say unto you by the word of the Lord, that we which are alive **and** remain unto the coming of the Lord shall not prevent them which are asleep. For the Lord himself shall descend from heaven with a shout, with the voice of the archangel, and with the trump of God: and the dead in Christ shall rise first: Then we which are alive **and** remain shall be caught up together with them in the clouds, to meet the Lord in the air: and so shall we ever be with the Lord. Wherefore comfort one another with these words."*

Moreover, Christ taught the Jewish people using the Old Testament scriptures that:

---

*"For as the Father raiseth up the dead, and quickeneth **them**; even so, the Son quickeneth whom he will. For the Father judgeth no man, but hath committed all judgment unto the Son: that all **men** should honor the Son, even as they honor the Father. He that honoureth not the Son honoureth not the Father which hath sent him.*

'Verily, verily, I say unto you, He that heareth my word, and believeth on him that sent me, hath everlasting life, and shall not come into condemnation; but is passed from death unto life. Verily, I say unto you, the hour is coming, and now is, when the dead shall hear the voice of the Son of God: and they that hear shall live.

'For as the Father hath life in himself; so hath he given to the Son to have life in himself; And hath given him authority to execute judgment also, because he is the Son of man. Marvel not at this: for the hour is coming, in the which all that are in the graves shall hear his voice, and shall come

*forth; they that have done good, unto **the resurrection of life**; and they that have done evil, unto **the resurrection of damnation**" (John 5:19-29)*

Christ used the word resurrection. The Greek word for resurrection is ἀνάστασις anastasis (*pronounced an-as'-tas-is*) From [ἀνίστημι anistēmi (*pronounced an-is'-tay-mee)* to stand up]. a standing up again, that is, (literally) a resurrection from death (individual, general or by implication by its author, or figuratively to get up from a dead state. In a moral sense of recovery in the spiritual truth or to be raised to life again, resurrection, rise from the dead, that should rise, rising again.[32] and not catching away.

The Greek word for caught up is **ἁρπάζω harpazō** [*pronounced har-pad'-zo*] means to *seize* (in various applications): [catch away or up], pluck, pull, take by force.[33] Paul, the apostle, did uses the word caught up. This is where the transcribers took liberties in the Latin Vulgate used the word [Latin: rapiemur].

Also, the Lord taught his disciples about the timeline in which the resurrection will happen. Was it in chronological order or just jumped around in Helter Skelter fashion? Let's see for ourselves. We need to look at the gospel of Matthew chapter twenty-four verses three through thirty-one in the New American Standard Bible.

There are two parts to these chronological calendars that gave by Christ Jesus: While Jesus was sitting on the Mount of Olives, the disciples came to him privately and said, *"Tell us, when will these things take place, and what will be the sign of your coming and the end of the age?" Jesus answered them, "'See to it that no one deceives you."—Matthew 24:3, 4 ISV.* These events were given in the order of how they are going to take place.

THE SIGN OF CHRIST COMING: _FIRST PART_—*"Because many will come in my name and say, 'I am the Messiah,' and they will deceive many people. You are going to hear of wars and rumors of wars. See to it that you are not alarmed. These things must take place, but the end hasn't come yet, because the nation will rise in arms against nation, and kingdom against kingdom. There will be famines and earthquakes in various places. But all these things are only the beginning of the birth pains.*

'Then they will hand you over to suffer and will kill you, and you will be hated by all the nations because of my name. Then many people will fall away, will betray one another, and will hate one another. Many false

---

[32] (Strong, 1890 [Public Domain]) G386 (John 5:29; Hebrews 6:2 ESV)
[33] (Strong, 1890 [Public Domain]) G726 (1 Thessalonians 4:17 ESV)

prophets will appear and deceive many people, and because lawlessness will increase, the love of many people will grow cold. But the person who endures to the end will be saved. And this gospel of the kingdom will be proclaimed throughout the world as a testimony to all nations, and then the end will come.'"

These have and are continually taking place throughout the centuries **in the Book of Revelation chapters two, three, and six** in the Church Eras and the seven seals of the Lamb.

___THE END OF THE WORLD: SECOND PART___—*"So when you see the destructive desecration, mentioned by the prophet Daniel, standing in the Holy Place (let the reader take note), then those who are in Judea must flee to the mountains. Anyone who's on the housetop must not come down to get what is in his house, and anyone who's in the field must not turn back to get his coat. 'How terrible it will be for women who are pregnant or who are nursing babies in those days! Pray that it may not be in winter or on a Sabbath when you flee, because at that time there will be great suffering, the kind that has not happened from the beginning of the world until now and certainly will never happen again.*

If those days had not been limited, no one would survive. But for the sake of the elect, those days will be limited. At that time, if anyone says to you, 'Look! Here is the Messiah!' or 'There he is!' Don't believe it, because false messiahs and false prophets will appear and display great signs and wonders to deceive, if possible, even the elect."

Notice what he said to his disciples, "If they shall say unto you, 'Behold, he is in the desert; go not forth: Behold, *"he is"* in the secret chambers; believe it not.' Also, notice the word "SEE" it had the connotation that the Apostles would see an antichrist, and they did through the Caesars. However, Jesus was talking about the Spirit of the antichrist and the actual man himself later; because his word is the same yesterday, today and forever.

The First Resurrection: The proof of what kind of resurrection he meant – *"For as the lightning cometh out of the East, and shineth even unto the west; so shall also the coming of the Son of man be. For wherever the carcass is, there will the eagles be gathered together."* (This is a parable about the word carcass means we are the symbolically the dead carcasses or we are dead to the world and the. But who is the eagle?

The Eagle in Christianity always symbolizes as the means to resurrect. So, the dead Church will rise into the body of Christ. Do these actions bring the revival of the body of Christ and usher in the 144,000?

"Immediately after the tribulation of those days shall the sun be darkened, and the moon shall not give her light. The stars shall fall from heaven, and the powers of the heavens shall be shaken: and then shall appear the sign of the Son of man in heaven: and then shall all the tribes of the earth mourn, and they shall see the Son of man coming in the clouds of heaven with power and great glory. And he shall send his angels with a great sound of a trumpet, and they shall gather together his elect from the four winds, from one end of heaven to the other (Matthew 24:29-31)."

This is something to think about, and I am only giving the facts of our doctrines. I don't want you to come to any conclusion yet. So, when thinking about when Christ returns for us, and he shall surely come back soon. This, I believe!

Could it be said then that in the disguise of religion, these men claim that this new Revelation, if not accepted, could condemn one to eternal damnation? Even the false prediction that came from these theories: Some notable predictions of the date of the second coming of Jesus include the following:

➢ **1844**: William Miller predicted that Christ would return between March 21, 1843, and (notice this prediction happen after the Catholic Apostolic Church movement in 1830). March 21, 1844, then revised his prediction, claiming to have miscalculated the Bible, to October 22, 1844. The realization that the predictions were incorrect resulted in the Great Disappointment. Miller's theology gave rise to the Advent movement. The Baha'is believe that Christ did return as Miller predicted in 1844, with the advent of the Báb, and numerous Miller-like prophetic predictions from many religions are given in William Sears' book, *Thief in The Night*.

➢ **1914: The New World Order** by Charles T. Russell

➢ **1918: Millions Now Living Will Never Die**! By Joseph Franklin Rutherford

➢ **1925**: **"Armageddon Immediately Before Us."** By Joseph Franklin Rutherford

➢ **1978: The Peoples Temple End of the World Sermon: by** Jim Jones

➢ **1993: Branch Davidians "The End Is Near!"** by David Koresh

> ➤ **1997: Heavens Gates Cult "Haley's Comet Is Our Spaceship!": by** Marshall Applewhite & Bonnie Nettles

Some notable predictions of the date of the Rapture include the following:

> ➤ **1978**: Chuck Smith predicted that Jesus would probably return by 1981.
> ➤ **1988**: Edgar C. Whisenant published a book called "[34] Reasons Why the Rapture Will Be in 1988."
> ➤ **1994**: Radio evangelist Harold Camping predicted September 6, 1994.
> ➤ **2011**: Harold Camping's revised prediction put on May 21, 2011, as the date of the Rapture.[35] [36] After this date passed without apparent incident, Camping made a radio broadcast stating that a non-visible "spiritual judgment" had indeed taken place and that the physical Rapture would occur on October 21, 2011—on that date, according to Camping, the "whole world will be destroyed."[37]
> ➤ **2017 September 23**: Christian numerologist David Meade motivated this date with astrological theories.

The Jehovah's Witness, along with the multitude, commanded their members to sell all they had to join them in a bunker. They would state if they did believe they would be damned to hell or rot in the grave, never to be resurrected. However, according to the doctrine of Christ, not trusting in Christ, Jesus was the only means of being eternally damned to hell and the Lake of Fire. Jesus Christ is quoted in the gospel of John says: *"Marvel not at this: for the hour is coming, in the which all that are in the graves shall hear his voice, And shall come forth; they that have done good, unto the resurrection of life; and they that have done evil, unto the resurrection of damnation."* (John 5:28, 29 KJV)

The same two resurrections are spoken of in **the book of Revelation chapter twenty verse four of the King James Version:** *"And I saw thrones, and they sat upon them, and judgment was given unto them: and I saw the souls of them that were beheaded for the witness of Jesus, and the word of God, and which had not worshipped the Beast, neither his image, neither had received his mark upon their foreheads, or in their hands; and they lived and reigned with Christ a thousand years. But the rest of the dead lived not again until the thousand years were finished. This is the first resurrection. Blessed and holy is he that hath part in the first resurrection: on such*

---

[34] (Strong, 1890) G726

[35] (Wikipedia Foundation LLC, 2008) Rapture

[29] (Lewis, 2016 [1890])

[30] (Wikimedia Foundation, 2018) Prediction of the Coming of Jesus Christ and their false Prophets.

[36]

[37] 31 Wikimedia Foundation LLC. (2008) Rapture

the second death hath no power, but they shall be priests of God and Christ and shall reign with him a thousand years."

Notice it does not give a third resurrection or Rapture. It only reads two, and neither does it bring up other resurrections for the living or the dead. The resurrections of Paul in 1 Thessalonians chapter four verses thirteen through eighteen never give a time, but that the resurrection will happen how do we know that the falling away won't happen first while we are here? *"Let no one deceive you in any way. For that day will not come, unless the rebellion comes first, and the man of lawlessness is revealed, the son of destruction..."* (2 Thessalonians 2:3 ESV)

The word that are used are "in the latter days," however, are we not in those times now? Then where did this doctrine come from, and is this true doctrine, or is it someone's traditions or philosophy? When the Holy Spirit was poured out again at the turn of the twentieth century. During the Azusa Street Revival, the Spirit of the Lord emphasized the fact of the nearness of the coming of the living Christ. The only thing was that the Pentecostals got no new revelation about the time on the specific event of his appearing, and neither did they try to sell literature on the subject.

Either the Pentecostal movement only carried over the same material that was from the Bible or from the things that were present from other Non-Pentecostal material. Does that mean that the material of the Irvingite movement was wrong, not Biblical, or immoral?

Now before we go on any further. I must ask my brothers and sisters of the faith to understand and forgive me if I have offended them. But I am doing this purposely to wake up the sleeping giant of the Body of Christ. It upsets me because this isn't a politically correct book trying to sound off about religion.

This book isn't trying to use the political and religious arena to get the Body of Christ out to vote for some politician either! I don't care if you vote or not. We need to save souls before it is night, and no one will be able to work. We need to be on the battlefield and fight.

I leave Christ to fight the Leviathan, and his *"Unnecessary dragons of government."* We should never have fought the King of England in 1775. Canada received her independence in 1982 and Australia in 1986 without firing a shot. We here in America have been rebellious ever since. Someone else can write that book! We needed to demand the House of Burgess and Parliaments and embargo our produce from England. We could have partitioned the one true King of kings. And yes, if God told us to go to war, then go to it.

As I told you earlier in the writing of this book that the purpose of this book isn't to destroy the Body of Christ, but to expose those elements that might be working against the very "doctrine of Christ." This is a warning from **the book of Hebrews chapter**

six verses one and two of the King James Version that was stated before: *"Therefore leaving the principles of the doctrine of Christ, let us go on unto perfection; not laying again the foundation of repentance from dead works, and of faith toward God, of the doctrine of baptisms, and of laying on of hands, and of resurrection of the dead, and eternal judgment."*

Point three— Does this theory or dogma bring unity? The only reason we argue and split churches is because we are immature and childish. We in the denomination are like little children in a schoolyard. And like children, we yell and taunt at each other like Christ said about the Jewish leaders.[124]

Now to some of you that aren't in the Body of Christ, this may seem somewhat harsh. I am not talking to you, so you can go to the next chapter! Now to the believers of the house, I must say that it doesn't matter who you are in the house of God. If the "DOCTRINE OF CHRIST" that is found again in Hebrews 6:1-2 aren't found in your ministry charter, and you are even preaching something else, then you need to look at your salvation again. Because you aren't even a part of the Body of Christ, nor are you mature enough to have a church.

According to the word, you may be doing the work of God in his name. However, it will fall in the end, and great will be your destruction. *"Thus, shalt thou say unto him, The LORD saith thus; Behold, that which I have built will I break down, and that which I have planted I will pluck up, even this whole land." (Jeremiah 45:4 [Matthew 7:24-27] KJV)*

You may be nothing more than an unfruitful leafy tree with no fruit that just takes up space in the God garden. However, in the eyes of God, you will be dealt with harsher than a sinner. That what denomination has become. In God's view, you are a heretic of apostasy; because you choose to believe the true Apostles, Creed found in Hebrews 6:1-2.

These watered-down versions of the Bible remove the scriptures that disprove the Trinity, the gospel of who Christ is being God, or the perfection of the doctrine of Christ. The Catholic Apostolic Church has removed all the Holiness of Christ making him a mere man and not the 100% God-and-100% man that he is that is error—a blasphemous attempt to do what Christ never did in his life and ministry, which is to divide himself from the body and speak another thing outside of the will of his Father. This is open rebellion, and a form of witchcraft at its core!

The very reason the country I served is weak, and the government officials don't see strength in their so-called Christian communities. Furthermore, the reason the Christian communities aren't strong is simple. They don't want to pray and fast to hear God's voice.

Instead, they'd rather sell T-shirts and hold concerts in God's House of Prayer and turning it into a den of thieves or Holy Coffee House. The reason there is no fasting and praying is that the leaders of the Church are fearful of losing members. Therefore, welcome to the spin addicted to religious insanity that hear nor tell the truth!

"You will know the truth, and it will make you free." (John 8:32)

Now, remember, at the beginning of chapter four, I told you about a tradition that arose in the wilderness of the Middle East, the town of Tadmur? Besides, I would prove that the worship of Ba'al has crept into the doctrine of Christ. Bringing in a false doctrine that may seem true, but it only brings people in a swinging pendulum of either a spirit of slumber or of the thinking that no matter what I do. I'll get into heaven, or the Spirit of bondage is in the person. And they act out in fear, thinking, I've got to worry about myself and forget witnessing to the lost and dying world. While hiding our gifts, we don't do the works of God.

The Spirit over the self-righteous is a haughty-spirit. This haughty-spirit is the Spirit that came into the Church during the Era of Philadelphia. The book of Revelation chapter three verse nine referred to spiritualist Judaizes. The leaven that was hidden in this Era known as the *"...synagogue of Satan, which say they are Jews..." (Revelation 2:9; 3:9 KJV)* Hebrew Roots Movement, which became of shoots of from the Seventh Day Advents founded May 21, 1863, by Ellen G. White. She came from William Miller, who in 1833 had started a movement called the Millerites or Millerism. But the Hebrews roots movement first three various times in Church History.

First was during the Pharisees becoming saved and demanding Gentile believers to become circumcised. Second, after the destruction of Jerusalem in 70 AD, the Ebionites moved throughout the empire spreading the heretical belief that John the Baptist and Jesus were Essenic believers. When Jewish proselytes traveled all over the Roman Empire converting Gentile Believers saying they were true Christians of Jesus. Finally, in the 19th, 20th, and 21 centuries with the Millerites, Seven Day Adventism, the Temple of Yahweh, and some Liberal Replacement Messianic Church Movement. These are all known as the Hebrew Roots Movement.

The Spirit over the self-righteous is a haughty-spirit was the leaven that was hidden in this Church Era Philadelphia (1791-1913). It is what the Catholic Apostolic Church did when they gave the doctrine of the Rapture. Looking at the counseling meeting on Monday and Wednesday night, which have taken the place of deliverance services of the sick and demon oppressed and prayer meeting in some churches. They are nothing but social pity parties meetings.

This is just what tradition will do, instead of worshipping God Almighty in Spirit and truth. We have the worship of our pastors and evangelist deep doctrinal messages on the Rapture, which this kind of worship brings in the Spirit of whoredom.

These ungodly acts cause men and women of God to covet the power that these leaders give the illusion of having true power, but it's not from the Holy Spirit. The people of God covet after families, lust after their money, and that brings into the church spiritual idolatry. Causing the leaders to become prideful and fall into sexual immorality.

This is a dangerous position to be in with God. Just like King Solomon fell into idolatry, with his five hundred wives and concubines. So, the leaders are the pastors falling with their many mistresses?

Even though Solomon built the temple, he also brought in the idols of foreign goes instead of worshipping God in Spirit and truth. Our modern-day pastors are the Solomon's of today. They, too, are bringing in idols of tradition, lust after money, calling themselves gods, and being self-righteous against the oppressed. This, as we can see, isn't the true purpose of the Church when we operate in the doctrine of Christ, but of men trying to imitate the worship and faith toward God.

The reality is that if we were allowing true worship of God, it would be according to the way it was designed in 1 Corinthians chapter twelve through fourteen. A lot of bondage would be broken out of the Church, as the scripture reads: *"Now the Lord is that Spirit: and where the Spirit of the Lord is, there is liberty." (2 Corinthians 3:17 KJV)*

A shadow of Jesus on a lampshade, prisms over a statue of the Virgin Mary, or blood coming out of her eyes isn't an example of the Spirit of God. These are nothing but illusional, nothing more than magical card tricks, which bring a sense of falsehood to who God the Father and Jesus Christ are with the movement of the Holy Ghost. They are God, and they are one!

This falsehood is nothing more than imitation of doctrines of devils that pose the tradition as being from the Biblical truths. These traditions are defined as another means by which their original Revelation is conveyed and mediated on by studying the word.

Tradition is then interrupted theme by some philosophers of theology, who state that tradition does precede scripture, and these traditions replace God's word. The many theologians with doctoral degrees from many American universities are quoted saying that these stories and teachings of the Patriarchs of the Bible were passed on by word of mouth to lessen the purity of Holy Scripture.

Henry Ford once said, *"History is more or less bunk, it's tradition. We don't want tradition. We want to live in the present, and the only history that is worth thinking about is the thing we do today and not the past...the history we make today."* In human history, we've only had a form of writing for the past five to six thousand years.

Scientists and archaeologists have proven that the theory of Biblical truth being passed by word of mouth is incorrect. As the historical sciences of both doctorates of linguists and archaeology have both agreed, the earliest known writing began in the Southern Mesopotamian area of the Sumerian in the city called Ur.

The area was south of the famed tower of Babel, around 3500 through 3000 B.C, in the Mesopotamian Empire of Sumer had their clay tablet cuneiform writing. The early evidence of writing was called cuneiform and consisted of making specific marks in wet clay. The professor I had at Oral Roberts University agreed with Professors Harold Brent timeline. Because Abraham was from Ur and did have the ability to write.

The name of the Sanskrit alphabet is Devanagari, which means and pertains to the city of the gods was created in the second or first millennium. The Egyptians even began their primitive forms of hieroglyphics. So, how can we prove when man started down the linguist trail of language and writing?

"Although human beings have been living and dying for millions of years," said René Etiemble, *"They have been writing for only six thousand years."*[38] So, we have gone from five thousand and five hundred years ago to now six thousand years. It's no different in the twenty-first century with the belief in tradition for some four hundred and thirty-five years, instead of believing in the Bible. We have educated ourselves right out of the will of God.

The Church, which Jesus Christ founded, was supposed to be the place for healing, restoration, and teaching mankind a better knowledge of God. The religions of mankind have made it a three-ring circus, and the pulpit is the sideshow for the new freak in town. We would rather bark-like a dog, or crawl on the floor like a snake. The people of God never use the nine gifts of the Holy Spirit of God, which We move by the fruit of the Spirit. When moving in these gifts allows the congregation to find out who they are in Christ. They end up dying of no spiritual growth.

Becoming the eternal audience for the pastor and the church members are ever learning and never coming into the knowledge of the power of God. Now, the question is, then, how do we change the one-man-rubber band syndrome we see and feel in the house of God?

First, move the pastor out of the forefront as the lone-wolf dictator and put him back in the pulpit as the conductor, by making him spend more time before Father God in the word, prayer, and serving the people. Have the elders of the Church take more responsibility for praying over the sheep and teaching home Bible studies. Instead of trying to compete for the next runner-up to be the preacher.

---

[38] (Descartes, 1637 [Public Domain])

Second, begin to move the other ministers of the Church to start home Bible studies in their neighborhoods, cutting out the program syndrome. This will do the service into a three-part form of Thanksgiving, praise, and worship that will give God the glory.

This will cut out or limit the TV and radio broadcasting, (nothing wrong with it just too much Hollywood programming) and make the whole media ministry assist the home-cell-groups in special tapes and video messages from the pastor and the ministers.

Finally, teach the congregation as a whole to begin to operate in the nine spiritual gifts of God. Also, we need to begin to study on the fruit of the Spirit in the home-cell-groups. These kinds of studies will bring unity to the faith, rather confusion and strife. This last statement brings an understanding of what is the spiritual gifts of God, and how do we, as believers, operate in the basic principles of Christ. How can we walk and do as he had done on earth?

Then let us go to the next chapter on what are the supernatural or also known as the spiritual laws of Christ. Because without the understanding of how to operate in the supernatural. We turn the movement of the Holy Ghost into another tradition of men that, if operating in the doctrine and traditions of men, will die, eventually.

And these lascivious actions will be turned into another denomination of works. Making or shall I say, trying to make God's law into actions of natural laws. That is why all of us, including me, have to repent from being an "AIN'T" and start acting like "SAINTS!"

CHAPTER 6
THE SUPERNATURAL (SPIRITUAL) AND THE NATURAL LAWS OF GOD

Because of the traditions of men have been interwoven into the laws of God. Humanity has tried to make God's laws into natural laws. These laws can often be defined as follows, first, as ethical philosophies that can judge actions taken by humanity. Second, theological considerations decide how God thinks toward humanity.

Third, legislative laws and rules of society moral code of what is right and wrong. Fourth, the social theory of how humanity has conducted itself through-out millenniums in history. Last, a set of principles that can govern society.

These principles are based on what are assumed to be permanent characteristics of human nature. These principles can also serve as a standard for evaluating conduct and civil laws. It is considered being fundamentally unchanging and universally applicable to human nature.

Because of the ambiguity of both the word "nature" and "natural," the meaning of these words may vary. As I said before, humanity having the natural laws interwoven with the traditions of men. The confused believer then sees the fundamental principles of both the natural and the spiritual that can give us a safety net to protect us from failure. However, the believer gets confused when seeing the natural and spiritual laws, not knowing the difference between the two.

The natural and spiritual laws can never stop us from sinning. No, my friend, that is a matter of choice. Following the natural and spiritual laws is designed to guide us in which way to walk on earth toward being like Christ.

Now, if we walk only in the natural laws. Then we find God left out of the picture, and humanity makes our religion and legalism. If we only try to operate in the spiritual laws only. We become in another form of religion called spiritualism. The balance is operating in both like Christ did on earth.

Now not to get off the subject, but I must digress for a moment to discuss with you, naturally, about what I talked about in the last chapter. It will help you later in the next five chapters. I never answered to my readers about how I felt concerning the rapture and the Second Coming of Christ. It is simple. I don't have an opinion!

You see, I do not care if we leave in the beginning, the middle, or the end. I do not care if we never leave, because God gave me an answer to this very question many years ago. God the Father had me read Matthew chapter twenty-four, which reads: "But he that endured unto the end the same shall be saved."

God the Father asked, "If you were to die right now, where would you be?" I said, "I would be in heaven with you." Then he continued, "If I called you home by splitting the Eastern skies, where would you be?"

"With you, my Lord," I shouted with peace.

Then God the Father said, "Then Michael, endure until the end, and let me be concerned when I am coming back, or when I will send my Son." The answer to that question was given to me a long time ago and has kept me out of spiritualism and legalism that is the traditions of mankind.

As for having power or authority, I can define that God is the author of all power, which I will be defining further about who can operate in this power. The supernatural and natural laws will be defining then by who can operate in them in these next following chapters.

Now I have already defined natural law, tradition, and spiritualism. As a consequence, the words "SPIRITUAL" and "NATURAL LAW" may also be considered an ideal to which humanity should aspire to live or a general factor how humanity usually act. The NATURAL LAWS is in contrast with favorable laws of nature, physics, and the enactment of civil society.

The supernatural laws are above the natural thinking of man, and the divine laws can only be used by God and those that are his friends in Christ.[39] Unless the person is holding the very character of God, which the person is promised to receive the infilling of the Holy Ghost.[136] Only a born-again believe will possess the supernatural power of God, but how can this be?

How can someone like Jim Baker, who, after all, he did wrong in his life by operating in the natural? Turning right around and operate now in the supernatural. And he is the righteousness of Christ Jesus?

First, we must look at two words before we go any further: the term "LAW" and "POWER" must be defined. The word law comes from three words. In the Hebrew meaning for "WORD" there is (דָּבָר) *dâw-bâr* or as it is [*pronounced da-var*] can

---

be defined as commandment, judgment. Oracles, and words.[40] Then there are the words for "LAW" that is (מִצְוָה) mitzvah [*pronounced mits-vaw'*] meaning a *command,* whether human or divine (collectively the *law*): - commandment), law, ordinance, or precept.[41] Then there is the Hebrew word for law (תּוֹרָה) tôrâh [*pronounced tôrâw*]. This word means a doctrine, decalogue, or the five Book of the Bible called Pentateuch.[42]

In the Greek, the name is **νόμος** spelled nōmōs [pronounced nom'-os] that means principle.[43] When I looked at the word "LAW" in the Merriam-Webster Dictionary, the concept was defined in the seventh clause, as "rule or principle stating something that always works in the same way under the same.

"Wherefore the law [principle] was our schoolmaster [instructor/tutor] unto Christ, we might be justified by faith." (Galatians 3:24)

In American English, the definition of law that works in the same way under the same conditions has always been misinterpreted as power. Therefore, in the United States, power is defined in the same way under the same circumstances. The United States government chooses to enforce the laws of the land that makes us justified in taking control or destroying if others do not operate in the shadow of democracy.

The power or authority given to governments comes from God, and the word power and *"AUTHORITY"* come from the Greek word ἐξουσία exousia [*pronounced ex-oo-'-ah*] means privilege, that is, (subjectively) given a force to rule with the capacity and competency to work in freedom, or keep token of control to delegated influence in authority or power.[44] And with this definition, the human mind can choose a course of action or make a decision.

The power "POWER" also is defined as the being without subject or restraints imposed by preceding cause by necessity or by divine predetermination of their free will. Now the definition of "FREE WILL" is determined as according to Oxford Dictionary is this: the will of a human being that is unrestrained by anything known that can be forced. This gives the human nature true liberty.

Understand this that the word "POWER" can in no way be confused with the concept and "AUTHORITY." Even though at the beginning of this paragraph, I used the word "authority," it was only for defining clarity. Because authority can only be given by God Almighty. He gives that privilege to Jesus Christ.[143]

---

[40] (Strong, 1890 [Public Domain]) H1697
[41] (Strong, 1890 [Public Domain]) H4687
[42] (Strong, 1890 [Public Domain]) H8451
[43] (Strong, 1890 [Public Domain]) G3551
[44] (Strong, 1890 [Public Domain]) G1849 (John 1:12 KJV)

However, the power can also be destructive as in the word δύναμις dunamis [*pronounced doo'-nam-is*] means a force that brings miraculous power.[45] The force used in this *miracle* itself brings the ability of the Spirit of God to bring abundance without limitations. It also has the meaning of mighty deeds), a worker of godly powers (worker of miracles), high strength, a violent force of destruction, mighty and beautiful work. This word is where we get the word *"DYNAMITE."* This is the closes word we have to explain the power of the Holy Ghost.

"And, behold, I send the promise of the Father upon you, but tarry ye in Jerusalem until ye be endued with power from on high." *(Acts 1:8 KJV)*

When I was in the United States Marine Corps, I was trained as an essential electrician, and I had to learn electrical theory in my trade school. While I was there in school. I learned that each component operated by two laws of physics. One was Ohm's law of resistance, and the other was the law of force, which states: Work is equal to the force applied (Ohm's law) to move an object multiplied by the distance the purpose will travel. Force, therefore, is the action on a body of mass that multiplied by the works done to cause acceleration on how quickly the work is done. These laws combined bring about power.

I learn that electricity is an immensely helpful power, and yet it is destructive and can kill you if this power isn't respected. So, the power of God needs to be respected. This power can't be taken lightly. For it is written in the scriptures:

"For the wrath of God is revealed from heaven against all ungodliness and unrighteousness of men, who hold the truth in unrighteousness; Because that which may be known of God is manifest in them; for God hath shewed it unto them. For the invisible things of him from the creation of the world are seen, being understood by the things that are made, even His eternal power and Godhead; so that they are without excuse... (Romans 1:18-20 KJV)

The power of God comes and flows from the spiritual laws of Christ, and if they are done in Christ Jesus, you transcend all that is natural. Then mankind must see and understand that if there are natural laws in physics at work for you to succeed. When the natural laws are design to work against us. Therefore, we must also assume that God made the supernatural (spiritual), which he runs his universe. These laws have

---

[45] (Strong, 1890 [Public Domain]) G1411

been doing all that we see in both the spiritual and natural realm. This has been here since the foundations of the world, and according to God's word, it reads:

"For by him all things were created that are in heaven and that are in earth, both visible and invisible, whether they be thrones, or dominions, or principalities, or powers; all things were by him created, and for him." *(Colossians 1:16 ESV)*

It is the same way in working God's spiritual laws. When we do something by the word of God. The Spirit of life goes to people by the power of the Holy Spirit. And God sends the Spirit of Christ to overtake the object of his creation, which, when we pray for, should be moved. It is not how long it took the goal or objective to be moved. Power isn't measured by how God moves things, but true power comes when God moves us.

Nevertheless, when will God move the purpose or goal being prayed for in life circumstances. As long as the purpose being moved is in God's perfect will (meaning the objective or object lines up with the word or plan of God). Therefore, it is the amount of time to move the objective or object, but God's timing.

God the Father isn't in time, for he is in eternity, and it is the representation of the timing of the Lord. We must wait on the Lord, and let patience have her perfect work.[148] This fact is what brings salvation, having nothing missing, and nothing broken.

"And count the patience of our Lord as salvation..."(2 Peter 3:15 ESV)

Remember, the word power has two meanings. This power means the ones with the power have the ability or privilege to act in the force given by the person or by God gives this authority. God provided this power for his people, and these people move in power through the spiritual laws that govern them. This type of power is the definition of authority. As long as we abide in the regulations of the spiritual laws. They have the Spirit of Christ dwelling into them. They won't work under the law of sin and death. They are weak, because of the works of the flesh. Matthew Henry said it best about Romans chapter eight verse three:

"It could neither justify nor sanctify, neither free us from the guilt nor from the power of sin, having not the promises either of pardon or grace."

Only the Son of God kept the law of the Ten Commandments perfectly. He even kept the Levitical and Sabbatical laws of the Old Testament. And The spiritual laws can't be maintained by a sensual person, but if we have the Spirit of Christ. Then we can walk in his perfect will of God. We walk in the Spirit when we walk in the spiritual laws.

The power of being in the Spirit of God's presence means being under the authority of being in the Spirit so as not to fulfill the works of the flesh. If we operate in the works of the flesh, and then we violate the law of sin and death. And we must repent by asking God to forgive us and pled the blood of Jesus over our sins and iniquities. The wages of sin we pay for these wages by the works of the flesh is death.

The Laws of God will either delegate authority or take it away. The spiritual laws give power by helping mankind being fulfilled with the Spirit of Christ to walk like Christ Jesus, or it will take away that authority to humanity.

It also delegates dominion, authority, and liberty, so the person rises above the natural laws of mankind. So, if there are invisible natural laws that run all influences of God's creation. Then there are supernatural (spiritual) laws that run the same universe, whether they are dominions, principalities, or powers. The supernatural, by definition, is above the natural realm of the natural things we see, smell, hear, and feel. The supernatural is governed by a different set of rules. Like the natural are governed by absolute laws/principles that we will discuss further in chapter eight.

According to the book of Genesis, the laws of God that moved the void over the earth, in the beginning, were the first spiritual laws that were the law of the Spirit of life in Christ Jesus. These laws were given to man, so he would operate in his dominion or authority in the Garden of Eden.

However, man gave all of that away in the garden to become a god! Mankind was the operator of the earth. And the Godhead wrote the laws/principles on the hearts of man by speaking it into man's heart in the beginning.

The Godhead will always give the ability for mankind to operate the laws/principles that formulate the foundations of the world. However, the Godhead will never let man, nor any of his creation violate these supernatural (spiritual) laws, which we will talk about further.

Now that we understand why I am making the statement I'm making about the supernatural (spiritual) laws versus the natural laws, and to break any of these laws/ principles would you have sinned or violated the functionality of how that law/principles operate. But if you serve in that law by enforcing another higher law/principle. (Like gravity that is a law of physics [what goes up must come down] like dropping a pencil, and the object will come down.

However, uses other laws/principle like lift (force), motion, power, and centripetal force by putting the writing object in an airplane or a spaceship, and it will float above the law of gravity.) The supernatural (spiritual) principles are a more divine law above the natural laws. You will die or sin by missing the mark. Leading to death! So, now that I explained the word supernatural means spiritual. I will use the word spiritual for now on.

What is a spiritual and natural law? Well, a spiritual law can be defined according to the word of God, which reads: *"It is the Spirit who gives life; the flesh accomplishes nothing. The words that I have spoken to you are spirit and life." (John 6:63 ISV)* The word of God is quick and powerful, and when spoken to an unregenerate soul or inanimate object can either be destroyed or moved out of the carnal realm into the spirit realm to operate in the power of God.

"Who also hath made us able ministers of the new testament; not of the letter, but the Spirit: for the letter killeth, but the Spirit giveth life?" (2 Corinthians 3:6 KJV)

It is this life that progresses the laws of God to move forward and not backward, adding never subtracting, yet multiplying never dividing whatever it overshadows. Darby states the things of God are spiritually discerned, and man is carnal; he has not the Spirit. The Lord does not go beyond the kingdom of God.

CHAPTER 7
THE SEVEN SPIRITUAL LAWS OF CHRIST

There are seven supernatural (spiritual) laws of Christ, and as I said in the previous chapter. They will move you to understand how Christ walked on earth, but they are never intended to make you into being a god!

Let's read Hebrews chapter two verses two through five to understand these differences between the Law of Moses and Christ Jesus, work in grace and truth. Picture if you will find two contractors and their crews building two mansions. One builds one out of stone and mortar, and the structure made with a dirt floor. The lighting is candles, and a well to get water with an outhouse in the back. This house constructed in stoned by Moses, and the only way to live in the house of Moses, you must pay rent. We'll talk more about this house later, and it's meaning.

The second structure of Christ Jesus, a mansion is built of gold, trimmed in silver. But this house is more modern structure presence built as a four-sided foundation, the framing and rafters, the electricity and wiring, the pipes to bring in water, and out the sewage, then the insulation, then the drywall and wood finishing's, and finally the roof. However, this house is owned and also built by the master Carpenter Jesus of Nazareth. This house will last forever and was here from the foundations of the world.

The first principle that was laid the foundation of the House of God that moves all of creation both the natural and the spirit realm. This principle was the law of the Spirit of life in Christ Jesus, and this foundation has the four gospel stones. This first law is found in Romans, chapter eight, verse two. Then there is the second principle called the laws of faith, and it is found in Romans chapter three verse twenty-seven. This law brings the framing of the house.

However, without these two laws, you don't have anything coming in like the power from the electricity and the water. The electricity is the laws of liberty found in the epistle of James chapter one verse twenty-five. Then the water and sewage is the law of kindness that is found in the book of Proverbs chapter thirty-one verse twenty-six.

Then there is the royal law of love found in the epistle of James chapter two, verse eight. This is the insulation the keeps the heat (fire) of the Holy Spirit inside. Next, there is the drywall and the wood finishing's, which this principle is the law of righteousness found in Romans chapter nine verse thirty-one. Finally, the roof that keep us dry and safe in the law of sin and death that is our protection to the body of Christ.

Having these spiritual laws, we can walk like Christ did on the earth. How can we do this, it's simple? It takes the Holy Spirit, and not our self will be trying to be good. This has each person in the body of Christ, putting on the mind of Christ. The word of God states in **Roman chapter eight verses three through five with the uses of the King James Version** that reads:

"For what the law [natural law] could not do, in that it was weak through the flesh, God sending his own Son in the likeness of sinful flesh, and for sin, condemned sin in the flesh."

Now what this means is simple. Putting in perspective what the word law means, which we have already defined as a commandment, judgment, word, or principle that comes from an authority or power that can't be changed or altered. Furthermore, the word "law" has two principles. Those principles are the spiritual and natural laws.

We have already defined the word "natural" in chapter two as carnal or fleshly, so naturally, the principles bring rules or commandments, judgments, words, or principles to the natural, carnal, or fleshly world. The spiritual laws bring to the commandment, judgment, words, or principle to the spiritual realm or world.

Because, the flesh or the natural realm can never have dominion over God's kingdom, simply put, you are either going to operate in the Spirit, which the Spirit will dominate over the natural, or you will operate in the natural. And the natural will war against the Spirit of God. We are born with iniquity, and we are conceived by our parent's sins.

"For I know that nothing good lives in me, that is, in my flesh. For I have the desire to do what is right, but I cannot carry it out." (Romans 7:18 ISV)

In the following verse, the Apostle Paul made it clear about why the natural laws were under the spiritual law of sin and death. When he said, *"When I would do good, evil is present with me." (Romans 7:21)* For Paul's delight in the law of God was after the inward man. However, he saw another law in him, which aggressively warred against the law of his mind.

"For the carnally minded is death; but to be spiritually minded is life and peace…"(Romans 8:6 KJV) The flesh envies against the Spirit, and the Spirit against the flesh. Because they're divergent, the one to the other so that we cannot do anything that we desire to do for God the Father.

Because the carnal mind is always going to be enmity against God, and it is not subject to the laws of God, neither indeed can it be. This was the result of Adam's fall in the garden when he rebelled by eating the knowledge of good and evil. Humanities soul was corrupted and became the dominating force over the Spirit of man.

Because the Spirit of man was created to communion with God and obey God's wishes. However, when man sinned, the soul became God ruling the Spirit of man. Making the Spirit of man dead or unable to hear or communion with God. So, then they that are in the flesh or carnal cannot please God.

Yet, many people use natural laws to enslave others, become rich, and gain the power to create other natural laws that make them successful. This can be seen in three vocations of entertainment, military, and religion. This is how the wealthy celebrities, the one percent, and generals of our military, uses the natural laws to conqueror weaker, poor, and ignorant.

Then how can the wealthy celebrities of politics, Hollywood, and the rich that we see in the limelight of society appear to be successful? Because, in the world system, they seem to be productive and not wealthy. Jesus Christ was wealthy because anyone that he encountered was changed, whether it was for the good, the bad, or the ugly. It's the difference between a pretty woman and a beautiful lady. If you're pretty it only on the surface, but if you're beautiful, then your character comes from the inside.

You were immediately changed and never the same after your encountering Christ Jesus. I guarantee if you were to meet any of the wealthy celebrities. You would be the same as you were before! Now your life might be enriched, but you would not become wealthy, nor would your life change.

Because you are only meeting these people at a natural level, and they can only operate on the sensual level of life. Moreover, they will only be able to use the natural laws to be successful. Case in point: in the gospel of John, where Jesus' meeting with the Samaritan woman at Jacob's well. All her life, she had rights to that well. When Jesus asked her for a drink, although she may have been rich in the rights to that well. When it came to her actions and judgments made her in poverty, because she couldn't even give a thirsty man a drink without being bitter at him.

Little did she know that the man she met. He was the creator of the water, the well, and the owner of the well. Jesus met Jacob nine hundred years before she was born. Christ was the God that showed Jacob where to dig the well while they were in a wrestling match. Jesus threw Jacob's hip out of joint, and he gave Jacob his new name of Israel.

Israel was the same lineage of the salvation that brought Jesus Christ to the earth, and this same Jesus of Nazareth was the same man that was standing in front of the Samaritan woman. Although the woman at the well of Jacob was rich in the well water. She was poor in the living water (the Holy Spirit), which only Jesus Christ had through the spiritual laws. He used in these spiritual laws all his life.

The Samaritan Woman to work in the natural laws would only help her soul and bodily needs. And she would never work in the spiritual realm, and please God like Christ Jesus did every day. This reason occurred, because the thinking of the rich is to become more prosperous, and they don't share their wealth, but the rich only do philanthropies get appreciation by others.

The rich people will always be getting more productive by purchasing some type of information, products, or media from them. You need to go jump through the same hoops they did to get rich, instead of God blessing you. The Bible states that the Lord orders the steps of a righteous man and woman.

The Bible reads: Receive ye the Spirit by the works of the law, or by the hearing of faith? Are ye foolish? Having begun in the Spirit, are now made perfect by the flesh? Now understand why many people don't prosper in the natural laws. We need to find out what these laws hold.

As the word of God has told us before, the person who works in the flesh under the natural laws are enmity against God, for it is not subject to the spiritual laws of God. Neither indeed can be, for as many as are of the works of the natural law are under the curse. For it is written, *"A curse on everyone who does not obey everything that is written in the Book of the Law!"(Galatians 3:10b ISV)*

Meaning there is only one person that can work under the natural laws successfully. The person is Jesus Christ, our savior. It doesn't matter how many times you try or try to use the natural laws. All of humanity will fail.

CHAPTER 8
THE NATURAL LAWS OF GOD FOR MANKIND

Now, if the spiritual laws keep you in Christ, and they allow you to walk in God's way. Then how are the enmity of the Natural Law against God? We see that these natural laws won't submit themselves unto to the spiritual laws of God. Neither indeed will the person be allowed to perform better while under the Natural Law. The person working under these laws will accomplish an end to the work, for as many that are of the work of the Natural laws, they are under the curse.

The design of the natural laws was created for a purpose. We will find out this purpose in a moment. However, what are the natural laws? These are the seven natural laws. The Ten Commandments (Exodus 20:1-17 KJV), known as the only natural law that God created for man. The Ten Commandments are known as "the Law," "the Commandments," and "the Schoolmaster." According to the Scripture, the law was designed to reprove humanity in sin, and correct us in our iniquity, and show humanity that we need redemption through a messiah.

The Levitical and Sabbatical laws (Exodus chapters 21-31, Leviticus chapters 1-26 KJV) will show us that we can never serve God without obeying and sacrificing to God daily, nor walk in his rest. There are over six hundred and thirteen minor laws. And we can't keep a one without Christ Jesus' power and His anointing!

Then there is the Law of progression (Deuteronomy chapter 28 KJV) will show if we obey God, we will be blessed, and we have life, and if we disobey him, we are cursed, and we have death. The law of reciprocity (the law of sowing and reaping [Genesis 8:22 KJV]) shows the principle of if we sow to our flesh, we will reap the whirlwind of destruction (Hosea 8:7 [Galatians 6:8 KJV]), or if we sow righteous seeds will have true eternal wealth in Christ Jesus.

Then there are the laws of nature and physics (Isaiah 40:12; Job chapter 38-41 KJV), which this law governs how nature and laws of physics move everything we see and don't see. Also, the nature, the natural and physical realm groan to see the power of God in the race of man. However, we fail the next law protects humanity from destroying itself.

The laws of authority and government (Luke 22:25 KJV) keep humanity in balance by not allowing our own destruction. This law also shows us how we are never to dominate over each other, and the consequences (to understand the judgments read (Revelations 5:1-8:1m KJV). They come forth seven judgments each era when humanity doesn't repent by the rise of a wicked leader, war, pestilence and famine, death and the curse of Hell, the martyrdom of his righteous, destruction of the unrighteous and revival, and Silence and calm.

Finally, natural laws are the authority of mankind over all creation (Genesis 1:26 KJV). This law shows humanity what we lost after the fall in the garden of Eden. In addition to this law allowing men to rule animals. It shows the wonder of nature and how nature praise their Creator (Romans 1:20 KJV), and how we don't if we are wicked.

Bringing the sinfulness of mankind under the curse and all that operate them. The whole purpose of the devil's mission to put humanity under the natural laws (the law of sin and death) He wants to keep you carnal, natural, and lost in the wilderness. It doesn't matter what position of the natural laws you can successfully operate in to get richer. You are still in poverty. Remember, it is all-natural!

Therefore, Christ has redeemed us from working under the curse of the natural laws and how humanity keeps operating under them. If we operate under the natural laws instead of being in the spiritual laws of Christ. We become the enemy of the kingdom of God, because to be carnally minded is death.

Bring us into the household of faith instead of being under the household of Moses. Paying the wages of sin, which the payment for working under the law is death. We need to be the household of faith by operating in the spiritual laws of Christ. In addition to operating in these principles, we become the house of prayer he designed us to be.

Christ as a son over his own house, whose house are we apart of in the world. A decision made by humanity to choose the natural laws. We will need to either stay in the house of the natural laws house of Moses' natural laws (principle) and be judged for our sins, or Come into the very presence of Abba by the spiritual laws of Christ and receive true salvation. If we stay in Moses' house, then you will have to pay a higher rent for staying in that house. Because you are under the law, and not to walk by truth and grace.

Some of you rebel with a cause, maybe saying to yourself like the Jews and Pharisees said, *"We are of Abraham, who is our father."(John 8:33 KJV)* However, it is another father we are working for and getting paid for our many deeds. You rebel, maybe saying, "I'm not working under any man's law, and much less any of God's laws made by some old dud name Moses!"

Well then, my friend, you're in worse shape because you're homeless, naked, and a foolish blind person. The transgression of the wicked said within their hearts that there is no fear of God before his eyes.

Matthew Henry said, "As one employed in serving the interest of God's kingdom among men more immediately and more eminently than any other in his day." _{xviii}

Mankind can't say in the heart that God is just some undigested bit of beef. This beef disagrees with our internal organs that we can get a 'Rolaids™' to make us feel better. Henry further said:

"The wicked, whether he means his persecutors in particular, or all notorious gross sinner in general, are not certain. But we have sin in its causes and sin in its colors, in its root and in its branches." _{-ibid}

The natural laws will remind all of mankind that they must pay the rent on earth. Because *"... the earth is the Lord's...(Psalms 24:1a NASB)"* Simply, the wages of our sinful nature are separation or to suffer in death. 'Death' means, that state of a being, whether human, animal, or vegetable, but more particularly human and animal.

Where there is a total and permanent cessation of all vital functions stopping. When the organs haven't only ceased to act, but the being has lost the susceptibility either of renewed and growth in actions, separation, or alienation of the body and soul from the presence of God. A being under the dominion of sin, and the person is destitute of grace, or the divine life of God is called being spiritually dead.

"For he said to Moses, I will have mercy on whom I will have mercy, and I will have compassion on whom I will have compassion." (Romans 9:15 MKJV)

Because you're on the outside of the house getting rained on by the wrath of God, and you are just waiting on death. You see, the ones under the natural laws are very sick, and they want to get well, fighting death, but they can't because they're too weak.

Now your silly thinking reminds me, which you resist the calling of God, for you to repent is like the sand-crab standing in the middle of the street, with its claws up. Daring the oncoming truck coming toward it, but it gets run over as the truck goes toward it.

Now being foolish is not afraid. When the landlord is about to evict you from the apartment [your body]. You are renting from God. Your lack of fear still doesn't change the fact that he has served you an eviction notice and dump your stupid tail outside withal your stuff. The same is true in dealing with Almighty God. The fact that you don't fear him never changes the truth about your day at the Great White Throne Judgment.

> *"But the fearful, and unbelieving, and the abominable, and murderers, and whoremongers, and sorcerers, and idolaters, and all liars, shall have their part in the lake, which burneth with fire and brimstone: which is the second death." (Revelations 21:8 KJVR)*

The truth be known, all who sin are under the law that states: *"Let no man say when he is tempted, 'I am tempted of God: for God cannot be tempted with evil, neither tempted he any man: But every man is tempted when he is drawn away of his own lust, and enticed. Then when lust hath conceived, it brings forth sin: and sin, when it is finished, brings forth death." (James 1:13-15 KJVR)*

So, the *"devil made me do it"* or *"I was born that way,"* maybe pure, but you have free will as it was stated in some previous chapters. Remember, our free will then is God-given nature, which the will is an organ of the soul. And our intention should rebel when it doesn't line up with. We choose to for God and our best interest.

> *"And whatever sins good men may themselves to be provoked to by their exercises and afflictions, God is not the cause of them."*[46]

This is the law of sin and death. There are six other supernatural (spiritual) laws that will be discussed in this book. Moreover, these seven spiritual laws will be explained incompletion, and they are all found in the Bible. Let's talk about some of these principles as we walk through this by faith.

---

[46] (Henry, 1662-1714 [Public Domain]) How am I good?

CHAPTER 9
THE LAW OF FAITH

> *Now faith is the substance of things hoped for, and the evidence of things not seen, but without faith, it is impossible to please him [God], for he that cometh to God must believe that he is and that he is a rewarder of them that diligently seek him. So, then faith cometh by hearing, and hearing by the Word of God, by what law; of works? No, but of [the] law of faith. (Hebrews 11:1, 6; Romans 10:17; Romans 3:27 KJV)*

Picture if you will, that you get a call from Los Angeles from a lawyer. He informs you that you are the inheritor of twenty billion dollars. Now the thing is that you own a wreck of a car. You must get to the lawyer's office in ninety days. You start the car, and it dies because the car began to smoke, as you heard the gasket blow, and the seizes up.

So, five miles outside of the town, you figure that you will start thumbing a ride across America. You will hitchhike your way to Los Angeles to the lawyer's office. Knowing you will do whatever it takes to get you there. Because you know your inheritance is waiting on you once you get there.

Think about it for a moment. Twenty billion dollars, and all you have to do is walk, run, thumb, or jump a train. And all the money your rich relative left is yours to spend. Knowing this, you would go through hell or high water to get that money. Because, you know, in the end, the reward be worth it, right?

Now picture, if you will, the same reward, but instead of unlimited cash to get whatever you want and need in the natural (I know that word, natural, has shown up again. However, you're reading me right, and you know where I'm going with this I hope, so just listen.)

Naturally, those twenty billion dollars would take care of you only, because you're the only one benefiting from your gain of success, right? You could buy an island, and you live the rest of your life free from the troubles until the next hurricane blew your way.

Maybe you could give the money to charity. That's mighty nice of you, but still, which one? Everyone is in need. How could you tell who a legit charity case was? Knowing nothing but what you know in the natural might help you keep your goals, but you can't cut through the truth.

You need more than just natural abilities to keep the $20,000,000,000 from driving you mad. And keeping you free to live, move, and have your existence to stay sane in this life and keep your liberty intact. In reality, the money you inherited was a gift, and you just focus only on your pursuit of happiness would be very selfish.

Maybe, this is why most people buy what they buy: the big fences, guard dogs, the bodyguards, and they have the scheduled mortal life that they lived. Blowing all the lottery money and becoming a bag-lady or homeless man holding a sign on the street.

When was the last time these well-to-do people, or for that matter, any of us? We left our wealth at home in the bank, and we fed five thousand people with a two-piece-fish dinner. Moreover, we used nothing more than a little boy's lunch, and we only their faith?

According to the scientist that uses the law of physic and mathematical equations, some miracles that Christ Jesus did of using faith were naturally impossible and defied these laws. Others in Christianity believe that you can't do what Jesus did without money, while others believe his miracles are fables or old wives' tales.

Jesus of Nazareth, who is the proven messianic Son of God, used these same principles to create the known universe. He used this same principle by operating in his earthly ministry, and he taught his disciples how to uses this one supernatural (spiritual) laws, and the doctrine he taught most on is the law of faith.

The question to all the scientists of every discipline, what did Jesus do in his life? Where he gets the power to do all the miracles and healings he preform? What principles worked while Christ Jesus was on earth. Can his disciples use these same principles? Can any person work his way to help humanity to be a success or save their life?

No, but in Christ by the law of faith, just like when a pilot uses laws of physics like lift, inertia, power, and force to move a plane in gravity. So, can a person handle the principle of faith to move through society and the curse of the natural? Is the law of faith a scientific principle like the natural laws of physics? We will find it here.

Because the scientist state that faith isn't a law or theory that can be proven in mathematical or a hypothesis. However, they are all wrong on all accounts. Reading the scripture at the beginning of the chapter, we find the articles of faith. These scriptures are the principle of the laws of faith. In this chapter, we discuss the foundation of the Bible. Also, these principles work according to the manual of the Creator of all we see and don't see.

Nevertheless, how do you define the word "faith"? Now faith in Hebrew is אֱמוּן 'êmûn (*pronounced as ay-moon'*) means to be established that is trusted or trustworthy and has truth.[47] Where in the Greek is (*pronounced pis-tis*) _{xvi} from the Greek word means to *convince or persuasion* to have *belief*; to have moral *conviction* of *religious* truth.[48] So, to Biblically have the fact, it is not in argument by it is a force.

"NOW FAITH is the assurance (the confirmation, the title deed) of the things [we] hope for, being the proof of things [we] do not see and the conviction of their reality [faith perceiving as real fact what is not revealed to the senses]." (Hebrews 11:1) When we look at the word faith, we see nothing, because you can't see faith, why? It's like gravity. Can you see gravity?

"And Jesus said unto them, because of your unbelief: for verily I say unto you, 'If ye have faith as a grain of mustard seed, ye shall say unto this mountain, Remove hence to yonder place; and it shall remove; and nothing shall be impossible unto you." (Matthew 17:20 KJVR)

We see the natural effect of other laws of physics and nature. Moreover, the natural laws, as we have proven, can work for or against us on this earth in the natural, earthly, and sensual realm. You may be asking, how does that establish that the law of faith is viable or authentic biblical principles, and how does it operate?

Let us look at the twenty billion dollars, which the inheritance is in the lawyer's office. You could see the money, but you have a letter, right? The money is there, according to the letter, isn't it? You don't know, do you? You have to trust a letter from a person that you have never seen, and you need to go by faith (trust) on what the person you can't see in front of you spoke or wrote in the letter. Working the steps of faith is the only way you will get the money, or you will never know the reward.

Then faith is brought about by equation that must plug into the word. Faith is of the first part of the equation by hearing The Greek word ἀκοή akoē (*pronounced ak-o-ay*) is a verb: meaning to give an audience of, come to the ear, to understand, be noised, be reported, to bring to understanding, or by hearing.[49]

Faith comes by hearing (understanding), and hearing (understanding) by the word of God. (Romans 10:17 [1 Thessalonians 5:23 MKJV])

---

[47] (Strong, 1890 [Public Domain]) H529
[48] (Strong, 1890 [Public Domain]) G4102
[49] (Strong, 1890 [Public Domain]) G189

The measure that a person understands the word of God. Plus, the measurable level of faith given by a person, whether great, little, or no faith, equal salvation. What is salvation? The Greek word defines it perfectly. The word **σωτηρία** sōtēria *[pronounced so-tay-ree'-ah]* that is a noun, which means to rescue from unsafe or hazardous situations both physically and morally. This rescuing brings deliverance to health, and brings salvation of the spirit, soul, and body.[50] of a person calls to God the Father through Jesus Christ the moment of salvation.

As the person receiving the Spirit of Christ. A humble child of God and friend of Christ will not think proudly of themselves, but they will operate in the measure of faith given to them. Because faith is in the evidence God's performance of the word that always moves in today, never in the impossibility of past failures, not operating in faith is sin.

Faith is never about the problem trying to change, which this type of thinking is stupid. That would be like God saying to the earth, which it was formless and void of life at the beginning of its creation. Then God just stares at his creation, and demand the creation creates itself with some light and become alive again. Without speaking any words to the creation to come to life.

Neither can the sick, possessed, or lost get salvation by themselves. That's not how faith words. If you have the Spirit of God living in you (the burden removing, yoke destroying power of God), it is your measure of faith that God will use to heal, deliver, or save the person and if you don't understand how to uses the law of faith properly. You have failed, not God or the person in need of help.

Remember the $20,000,000,000.00 problem? Think about it. I mean, really think about it. You can ask yourself, is this money all a bad joke? You'll never know unless you step out the door. The definition of faith is in the spiritual realm. Because without faith it is impossible to please him (God), for he that comes to God must believe that he is and that he is a rewarder of them that diligently seek him.

The formula parts of faith move and operate in cosmic powers without natural explanations. But like all laws of physics, act and progress in our universe in repetitive constant motion. Natural laws mean when we move all things. To define these natural things, they are circumstances, and problems the negative forces, and in beliefs. When we trust the real authority of God's word, God puts his trust in us by giving uses his blessings, both natural and spiritual. God said, *"The just shall live by faith."(Habakkuk 2:4 MKJV)*

We must diligently seek his face, and we need to veil ourselves in the shadow of his counsel and might, in which this spirit (characteristic) comes from the Holy Spirit.

---

[50] (Strong, 1890 [Public Domain]) G4991

Who is he, you ask? He is the Father (ABBA) of all creation, and he is all that we see and don't see.

In the Body of Christ, he is our Provider ([יְהֹוָה יְרֶה]ᵃ Jehovah Jireh), which this interpretation means: THE LORD OUR PROVIDER. Then there is God is our banner, ([נִסִּי יְהֹוָה]ᵇ Jehovah Nissi) which this interpretation means: THE LORD OUR BANNER. Then there is God who is our sanctification, ([מְקַדֵּשׁ יְהֹוָה]ᶜ Jehovah M'kaddesh) the definition means: THE LORD OUR SANCTIFICATION. Then there is God who is our shepherd ([רֹעִי יְהֹוָה]ᵈ Jehovah Rō'yē), which this interpretation means: THE LORD MY SHEPHERD. Then there is God being our righteousness, ([[יְהֹוָה צִדְקֵנוּ]ᵉ Jehovah tsidkenu) which this interpretation means: THE LORD OUR RIGHTEOUSNESS. He is always there in our presence today, yesterday, and forever. The Lord God being present is, ([יְהֹוָה שָׁמָּה]ᶠ Jehovah Shammah), which this interpretation means: THE LORD IS THERE.¹⁹¹ Then the Lord God is our peace, ([יְהֹוָה שָׁלוֹם]ᵍ Jehovah Shalom) this interpretation means: THE LORD OUR SHALOM⁵¹

In the very presence of God, Almighty is all of these names that describe the real character of Jesus Christ, who is God Almighty warns not to take him lightly, and these attributes he is in Christ Jesus. The names of God, most of the time, found on altars, and these altars were places of worship in the times of Abraham's, Isaac's, and Jacob's.

As Paul stated that Jesus was the shadow of things to come, so these names were also the shadow of things to come. Jesus was the good shepherd (I AM the GOOD SHEPHERD). Jesus was our righteousness (I AM the Great I AM). Jesus was the great physician ([רָפָא יְהֹוָה] Jehovah Rafah) THE LORD OUR HEALER.⁵² These names of God Israel labeled on the altars of God Almighty ([אֵל-שַׁדַּי] El-Shaddai), which this interpretation means: - the mighty one that satisfies.⁵³

"So, then faith that comes by hearing, and hearing through the word of Christ." (Romans 10:17 ESV)

The word hearing is the Greek word: ἀκοή akoē (*pronounced ak-o-ay'*) from the Greek word [ἀκούω (*pronounced ak-oo'-o)* A primary verb; to mean to hear in various senses. Give in the audience (of), come to the ears. One shall listen to or hearken or listen to a noised—one person to give a report. A person gave understanding.⁵⁴

---

⁵¹ (Strong, 1890 [Public Domain]) a.H3070; b. H3071; c. H3068 & H4720; d. H3068 & H7473(H7462). e.H3072 f. H3074 g. H3073
⁵² (Strong, 1890 [Public Domain]) H3068 & H7495 (Exodus 15:26 KJV)
⁵³ (Strong, 1890 [Public Domain]) H7706 (Genesis 22:14 KJV)
⁵⁴ (Strong, 1890 [Public Domain]) G189

Mainly the definition means to hear in the act, the sense of a person listened to what you said and understood it …by the Word of God…by what law does faith operate in or under; of works willing it to happen or that faith help objects just falls out of the sky?

No, the law of faith is a principle that works like any other law of physics or nature. Calling those things into existence, is what produces faith: hearing or understanding the word draws faith into the open. Then getting agreement with God and another person, and then the manifestation of what you want.

Look closely at what Jesus did with feeding the five thousand. He heard the problem of these hungry people, and Jesus wanted agreement from his disciples. The three disciples gave a solution to the problem. The first said to send the people away, but the second person wanted to collect money to buy bread. And the third got a little boy's lunch and getting the boy lunch was the right answer. Getting agreement from God, the Father, and Andrew, with the bringing of the little boy's lunch, got faith to work.

Even though there is a law or principle of force that will help humankind work. Humankind will work in the doctrine of faith toward God, and we can have the same capacity for the more excellent work, and we can operate just like Christ did when he walked on earth.

Even though we are his creation, we are the only creature designed to be like God and not trying to be God. However, we individually created to be like him. Better, known as his offspring.

I have a hard enough time being a man, so how do I become like God? The answer is simple. Be like Jesus. Operating in the law of faith is the first step you take action to be like a child of God. Jesus stated we must come to God in the spirit of faith, and the truth of the word of God.

Therefore, knowing who He brings the spirit of the knowledge and the fear of the Lord. Meanwhile, the believer has a fear of the Lord. The fear brings the believer to a reverential fear towards the Lord. This reverent fear produces the beginning of wisdom and knowledge. Having this wisdom is your life in total rest in Christ Jesus.

Having the Holy Spirit will bring the character of the spirit of faith, which this spirit is one of seven Spirits of God. I lose myself in this fact that God wants me a sinful empty man that he wants his life-force in me, and it makes me more than just a Christian. I am a friend in Christ and a child of God.

The Godhead of the whole universe gave us evidence of this so-called mysterious God of the heavens. All we have to do is read the Bible to have to understand him. Faith isn't a mystery, but a simple principle act of reverence to the one that created us.

It seems that this very act of blind faith to some that don't know a father's love is crazy but do not have confidence in the heavenly Father seems more foolish than fearless. Faith is, therefore, the glue that brings him that would appear to be distant closer to the evidence that he (God) is real.

God is always going to be first God the Father with Christ Jesus through the Holy Spirit (by not know who God is and what he is capable of doing), it would be impossible to believe that he is, and that's why none can seek him diligently without faith. The reward is not in getting stuff or going into heaven. It is the fact that he has so much faith in man. If we honestly look at what he has done for man, and I'm not talking about showing mercy to all the wicked people in the world.

God has so much faith in a man that Jesus Christ, after taking back the dominion that Adam lost in the Garden of Eden. He said he wouldn't return until his body had completed his mission of the Great Commission.

This fulfillment of the Great Commission is why he asked the question to his disciples, *"When the Son of man returns, will he find faith (meaning will Jesus see the law of faith in operation) on the earth?" (Luke 18:8 KJV)* The answer is, without a doubt, yes! That is why works alone can't save you, and what does it mean in the scripture, "by works?" So, the question I am asking you. What is the actual work of faith?

CHAPTER 10
THE ROYAL LAW OF LOVE

Now abideth faith, hope, charity, these three, but the greatest of these is charity. (1 Corinthians 13:13 KJV)

So, I will answer the question I am asked you in the last chapter. What is the real work of faith? The answer is love, and love is the work of faith. However, how does the principle of Love work? We need to define the word, love. And in this definition, we will get what real love is and how to work the principles of love.

When Christians define the word love, we have a habit of making love symbolize in everything. I love cake. Instead of saying I am fond of cake. I love this music; to mean, I like a preforming and dramatic action. I love how you make me feel—instead, a statement to an emotion of fondness.

Moreover, the misinterpreted affection of love as an animated object that can never receive significance, and we don't understand what the person tries to tell us. The fondness of the person or inanimate objects doesn't draw you to get into a relationship with the person and inanimate. And you are confused by what they are saying to you. I mean, can you have a relation with cake, music, or a performance? No, of course not using mindfulness you can enjoy the pleasure of the objects. You don't have a relationship with these objects or inanimate objects. We have a relationship with people and with God.

However, with pets, you will take care of them and show fondness towards them. Nevertheless, what is the feeling you have towards them? It is a form of love. In the Hebrew, there are many meanings of love. But only in the Greek, do we get the understanding of the true meaning of the word love. In Hebrew, the name Loves definition of one that shows fond of someone like a friend or in a sexual sense. Simply we are fear that's why we perceived because God was feared, so he was only a feared friend to keep at a distance: *"Therefore thou shalt love [Great fondness of God in fear] the Lord... (Deuteronomy 6:5 KJV)"* (the word used here is in the Hebrew אָהַב 'ahab (*pronounced ah'hab*) is love like a friend.[55] This is the same word Peter used when he told the Lord he loved him φιλέω in the Greek phileo (pronounced fil-eh′-o) to be a friend or fond of a person).[56]

In the Old Testament, you could only fear the Lord God. However, in the Greek the new meaning of how God wanted to love, and with the rejuvenated heart through salvation, there was a new form of love that Christ Jesus introduced, and that was the complete form of love, which is where the Royal law of love gives new meaning to the word love.

In the Greek, there are several meanings of love that we will study. We will explore all of them starting with the most critical first unconditional love first in the Greek is ἀγάπη agapē (pronounced ag-ah′-pay) that is from the word ἀγαπάω apapaō (pronounced ag-ap-ah′-o) defined as to love; however, ἀγάπη agapē is as affection or benevolence; specifically, or plural a love feast or charity.[57]

Now the word love has several meanings, and it is dealing with the fleshly or carnal type of love, the soulish kind of love, and the spiritual type of love. The Greek word θέλω thelō (pronounced thel′-o):- means to delight in or to desire in anticipation of love.[58] Then there is the Greek word ἔρως Eros (pronounced erōs):- is the meaning of falling in love in a sexual sense, or a humankind of Love.[59]

The Kinds love's you could find fondness

Meanwhile, phileo is of the soulish nature of being found. Here is some example of having the soulish form of fondness. Notice that all are using the word liking.

1. Philagathos (fil-ag′-ath-os) fond of good, that is, a promoter of virtue:- the love of good men.
2. Philadelphia (fil-ad-el-fee′-ah) fraternal affection:- brotherly love.
3. Philandros (fil′-an-dros) fondness of your husband.
4. Philanthrōpia (fil-an-thro-pee′-ah) fondness of humankind: - a love of philanthropy.
5. Philarguria (fil-ar-goo-ree′-ah): - Love of money.
6. Philautos (fil′-ow-tos) fond of self: - lover of own self.
7. Philēdonos (fil-ay′-don-os) fond of pleasure, that is, voluptuous: - lover of fun.
8. Philoteknos (fil-ot-ek-nos) fondness of one's children (maternal).

---

[55] (Strong, 1890 [Public Domain]) H157
[56] (Strong, 1890 [Public Domain]) G5368
[57] (Strong, 1890 [Public Domain]) G26 [G25]
[58] (Strong, 1890 [Public Domain]) G2309
[59] (Random House Publisher Group, 1833)

9. Philippos (fil'-ip-pos) fond of horses: -a love of horses.
10. Philoproteou (fil'-op-rote-yoo'-o):-to be fond of being first (ambitious of distinction).
11. Philotheos (fil-oth'-eh-os) fond of God that is, pious: - lover of God.
12. Philologos (fil-ol'-og-os) fond of words: - a lover of talking.
13. Philoneikos (fil-on'-i-kos) fondness of strife, that is, disputatious: - a love of contentious.
14. Philoxenos (fil-ox'-en-os) fondness of guests that is, hospitable: - lover hospitality.
15. Philosophos (fil-os'-of-os) fondness of wisdom: - a lover of philosopher.
16. Philotimeomai (fil-ot-im-eh'-om-ahee) fondness of honor: - a love of labor.

Once again, the Greek that is firmly dealing with soulish Love. The Greek word φιλέω phileo (pronounced fil-eh'-o): - defined as a fondness in the feeling of liking a person that has several terms of tenderness, which are as follows:[60] As you see the difference is that when we say I love chocolate. You are only really saying I like this pleasure of chocolate (*Philēdonos [fil-ay'-don-os] fond of pleasure fond*). People in history report, *"I am falling in love with you."* You are actually saying: *"I like them."* (*Philandros* [fil'-an-dros] fondness of your husband). All the religious people in the house say amen when they say, *"I love God."* No, you only like God with (*Philotheos* [fil-oth'-eh-os] fond of God, that is, piously liking God.)

It is the in the Greek is ἀγάπη agapē (pronounced ag-ah'-pay) that best suits the unconditional love is what the Royal law of love is referring to.[61] Still, the Greek word used to state in the scripture: *"Thou shalt love"* (the name is the Greek word ἀγαπάω apapaō [pronounced ag-ap-ah'-o] defined as to love in a social or moral sense, which come

In comparison to the Hebrew word עָגַב 'âgav *(pronounced aw-gab')* is defined as to breathe after that is to love worshipped as a lover.[62] So, the name is too beloved, but the concept is not the Greek word Love φιλέω phileo, which is to be fond of one's self. In the commandment, it demands that we *"love our neighbor as thyself."(James 2:8 KJV)*

Now we can understand the principle of the Royal law of love. You can do this spiritual law without Christ Jesus and the power of the Holy Spirit. But, why can we love God with all our heart, mind, and soul? And do the second like the first, which this commandment is to love your neighbor, as yourself?

Because our love has conditions, rules, and hidden agendas, we can love our selves, that's easy. We love ourselves so much that we would kill ourselves for the shamed,

---

[60] (Strong, 1890 [Public Domain]) 1]G5358 2]G5362 3]G5363 4]G5364 5]G G5368 6]G5367 7]G5369 8]G5383 9]G5376 10]G5383 11]G5377 12]G5378 13]G5380 14]G5382 15]G5386 16]G5389
[61] (Strong, 1890 [Public Domain]) G25
[62] (Strong, 1890 [Public Domain]) H5689

dishonored, or violation done to us. However, when we kill ourselves, we careless how that would impact others around us.

What does love to have to do with anything?

Learning the spiritual law of love is found in **the Epistle of James chapter two verse eight in the Amplified Bible,** but also reading poems nine and ten gives us a clue: *"If indeed you [really] fulfill the royal law following the Scripture, You shall love your neighbor as [you love] yourself, you do well. But if you show servile regard (prejudice, favoritism) for people, you commit sin and are rebuked and convicted by the law as violators and offenders. For whosoever keeps the law [as a] whole but stumbles and offends in one [single instance] has become guilty of [breaking] all of it."*

Those who act in prejudice and favoritism are not following this spiritual law. When you operate in bias just because of a person's skin color or belie, God will throw a monkey wrench into that machine of bondage. The word says its mode of operation Prejudice: - a noun that means when people have a rigid opinion not based on truth or experience around an ethnic group. This kind of judgment shows another form of the tree of the knowledge of good and evil, which we prejudge others with no logical reason for what is truth.

I remember when I was in the Portsmouth Public School System segregation 1969, and they were starting discrimination in all the schools in 1969. When I was a young boy, the school desegregation program began already since 1958; however, the schools in South having stubbornly resisted desegregation caused problems with their mayors because of Jim-Crow laws. Eleven years later, all schools started desegregation, and while children were sent to Lakeview Elementary School when I started the third grade.

One day as I was walking down the hall. I passed a group of boys,' and they were looking at me funny and pointing at my rear-end. They did this every day, so finally, I came up to them in the playground, and I asked, *"What was funny?"*

One boy with red hair and freckles said, *"You must be one of the monkeys without a tail."* I asked my mom why white people think that black people are monkeys. She said, *"That was what the Southern believed about us ever-since we came over from Africa."* The Dutch and Portuguese Sailors told the Europeans and American's that they cut off our tails because we were monkeys.

The story was a fairy tale about: *"How a race of people, the Cainites, who were from the 'Great Flood' hide themselves in the Ark-Of-Noah clothed as monkeys. Because they deceive God and the prophet Noah their skin turned dark, and they grew tails."*

They were bringing to light this factor of the prejudices of my people. We must study the true nature of the royal law of love found in James chapter two, verse eight.

Learning this supernatural (spiritual) law of love, you see the evidence that a person has the God-type-faith when the person works in the God-type-love.

Remember, in chapter one that we talked about the two laws working together to create the law of righteousness. Meet the second part of this law, called righteousness. Now, the royal law of law states: *"If thou shall love thy neighbor as thyself, ye do well."(James 2:8 KJV)*

If you say you love God, and you have respect person or prejudice, then you are a liar. Because if you love yourself more than your neighbor, then you don't love God! Owe no man anything, but to love one another, for he that loves another hath fulfilled the law. *"Love doesn't work badly toward his neighbor; thus, love fulfills of the natural and spiritual laws."(1 John 4:9-17 KJV)* To fulfill the divine law, and to love the *"self"* must be put to death.

Because the work is loving your neighbor, and the work according to the scriptures, is serving your neighbor. Moreover, your neighbor is the person you show mercy to in the act of Love.

The royal law of love will never work ill, which the word ill means your action will not result in suffering, distress, to act in hostility or unfriendliness, and your response will not be unpropitious: and ill omen. The treatment towards another person will not be up to the standards of kindness toward another person: ill-treatment is defined as scarily or with difficulty to an evil act, disaster, or harm.

The True Meaning of Love.

Something that causes suffering, or the Greek word κακός Kakos (*pronounced kak-os*) Apparently a primary word: that is, (subjectively) *depraved*, or (objectively) *injurious:* - harmful, evil, harm, ill.[63] Operate in the law of faith and the royal law of love, which will keep you God's righteousness, bringing peace, and strengthen you in joy in the Holy Spirit.

The precepts of the royal law of love can be found and studied **in 1 Corinthians chapter thirteen, verses four through eight, which these verses will be in the Amplified Version Plus notes**:

> *"Love endures long and is patient and kind; Love never is envious nor boils over with jealousy, is not boastful or vainglorious, does not display itself haughtily. It is not conceited (arrogant and inflated with pride); it is not rude (unmannerly) and does not act unbecomingly.*

---

[63] (Strong, 1890 [Public Domain]) G2556

Love (God's Love in us) does not insist on its rights or its own way, for it is not self-seeking; it is not touchy or fretful or resentful; it takes no account of the evil done to it [it pays no attention to a suffered wrong]. It does not rejoice at injustice and unrighteousness but rejoices when right and truth prevail.

Love bears up under anything and everything that comes, is ever ready to believe the best of every person, its hopes aren't diminished under all circumstances, and it endures everything [without weakening].

Love never fails [never fades out or becomes obsolete or comes to an end]. As for prophecy (the gift of interpreting the divine will and purpose), it will be fulfilled and pass away; as for tongues, they will be destroyed and cease; as for knowledge, it will pass away [it will lose its value and be superseded by truth]."

There is the gift of speaking what God has revealed, but revelation from God stops. There is the gift of speaking in other languages, but it will stop by myself. There is the gift of knowledge, but it becomes worthless and powerless.

Now for all of my charismatic brothers and sisters, beware because you may have all of these gifts. However, if you don't have love, your pew jumping, running around the church, tongue-talking-self will be worthless to God in heaven.

The word love in bold was describing the agape (pronounced ag-ah'-pay). This kind of love is unconditional, which this kind of love has a deep affection or benevolence toward all humankind. This word love defined explicitly as a love feast because you may find yourself sitting right next to a drunk. Praying for him or her through that hang-over.

The reason people have a problem with Christianity is simple. We only show love when it benefits us. Jesus said to the man who had invited him, *"When you give a dinner or a banquet, do not invite your friends or your brothers or your relatives or rich neighbors, lest they also invite you in return and you be repaid. But when you give a feast, invite the poor, the crippled, the lame, the blind, and you will be blessed, because they cannot repay you. For you will be repaid at the resurrection of the just."—Luke 14:12-14*

And that kind of love is conditional. The Spirit of God can sober them up. Jesus Christ paid for this feast already. The love feast is inside of you through the fruit of Spirit.

We just need to cultivate our love of unconditional embracing others as Christ embraced us. We need to throw a love feast party for some undeserving soul. So, get out the party hats and balloons. Go blow the birthday horns. Go invite the most unlovable slob other than yourself. Throw them a love feast!

CHAPTER 11
THE LAW OF KINDNESS

The Holy Ghost inside of you will help to cultivate a daily love-fest party for some undeserving soul, and by working the principle or law of the Spirit. This law is both a characteristic of God and a principle of Christ covenant, the law of kindness is the essence that both fulfills both the LAW (Torah) and the PROPHETS.

The heart of this sympathetic nature is for people to act in friendship or to have a forbearing and gentle nature. Stems from this law in action and is a characteristic that comes from the spiritual character of the Spirit of grace and supplications, which this law of kindness comes from grace the and mercy of God. The understanding of grace and mercy has its roots in the Old Testament and the dealings God shows to the children of Israel.

"She opened her mouth, wisdom, and in her tongue is the law of kindness." (Proverbs 31:26 KJV)

The word kindness and grace are twisted; the word grace is חֵן (pronounced *khane)* it meant graciousness and for one to show kindness *or* favor. It can also mean beauty.[64] So, if you got the unmerited favor of God through an act of kindness, it was this Hebrew word. Where the Hebrew word for mercy is defined the Hebrew word chehsed חֶסֶד(*pronounced kheh`-sed)* as kindness to bring piety toward God.[65] Notice that both definitions are actions of kindness.

In fact, the very character of God will prove that he is in your operating and demonstrating the law of kindness. As you begin to mature into the very nature of God. The born-again believer will begin to show signs of this principle of Christ.

---

[64] (Strong, 1890 [Public Domain]) H2580
[65] (Strong, 1890 [Public Domain]) H2617

When Jesus Christ sat on a grassy hillside. He gave the precepts of the law of kindness. The speech he gave could've anywhere from one or two and a half hours long. Moreover, this speech gave the blueprint of how a believer conducts his life. And how this principle brings deliverance and salvation to the lost and all that is around them.

The law of kindness will bring deliverance and salvation to those who will operate in the kingdom of God's principles of righteousness, peace, and joy in the Holy Ghost. The believer will tighten on the armor of Christ.

The believer must release all ties with the world. The believer fixes their eyes where Christ is seated, keeping their minds on things that are above, and not on things that are on earth (Colossians 3:2 KJV). As Matthew Henry declared about 2 Corinthians chapter ten, verse six. When he stated:

"The apostle's power to punish offenders (and that extraordinarily) is asserted in [... and being in readiness to avenge all disobedience, when your obedience shall be made full.] The apostle was a prime-minister in the kingdom of Christ, and chief officer in his army, and had in readiness (that is, he had power and authority at hand) to revenge all disobedience, or to punish offenders in a most exemplary and extraordinary manner.

The apostle speaks not of personal revenge, but of punishing disobedience to the gospel, and disorderly walking among church-members, by inflicting church-censures. Note, Though the apostle showed meekness and gentleness, yet he would not betray his authority; and, therefore, intimates that when he would commend those whose obedience was fulfilled, or manifested others would fall under severe censures."[66]

The law of kindness will cause you to go and start praying and supplicating towards the Lord Jesus about a person. This petition will bring both deliverance and salvation to the people you are praying about. The law of kindness must be wielded with the sword of one's tongue, and the edges are the Word of God... alive and active, sharper than any double-edged sword. It can cut all the way... penetrating to the division of soul and spirit, both of joints and marrow, and a discerner of the thoughts and intents of the heart.

For the bride of Christ must bring her water out of the wellspring of the belly, and it must be living... He that believes on me, as the scripture has said, out of his inward being shall flow rivers of living water. As it is written of the virtuous woman— *"She opens her mouth with wisdom; and upon her tongue is the law of kindness..." (Proverbs 31:26 MKJV)*

---

[66] (Henry 1662-1714 [Public Domain]0

Understanding must be our pillar, and the seven Spirits [characteristic] of God the Holy Ghost. This is the true essence and power of God in us. The law of kindness moves by the leading Spirit [characteristic] of meekness.

"Brothers, if a man is overtaken in a fault, you the spiritual ones restore such a one in the spirit of meekness, considering yourself, lest you also be tempted." (Galatians 6:1 MKJV)

You may remember the phrase: *"So whatever you wish that others would do to you, do also to them, for this is the Law and the Prophets."(Matthew 7:12 ESV)* as the golden rule. Well, this phrase comes from the above scripture. Many without the Holy Spirit have tried to do this in their own power. However, trying to fulfill the very nature of Christ without Christ, Jesus in vain.

Remember, in the precepts of the royal law of love: *"And if I shall bestow out all my earthy goods in food, clothing, and riches to the poor, and if I sacrifice my body that I'm burnt alive, but have not love, I profit nothing."(1 Corinthians 13:3 NLT & AMP paraphrased)* Bathing kindness love is more powerful than that random act of charity.

You need to picture a master teacher washing the feet of his students to prove he was a real master of all of them. *"It shall not be thus amongst you, but whosoever will be great among you, shall be your servant..."(Matthew 20:26 KJV)* So, a true teacher will serve his students and not just teach them his principles.

This is what Jesus did in John 13:5-20, and he even washed the feet of both Judas and Peter. They are the ones that would betray and deny him. Now that's power! Christ Jesus would even consider himself a great servant. He exercised this by holding his peace for their misconduct.

We find that precept of the law of kindness is found in Matthew chapter five, verse two, through chapter seven, verse twenty-seven. The Holy Spirit with the law of kindness makes the desire of the spirit of man (led by the Holy Spirit) to show compassion (love in action [Matthew 6:1-34]), mercy (love a defensive mode by forgiving [Matthew 7:1-6]), and the most important of them all acts of grace (the unmerited favor to give salvation and love by the power of Father God [Matthew 7:12-27]).

The law of kindness will always destroy the Spirit of haughtiness, and it reminds his people where they got their wealth from, and who gave them the love in their heart. In fact, the next law allows us to witness to the lost and deal with the immature and weak saints. All of this must be crowned in the vision of who Christ Jesus is, and what is his purpose for our lives.

CHAPTER 12
THE VISION

"And Jehovah answered me and said, Write the vision, and make it plain upon tablets, that he may run that readeth it. For the vision is yet for the appointed time, and it hurries toward the end, and shall not lie: though it tarry, wait for it; because it will surely come, it will not delay. Behold, his soul is puffed up, it is not upright in him; but the righteous shall live by his faith." (Habakkuk 2:2-4 ASV)

Now that we have learned to operate in some of the spiritual laws, why do we need these laws? It all goes back to the vision [I want all of you to know I don't know what else to call this because I sat down touched things and saw colors and unbelievable things.] I had while I was under sedation in the hospital. Jesus Christ spoke to me, plainly, saying, *"Michael, my word is in you. Go, tell my people that they have forgotten me and my covenant."*

The vision has to do with the love of the Father, not mine, or your vision to start a ministry, church, nor a non-profit business in the name of the Lord. No, it is the vision that was spoken in **Malachi chapter four verse six written in the King James Version**: *"And he shall turn the heart of the fathers to the children, and the heart of the children to their fathers; lest I come and smite the earth with a curse.— Malachi 4:6 King James Version"*

God, the Father, need us to do the bidding like Elijah (John the Baptist), and bring healing to the nation of the world. We have a duty as the Body of Christ to bring in the harvest of the world. We will bring in this harvest and lay. Moreover, we will lay the reward of the harvest at our master's feet, and we are not called to sit down eat, drink, and beat our fellow-servants waiting on the rapture!

Let us consider what regard we ought to have to our own duty and to the grace of God. Some would separate these as inconsistency. When it comes to your duty in the world, we live in saying, *"We can't be a Christian and work in the worldly of business."*

For four centuries, humanity only does the natural, but we will only the fulfilling of a holy call while in church.

Saying, "There is no room for grace in the world, and if it is the result of grace there is no place for duty (when I speak of duty I mean "religion": because religion is a form of loyalty and a sense of duty towards their God.).

So, we bring in our sense of duty into the industrial, logical, workplace, and we have to conform instead of conforming to the work environment. Because our duty and God's grace are nowhere opposed in dealing with matters of sanctification. It isn't the duty that please God, but the righteousness on has in action toward God.

The same with a vision, the vision is a form of the Word of God. And the vision is spoken to the person or people to go back and refer to the Word of God; it is truly from God. *The vision will still happen at the appointed time. It hurries toward its goal. It won't be a lie. If it's delayed, wait for it. It will certainly happen." (Matthew 25:14-30 [Luke 12:45])*

A vision is only as good as the purpose the Lord Jesus gives us, and we must remember that we are his building. We must be on guard as his watchmen on the wall of this building. We need to watch and wait for his coming. We, as the Body of Christ, should be aware of false-vision and the true vision from the Bible. We need to do our part by watching and praying.

"Unless the Lord builds the house, its builders labor in vain. Unless the Lord watches over the city, the watchmen stand guard in vain. It is vain for you to rise up early, to sit up late, and eat the bread of sorrows. For so He gives His beloved sleep. Lo, children are the inheritance of Jehovah; the fruit of the womb is a reward. As arrows in the hand of a mighty man, so are the of the young. Blessed is the who has his quiver full of them; they shall not be ashamed, but they shall speak with the enemies in the gate." (Habakkuk 2:3KJV)

As arrows in the hand of mighty, so are the sons of the young... means that we need to have our time of prayer over the son of the ministers of God. And praying and fasting will enhance the word of God!

The vision of the Lord is built brick by brick by the hands of his body, and the five fingers of the five-fold-ministry. The apostles, prophets, evangelist, pastor, and the teacher are the appendages that will assist all in the Body of Christ to come to the unity of the faith and of the full knowledge of the Son of God. So, what is the purpose of the five-fold ministers?

Fully mature believers who operate under one adjunct member of the Body of Christ must be content in their gift, they were given and know that unless the Lord builds there to mature as a believer. The fully mature believer's labor is in vain.

The Apostle *is the only member that is complete, and the spiritual character of the word echoes the voice of the prophets of the Old Testament. And It doesn't need to be given to another person to continue. However, the missionary, the Chief Elders, and church planters take that role. As long as they are following the teachings of the Apostles and the Doctrines of Christ, they can be considered apostles, and if one of them has a vision of Christ, he needs to be mentored and disciplined like any other believer.*

The *intercessors/prophets* *who prays over a ministry or city must remember that unless the Lord watches over the city, the petitions, confession, supplications, thanksgivings, and prayers are made on behalf of all men the watchmen stand guard in vain. The purpose of the watchmen is to make sure that the leaders and all the ones in the high position may lead a tranquil and quiet existence in all godliness and dignity.*

Because *the evangelist and pastor* *have a bad habit of getting ahead of God's plan by implementing new programs or tradition that our unbiblical in nature. When this happens, the elders of the pastoral leadership will begin to experience the sleepless nights of worry. This is the vanity talked about for those who rise up early in prayer. The church will eat the bread of sorrows because of the pastor actions.*

An evangelist *will get restless by trying to be a pastor instead of preaching the word to the lost on the streets. The church will begin to experience rest once the presbyteries of the watchmen begin to advise the church leaders. "Then he gives his beloved sleep. For this is good and satisfactory before God, our savior, to the appraise of the prominence of the fullness of Christ." (1 Timothy 2:1-3 KJV)*

The teacher *must know the word and study diligently to disciple others the basic understanding of the Doctrines of Christ (Hebrews 6:1-2), and they should be disciplined and under church leadership. Furthermore, they must hear the voice of the Lord.* Because part of walking in your purpose is to the agony of letting the vision mature, it will certainly happen. We as Body of Christ must do as it is written in Matthew chapter twenty-four verse thirteen that reads: *"But he that shall endure to the end, the same shall be saved."*

CHAPTER 13
THE LAW OF SPIRIT OF LIFE IN CHRIST JESUS

"Being then made free from sin, ye became the servants of righteousness. But now being made free from sin, and become servants to God, ye have your fruit unto holiness, and the end everlasting life." (Romans 6:18, 22)

In this scripture, we must become servants of righteousness, or we as mankind will never be free from sin. This fact keeps us in the spirit of bondage. The spirit of bondage is an addiction (sex, drugs, overeating, drunkenness, self-righteousness, religious traditionalism, excessive compulsive behavior, and gambling), and these additions can only come out by a person crying out towards the Father in Heaven.

We must receive the freedom that can't come by a Declaration of Independence of any nation away from God. Because, true freedom comes by your life totally hidden in the Lord God. And not by the physical nature of action written in the charter that states we are free and endowed by our Creator. We, as a people, never want to believe in the one that can give us true liberty.

In the Garden of Eden, there were many fruit trees, but only two fruit trees were unique and had special powers. The first one was in the midst of the garden, this tree was called the Tree of the Knowledge of Good and Evil, and then there was the Tree of Life. The fruit of that tree is called holiness, which this tree a bear fruit by this means according to the word *"...a living sacrifice, holy, acceptable unto God." (Romans 12:1b KJV)*

Then to live in (under) the law of the Spirit of life in Christ Jesus makes you separated in holiness, accepted by deliverance, and sanctified unto life. Moreover, to have anything else would cause the person to work under sin, death, and bring justice to all who don't operate by this principle in Christ Jesus, and none are indeed free without salvation.

God will give all things to those willing to obey his command because of the covenant of the blood of Jesus. And he is ready, by the anointing of the Holy Spirit, a famous preach of the charismatic movement would say, *"We need to put God's excellent of spirit on our natural to make the supernatural happen in our lives,"* and you'll be able to do the works of God in righteousness.

You'll be able to accomplish *"His Will"* supernaturally in your life, and you will be able to stand and never fail. And will operate in the grace of the Spirit and not the deeds of works by the law. We can facilitate mercy to people. Even in our weakest moment, Jesus Christ did on the cross.

Life then is not the essence, but life is to provide the means by faith in Jesus Christ's Blood through the grace. Know that God Almighty has given man his grace by the Spirit of God, which this Spirit is known as the Holy Spirit. Humanity truly sees that there is more to the person of God...

Now cross-reference over to the book of Zechariah 3:8-9 with the King James Version: *"Hear now, O Joshua the high priest, thou, and thy fellows that sit before thee: for they are men wondered at: for, behold, I will bring forth my servant the BRANCH. For behold the stone that I have laid before Joshua; upon one stone shall be seven eyes: behold, I will engrave the graving thereof, saith the LORD of hosts, and I will remove the iniquity of that land in one day."*

Now let's find out who is "THE BRANCH" the Lord God is talking about to the prophet. This reference is found in Isaiah 11:1-2, which reads: *"And there shall come forth a rod out of the stem of Jesse, and a Branch shall grow out of his roots: And the spirit of the LORD shall rest upon him, the spirit of wisdom and understanding, the spirit of counsel and might, the spirit of knowledge and of the fear of the LORD..."*

Notice that the same branch that is in the person of Jesus of Nazareth, is referred to in John the fourteenth chapter, but in that case, he is called branches. Christ Jesus, the anointed one, has shown in revelation in the Word of God. We need to see what the seven spirits of God are listed. Each of the lamps only symbolizes who Christ is in the Godhead, and these Spirits are the Spirit Christ's Character.

These seven characteristics are what you would see in God. The Spirit of wisdom and understanding, the Spirit of counsel and might, the Spirit of the knowledge and the fear of the Lord, the Spirit of faith, the Spirit of meekness, the Spirit of grace and supplications, and finally, the Spirit of prophecy.

And out of the throne proceeded lightnings and thundering's and voices: and there were seven lamps of fire burning before the throne, which are the seven Spirits of God.[67]

Figure 2

Look at the drawing above (Figure 2) that shows each bowel. This is the same lamp that was once in the Old Testament Tabernacle and Solomon's Temple. Look carefully at the picture and see the symbol used. The drawing is the menorah that is found in the Holy Place

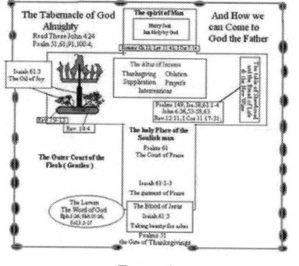

Figure 3

Now, look at where the menorah was in the Temple of Solomon and the Tabernacle. God is always facing in the Northern direction, that is where the Altar of Incense is

---

[67] The Seven Spirits of God a] Isaiah 11:2; b] 2 Corinthians 4:13; c]Galatians 6:1; d] Zechariah 12:10; e] Revelation 19:10

located. The menorah is facing the Western. The Table of Shewbread is in the Eastern, and the Brazen Altar and the Lavern are in the Southern portion of the Temple.

The menorah was symbolic of the tree of life, which bears the fruit of the Spirit. Figure 2 is the menorah that is also what Moses saw in the throne room of God, and the menorah and all of the items in the Holy place is a shadow of the Spirit of Christ. We, being Christ offspring, can freely eat of this tree now because of the Blood of Christ.

This symbol gives some clarity to the Tree of Life, and to what the Apostle John must have seen in the book of revelation. Please keep in mind that these are only drawings of what I saw while I was in heaven being judged. Yes, that right, I said, judged. The commission I was given was a judgment. I have forgotten him, and his covenant, so he wants me to go tell his people that we have forgotten him and his promise.

This covenant starts with the law of the Spirit of life in Christ Jesus, the law of faith, the law of liberty, the law of kindness, the royal law of love, the law of righteousness, and the law of sin and death. The Seven Spirits of God were also talked about by Paul when he referred to the Spirit of faith and meekness, and Paul also referred to four of the spiritual laws in Romans chapter three verse twenty-seven, chapter eight verse two, and chapter nine verse thirty-one.

The law of the Spirit of life in Christ Jesus that reads: *"For the law of the Spirit of life in Christ Jesus hath made me free from the law of sin and death."(Romans 8:2 KJV)* Laid the foundation for giving life and freedom to all of God's being. And this principle gave power to mankind to offer experience. Therefore, as Paul wrote about this law, it is what allows true freedom to take place in all creation.

Everything in God's creation must operate by this same principle, and this principle of God's creatures have their own glory. This glory allows us to live, move, and their own being. If we, as humans try to operate in another kind of beauty.

We violate this principle law of the Spirit of life that was established before the foundations of the world. *"Father, I will say that they also, whom thou hast given me, be with me where I am; that they may behold my glory, which thou hast given me: for thou lovedst me before the foundation of the world."(John 17:24 KJV)*

This violation of trying to take the glory of God and make it your own is what Adam did in the garden. Trying to be like a god when he could only become a Son of God. Both Adam and Eve were created beings like Satan was an angel. Humanity was still a created; furthermore, Adam wanted to receive worship and knowledge that wasn't his to own.

The old-timers in my youth use to say it best: *"Stay in your own lane."* He was trying to be something that he was never called to be, and that was a god. Both Adam and Eve operated in doubt, which the doubt came in the form of fear when Satan asked

Eve (while Adam was standing right there. He didn't interrupt the conversation because he might have made Eve angry.) *"Did God actually say, 'You shall not to eat from any tree of the garden'?" (Genesis 3:1 ESV)*

They walked out of faith, as it is written: "For whatever does not proceed from faith is sin." (Romans 14:23 ESV) After sinned came death, the separation of the spirit of man connected with the Spirit of God. So, to better understand sin and death, we need to read further.

CHAPTER 14
THE LAW OF SIN AND DEATH

This chapter we will be studying will make short and sweet, because to be honest with you. All of us already know how to sin or the operation of sin. It's the mechanism or the infestation of crime into a person's being. And once it is explained through the Holy Spirit to you, the reader, how Satan uses our own glory (authority) steal our strength, kill life to send you to hell, and destroy your legacy by you winding up in the Lake of Fire.

Once you learn this about the principle of the mechanism of sin and death. You will never let him get away with it again. Just think of Satan's mode of operation like that of a seed being planted. There is the planting of the grain, then the germination of the seed into the root system, and the plant that produces the fruit. We will study the Genesis account of the fall of mankind found in Genesis chapter three, verses one through seven.

First, let us understand how the principle/law works. To that, we must go to the Word of God: *"Let no man say when he is tempted, I am tempted of God, for God cannot be tempted, neither tempts he any man; but every man is drawn away of his own lust and enticed. Then when the lust is conceived, it bringeth forth sin, and sin, when it is finished, bringeth forth death." (James 1:13-15 KJV)*

Now, do you see what Satan does to us? He studied our nature, and he used our own power (authority) against us. You say, how so? It is simple, first invade the natural to control the spiritual.

Second, the mechanism of this principle/law carrot and stick philosophy. The carrot tempted Eve when Satan told her she would be like gods knowing both good and evil [verse 5]. Then when she saw that it was good for food (the lust of the flesh), and (the fruit) was pleasant to the eyes (lust of the eyes), and could make one wise [verse 6] (like gods [pride of life]). The stick both Adam and Eve intuitively knew they had sinned, and they saw they were naked [verse 7].

The law of sin and death was brought about because Satan was so wicked in his attempt to overthrow the Kingdom of God. There had to be a final solution for rebellion, and the answer was death. However, God isn't bound by these supernatural (spiritual) laws (because he doesn't tempt humanity, nor is he tempted by evil), and God never uses the carrot and stick method to teach us anything.

The spiritual laws are to guide humanity and mankind into a greater understanding of becoming and walking like Christ, as he did while among all of creation. We aren't under the curse of the (natural) law, in which this natural law of the Mosaic law is both carnal and spiritual, as we studied in past chapters.

The Ten Commandments were written by the finger of God in Mount Sinai. God never intended for mankind nor humanity to live by the carnal (moral code) laws of the commandments. *"Christ (Jesus through his sacrifice) hath redeemed us from the curse of the law, and being made a curse for us, for it is written, cursed is every one that hangs on a tree." (Galatians 3:13 ESV)*

What is the real purpose of the law? Being under the law of sin and death, uses the Ten Commandments, the Lord God wrote, and the six hundred and thirteen Levitical and Sabbatical that Moses wrote. They became guidance to Israel and was a light to make human beings cry out to Christ. The Lord God, who is Jesus when he spoke to Moses, knew we never could keep the law. Christ death justified us by faith, but after that faith is come, we are no longer under a schoolmaster.

According to the scriptures, the schoolmaster is the Mosaic law. These laws put mankind and humanity under bondage. Now we have received, not the Spirit of the world, but the Spirit, which is of God. The power that Satan uses is the fact that he knows our power (authority) that glory or power (authority) given by God Almighty. And when we receive his Spirit, we might know the things that God will freely give to us by the fruit of the Spirit, the seven characteristics of God, and the gifts of the Spirit.[68]

Wherein, by using the act of worship, meaning, God is to be worshipped in Spirit (the things mention in the last paragraph,[254,] and in truth, our words are the power.[255] Satan knows about the second factor, but he doesn't understand about the first factor.

Because he is blinded by pride, thinking deserves the same worship as God Almighty. He will plant false visions, thoughts, and dreams in our imagination. When he does that, our soul begins to order our emotions, mind, and will order our flesh to move out of fear, and not act by faith.

"And [that He] might free all those who through [the haunting] fear of death was held in slavery throughout their lives." (Proverbs 18:21 ESV)

---

[68] 2 Corinthians 3:17 a] Galatians 5:22-23; b] Revelation 4:5 (Isaiah 11:2; Zechariah 12:10; 2 Corinthian 4:13; Galatians 6:1; Revelation 19:10); c] 1 Corinthian 12:8-10

It was by the misuses of the law of sin and death; which Satan launched his Coup D'ètat to take dominion over the earth. And make the world his as a ransom. Satan's weapons are always the same fear, bondage, and death.

Man was given the authority to curse sin with the action of death. This action was what we should be doing. Now we are in Christ Jesus we should by using the act of worshipping God is to be worshipped in Spirit and in truth, our words have the power to curse temptation, and Satan's power would reflex back at him. He sees his dark mirror image and runs away. We reflect the power and light of Christ Jesus. The Discussion of this authority and how the body of Christ will one day victoriously move is discussed in chapter nineteen.

When you are beginning to walk into the enticement of lust, remember, sin is coming with the obsession of the soul's foolish enjoyment of bondage. Then fear will come toward you with its chains to collect. When it's time to pay the debt of your blissful days of pleasure of working in the flesh, for the earnings of sin is death. We now know what this means. So, how do we operate in liberty to be free from sins chains?

CHAPTER 15
THE LAW OF LIBERTY

But whoso looketh into the perfect law of liberty, and continued therein, he is not a forgetful hearer, but a doer of the work, this man shall be blessed in his deed. So, speak ye, and so do, as they that shall be judged by the law of liberty. (James 1:25; 2:12)

Reading the above scripture informs the saint of God that they cannot operate just in the natural realm. When it comes to coming into the salvation of just mentally assenting or just merely hearing the word with no action.

We need to read and do the Word of God by operating in the law of liberty. This person becomes a doer of the work of God. We will abide in the promises of the master, and the whole being of a person will bring the very blessing of man in Christ to ourselves.

Now to I want to side-bar this subject of blessing for a moment, and look at a scripture that comes from the natural law of progression will assist the believer in operating moving forward in the spiritual law of liberty. Progression [pronounced prəˈgreSHən] noun: the process of developing or moving gradually towards a more advanced state of being whole.[69]

The process can also affect the events of a person to move in a backward in the opposite direction, cursed and towards death. And the person can move toward the blessing of God, and having a life, and more abundantly. This was how THE LORD GOD dealt with Israel, the two scripture we are going to look at.

The first scripture is found in **the Amplified version Deuteronomy chapter thirty verse nineteen, which it reads:** *"I call heaven and earth to witness this day against you that I have set before you life and death, the blessings and the curses; therefore, choose life, that you and your descendants may live."* So, what does this mean? God wants to choose life, and with life comes obedience to his laws.

---

[69] (Random House Publisher Group, 1833) paraphrased

Second, we need to know what happens. We don't obey the laws of God. The answer is in the whole chapter of Deuteronomy twenty-eight that reads, so let's begin our study.

(Verses 1-6) You will receive the blessing of God that when you obey the Lord God, who will make you highly favor before humanity to worship God. When they ask you, why are you blessed? You will be blessed in your city and the countryside areas. Your children and your crops won't die before their appointed time to be harvested, and your herds of cattle, your flocks of sheep and goats, and flocks of chickens, ducks, and geese. What you store up as food will not rot or mildew. You and your family will be blessed to come into any country you conquer and blessed when you leave the country to your heirs.

(Verses 7-11) When you attack an opposing enemy, whether foreign or domestic. The attack will come at you one way, and the angels of the Lord and your armies will outnumber them to make them flee seven ways. You will never go through a famine in your body, domesticated animals, or your crops.

(Verses 12-14) It will always rain at the proper time, and the Lord God will bless the work of your hand. You will lend to many nations and never borrow from them, so they can extract interest on you and put you in slavery. The Lord God will keep you as long as you never go, and you or your family backsides from the law of the Lord God.

Now take these twelve verses of blessing and apply a curse to it. And these courses are designed to make you repent. And if you don't repent, and you choose to rebel, then these curses will bring death.

(Verses 16-21) You are cured in the city and the countryside. You're cursed in the storehouse. You animal, crops, and even your children are cursed. You will feel bitter anger, and the world will rebuke you. Hatred will fill your life, and all that you do in your work. Cursed coming in a country that is fleeing to and cursed are you when you leave any country. Your destruction will come through pestilence to drive you off the land.

(Verses 22-23) You and your heirs will be plagued with cancer, influenza, unbearable heat, and the plague of mildew blast you and your crops. The sword of war will chase you and your successors. The heavens won't bless you with rain, and your prayers will have iron over your head.

(Verses 24-30) Your corpse will be food for both the bird and animal. Every plague that destroyed Egypt will consume you. Blindness, insanity, heart failure, because of the horror of everything that is happened to you. Poverty will overtake you, and no one will help you out of the pit you dug for yourself. You try to marry a wife, and another man takes her for his own. You build a house, and someone else lives in it. You plant a vineyard, and someone else benefits from the fruits of your labor.

(Verses 31-43) The slaughter of your livestock will overtake you. And your cities will overwhelm you as well. Your son and daughter are taken from you, and even the fruit of your land is eaten up then burn down. All you can do is weep in front of the destruction that is before you. Cancer sores on your head and gangrene sore grow on your feet, causing you to grind your teeth and gnawing of your tongued. Herds of locust with devour your land, and all types of worms blight the land. You will have a wicked king that will force you to serve his gods. None of the fruit trees of the olives, grapes, or any fruit trees will be harvested. The stranger than is invited into your country will become successful while you fall into poverty.

(Verses 44-52) You will become the borrower and have to give back in high interest. You always be a servant to other nations. Other kingdoms will chase you; you will serve your enemies. You die of hunger, feel nakedness, and be put under the yoke of bondage. Your curse will be so bad that other nations will eat the fruits of your labor. Those nations will besiege your homeland and tear down everything your countrymen built.

(Verses 53-59) These curses will cause you to eat your own children, to the point that your neighbor will fight you for the flesh of his children he has for food. Even a graceful lady will become an evil woman to practice cannibalism with her own children. Because the war is so violent and fierce.

(Verses 60-68) If you don't keep the natural law of progression every plague, the Lord God did to Egypt will be done on you. Even the Lord God promised to bring an enemy that will put you and your countrymen in chains. And you shall go one ship in far countries in chains. And unless you repent, you will never see your country again.

This was what THE LORD GOD required from Israel these natural laws were based on the other natural laws of the Ten Commandments, the Levitical and Sabbatical laws, and the law of reciprocity (sowing and reaping). It being a conditional law of either showing grace if you obey or judgment for disobedience that progressively gets worst if the person doesn't repent. The Jewish people had no room for error because it was a conditional covenant. You do right, and you get a life and blessed. You do wrong, you get death and cursed.

So, we are blessed in the Church Era by the Christ deeds and not ours. Because as I said before, we can't keep the laws of God in word or deed. However, in Christ, we can work in the spiritual laws of life, liberty, faith, love, kindness, and righteousness. Because show all humanity unconditional love by the sacrificial deed of Christ death on the cross.

In the Old Testament Covenant, the Jewish people lived in a sacrificial progression of fear. Still, in the New Testament, Humanity could receive the love of God through Christ Jesus and have the liberty to obey by grace God the Father with the Holy Spirit correcting his child.

Thus, this is what blessing really amounts up to. Blessing doesn't always have to be monetary. Because deeds of obedience bring not only a blessing but life, liberty, and the pursuit of happiness. However, deeds of disobedience will bring cursing and death, which disobedience will bring death (both spiritual and naturally), bondage, and an overwhelming feeling of depression.

People speaking or acting in the law of liberty will fully understand that they can still be judged by their actions and deeds while the law of liberty changes into a moral decision; because they will violate the royal law of love and become selfish in their deeds.

The instruction given by Christ was simple when he said, *"Therefore all things whatsoever ye that men should do to you, do ye even so to them: for this is the law and the prophets." (Matthew 7:12 ISV)*

This law is a principle of the law of kindness, but you are instructed not just to respect them in their beliefs, ideologies, or even their sin.

Because law centers on both love and respect for the other's sinner or saint's maturity and growth. Trying to understand how God the Father views us as a family is a mystery, yet believer's and religious people alike will see others through carnal eyes of being an adult has caused much strife in the body in Christ Jesus. This new creature isn't like the sinner (old man) that is under the laws of humanity, but he should operate much like Jesus of Nazareth did in the spiritual realm, which this realm is the supernatural.

The newborn-again Christ-like-baby must mature the very image of Christ Jesus himself. He must die to self, hate sin, and love all mankind. Because this person knows that they were delivered from becoming a prisoner of this world (POW) that needs to see the mater, who is their redeemer.

The mature believers must help the human to make their eternal choice that choice is every right. We are like flying fish with the law of liberty; eventually, we will have to return to the water that birthed us.

According to their will and liberty, the believers are to move in the character of God's Spirits (see chapter thirteen, the law of the Spirit of life in Christ Jesus), and that moving in liberty is what this law is all about. I will explain to you in these next few pages how to read and understand these principles work. To learn the practicality of the law of liberty. We must learn through the Apostles Paul.

Although he never mentions this particular supernatural law by name. Paul did define it for us in 1 Corinthians 6:12; 10:23, 26 that reads: *"All things are lawful unto me, but not all things are expedient: All things are lawful for me, I will not be brought under the power of any."*

In the reading of the first phrase, "... All things are lawful unto me, not all things are expedient..." While I was serving in our country, I learned even shouted that "Discipline is the obedience order!" So, it is with the disciple of Christ, it is understood the disciple of Christ has the right to anything, and where the Spirit of the Lord is, there is liberty. However, with this liberty, comes the discipline to know the difference to do or not to do.

Mankind may have the liberty to do anything, and everything in Christ, but these freedoms come with the price of both your witness and your health being damaged. The word "expedient" is an adjective, which means to act to bring about to a particular purpose, or to serve a narrow or selfish interest. Yet acting this way will never be profitable. All things are lawful for the man of God, or will this natural thinking make you a sellout?

You can choose to give your dominion, and lose your authority toward the flesh, the world, or Satan. When you act like Adam, who knew the truth but did honor it. When you act like this, you just put a price on your head, for the devil to sell your earthly goods, which the body, soul, and the spirit of man are now worthless. Matthew Henry is quoted:

"He tells them that many things lawful in themselves were not expedient at certain times, and under particular circumstances, and Christians should not barely consider what is in itself lawful to be done"[70]

He has also said, *"Note, there is a liberty wherewith Christ has made us free, in which we must stand fast."*[71] Satan may be the commander of the armies of hell, but it is the works of the flesh that are the pawn driven by the hordes of hell. It is deliverance by the blood of Christ, verses to tempted God hand to discipline.

Surely Paul would never carry this liberty, so far as to put himself into the power of any bodily appetite. All things are lawful for mankind, but all things are not constructive to the character and edifying to the spiritual life.

The law of liberty works against selfishness, which selfishness is the working two accomplishments towards your personal goals? The law of liberty doesn't allow anyone to work for a self-center goal. Moreover, if those goals aren't met, the person will want revenge.

And in the body of Christ is never the option. We are to love our neighbor as ourselves. The story of the Good Samaritan is a classic parable on how to treat those in need or hurting.

[70] (Henry 1662-1714 [Public Domain])
[71] (Henry 1662-1714 [Public Domain])

The law of liberty works against idolatry, which this sinful action is the breaking of the tenth commandment that is covetousness. And this is the operation of the spirit of whoredom. This particular spirit can only operate under the root of stubbornness and the seed of iniquity, which this seed produces the fruit of idolatry.

Therefore, the Holy Spirit uses the law of liberty to remind the believer that the earth is the Lords, and he has the liberty to do with his creation as he wills. He can test our faithfulness by allowing Satan, the world, or even our own flesh with sins or iniquities that are hidden on the inside of us. He does to prove his children and to prune dead and unwanted things in a person's life that is a believer.

He is giving through blessing to us to see if we will be good stewards of the blessings. We need to remember that everything we have belongs to God and the scripture: *"I can do all things through Christ Jesus, which strengthened me... My God will supply all my need according to his riches and glory through Christ Jesus."(Philippians 4:13,19)* Everything in the earth has been given to the race of man to be a steward of Gods property. Knowing these facts, we must ask the question. How do we operate as stewards of what God has given us?

Therefore, the Holy Spirit (Ghost) uses the law of liberty to remind the believer that the earth is the Lord's Everything in the earth has been given to the race of man, who is the steward of God's property. We must never violate the seventh natural law that is defined as: the authority of mankind over all creation. Knowing this fact, we are to not strive to only give 10% of just money, but we must give sacrificially both the natural and the spiritual.

Now we come to the principles of how to operate in the law of liberty, remember this as I said before: "I can do all things through Christ, which strengthened me. This strength can only come and takes place when we read the masters manual from the Chief Shepherd.

How to deal with the strong and weak Christian, even if that weak belief is you? This how-to-be-like-Christ help book can't be found in any bookstore unless you look in the Bible under Romans chapter fourteen, which this chapter is free to all.

In verses 1-5: Paul tells the pastors and the people of Rome to let the meeker uphold, the weaker in faith and not judge them in their fleshly and soulish deeds. However, they should sustain those who are weak by teaching Christ's commandments (the spiritual laws) to them, and then covering them in prayer and forgiveness when they sin.

The next five verses in chapter fourteen of Romans reminds us that whether we are saved or lost, and whether we live or die, it is God that sustains all of mankind. Only God the Father can hold us in judgment, so we are warned not to criticize or pass judgment.

They will all stand before his judgment-seat; much like I did in the vision I had of "the passion" We either honor God with what we confess out of our mouths, and bless those who are weaker, or condemn them. When we actually do either bless or condemn them, we are also doing the same to God. I much like communion when we don't discern the body of Christ correctly.

As Matthew Henry said, "They shall **be guilty of the body and blood of the Lord***,' of violating this sacred institution, of despising his body and blood. They act as if they...* '**counted the blood of the covenant, wherewith they are sanctified, an unholy thing,'** *They profane the institution, and in a manner crucify their Savior over again. Instead of being cleansed by his blood, they are guilty of his blood. It is a great hazard which they run:* '**They eat and drink judgment to themselves***.' They provoke God and are likely to bring down punishment on themselves.*

No doubt, but they incur great guilt, and so render themselves liable to damnation, to spiritual judgments and eternal misery. Every sin is in its own nature damning, and therefore, surely so heinous a sin as profaning such a holy ordinance..." In verses 6-12: We can't use our liberty to spawn hatred towards humanity. Thereby, we pronounce over both humanity and God our judgment over both. Sitting in the seat of a god. The only reason we criticize others or even God is to justify our own selfish nature. You can't judge others based on what they eat or when, what, how, or why they worship God.[72]

In verses 13-17: According to Romans, to be accepted in the kingdom of God isn't based on our carnal aspiration of being a good person. This aspiration is based on legalism and not righteousness. Legalism states: If one does good by deeds; then one is good. However, I one doesn't do good by deeds, you are evil.

So, this person needs to be righteous. Being righteous is to have faith and love towards God. To have that kind of faith and love. We must be born again and receive the power of faith and the gift of love.

This is why the kingdom of God isn't based on the natural thing of possession. Still, it is righteousness (faith & love, which is what Jesus Christ operates under the laws of righteousness), peace (the state the soul is in regardless of circumstance or surroundings), joy (which the strength of joy operates through the law of liberty), in the Holy Ghost.

---

[72] (Henry 1662-1714 [Public Domain])

Operating in these characteristics of the fruit of the Spirit of God, you will be pleasing to God and approved by men as you move in true liberty. True liberty can only be defined as peace and joy in God that will make harmony for the mutual upbuilding edification, and the development of one another.

Finally, true liberty isn't to do what you want when you want at the expense of others, but it's not to do anything that would cause your brother or sister to stumble, and the person turns away from God. The person that causes them to stumble in sins of offense or weakening them has done the greater sinning. First, we can prove all of this by knowing that your personal convictions should be done in the presence of God. You must have enough self-control to keep them to yourself. Secondly, strive only to know the truth and obey Christ Jesus' will for your life in faith.

Therefore, doubts about what to eat, drink, smoke, the wearing of clothing, or other confusing convictions aren't an act of faith. As it is written, for whatsoever is not of faith is sin. We, as the body of Christ, have been called to liberty; we get this liberty by humbling ourselves and receiving the adoption through the spirit of grace and supplication by calling on Abba, Father.

Therefore, operating under the law of liberty allows love to serve one another, not to seek us but each other instead of striving and bickering. Striving stops the liberty of God moving to help in a time of provision. The law of liberty allows a person to walk habitually in the Holy Ghost, which will break the spirit of bondage to fear and freedom from the sting of death.

Sinning can only assist a person in gratifying the cravings and the desires of the flesh; it allows mankind's nature to be formed without God. Being led by the Holy Ghost or the carnal nature is a choice which brings two things: with the Holy Spirit, you will be led to operating in the law of the spirit of life in Christ Jesus and will free you from the law of sin and death.

Finally, being led by the carnal nature, you will only fulfill the works of the flesh. The works of the flesh are a consequence of the law of sin and death, and walking in the spirit results in the law of the spirit of life in Christ Jesus and the law of liberty.

The fruit of the spirit are the rewards of our not operating in the sensual nature of the world, which makes a disciple a prisoner of this world. Operating in the consequences of these laws will bring both supernatural and natural results, but the fruit of the Spirit, which is the reward of the law of liberty (which is the result of righteousness, peace, and joy, which brings the moving of the Holy Ghost).

Where the Spirit of the Lord is there is liberty, which will never allow the law of sin death is now an offensive weapon for the believer that at one time was the force that bound you to the flesh, the world, and Satan's control.

Now the forces that will protect you because you are the righteousness of Christ Jesus, which is the Tree of Life. Matthew Henry states: *"The covenant of grace made with us in Christ is a treasury of merit and grace, and thence we receive pardon and a new nature, are free from the law of sin and death, that is, both from the guilt and power of sin - from the course of the law, and the dominion of the flesh. We are under another covenant, another master, another husband, under the law of the Spirit, the law that gives the Spirit, spiritual life to qualify us for eternal." (Hebrews 10:29 AMP)*

The resurrected power of Jesus Christ can and does bring the hardest sinner to their knees, but if you continue to rebel by seeking the laws of the natural and nature. You can open the door of the works of charismatic witchcraft and the spirit of divination, which in the body of Christ at this moment.

CHAPTER 16
CHARISMATIC WITCHCRAFT AND THE SPIRIT OF DIVINATION IN THE BODY OF CHRIST TODAY

Is the purpose of being Spirit-filled is so we can conduct a worship service that resembles a three-ring circus? Should we turn God's house into a house of merchandise? Should we entertain each other with magic shows and concerts?

Now you've read some interesting things, and now you're saying, Well, Mr. Tsaphah, all this information is nice, but how does all of this tie in with the title that you have given this particular chapter? Well, it's simple; this statement from the Bible reads, "… rebellion is as the sin of witchcraft."—*1 Samuel 15:23 KJV.* The word, "witchcraft," comes from the Hebrew word, קֶסֶם Qesem (*pronounced Keh'-Sem*), a lot or by magical scroll, also divination (include its fee) an oracle, divine sentence that seeks for a reward.[73] Notice the word, "divination," which shows up in the book of Acts chapter sixteen, verse sixteen.

The word, "charismatic," comes from the word, "charisma," from the Greek, χάρισμα charizomai (*pronounced Khar-id'-zom-ahee*) to grant a personal favor, that is, gratuitously, in kindness, pardon or rescue and in passion. [74]

But Satan has perverted this free gift to a movement that is now turned into the church era of the Laodiceans. Embracing those who work in divination, and producing a false miracle. Like throwing coins on the floor, and they say it fell from heaven.

The chapter you are reading is not a witch hunt, but it deals with the spirit of divination, and the new form of the Catholic Apostolic Church from the eighteenth century. Paul ministered to a woman that had a demonic spirit, known as a spirit of divination.

This very same spirit that has crept into the church of the body of Christ, which unknowingly to most Christians, are calling themselves oracles, miracles works, ministers, and now gods that are wielding the deadly divine sentences of death in

---

[73] (Strong 1890 [Public Domain]) H7081
[74] (Strong 1890 [Public Domain]} G5483

others' lives. Some of the miracles, signs, and lying wonders that have been used to fool the very elect of God into following their magic shows that charge many for a fee to be healed.

It goes by many names, but this movement had its start in the late eighteenth century and early nineteenth century. In the gospel of **Matthew chapter twenty-four verses twenty-four:** *"For there shall arise false Christs, and false prophets, and shall shew great signs and wonders; insomuch that, if it were possible, they should deceive the very elect."* These lying wonders, as the reads, are only the start of the charismatic witchcraft movement. Still, the hidden spellbinders are the prayer of those thinking that they are praying to God. When only Satan is answering prayers through a familiar spirit.

And any Christian could be guilty of this example of a mantis-type prayers of death and sickness over a rebellious loved one. Once these prayers are done, the victims find themselves are revived by a preacher-like-voodoo-witch doctor who saves the humbled, loved one from destruction. And a person doesn't have faith in God, but a fear that they will do something, so bad they God will kill them.

So, what is the difference between this and grandma's prayer for her son to come to Jesus? She will state, *"Even if you have to kill him!"* Show me if Jesus prayed any of thought type of prayers over the unrighteous of his day. (Read John chapter seventeen)

Now on an interesting note about the Greek word for "divination" the word Πύθων Puthone (pronounced poo-thone) was the seat of evil in the region. The temple of Delphi in Greece is where the famous oracle was located. A (talking like Genesis 3:1) python that was supposed to be a diviner or soothsayer used to foretell the future for a fee. This python was a mythological giant snake in Greek mythology, and he was the son of the goddess of mother earth Gaia, and he came from the slime that was produced after the Great Flood.

This belief came to the surface once the philosophers had covered up their idolatry by making themselves the new order of priesthood. They started schools, much like the school of the Heraclitus of Ephesus (535-475 BCE). He continued the search of the Ionians for a primary substance for the force behind all power.

Heraclitus claimed it to be about the fire of the gods that came from heaven. He also said, *"Listening not to me but to the logos it is wise to agree that all things are one."*[75] Many of the other noted philosophers (Socrates, Aristotle, and Plato) noticed that the logos doctrine of Heraclitus, which identified the laws of nature with a divine mind, developed into the pantheistic theology of Stoicism, which formulated the doctrine of metaphysics that they believed the study of metaphysics could answer the cosmic riddle.

---

[75] (Non-Profit from Wikipedia, the free encyclopedia, 2020) "Heraclitus quote on Logos"

So, the worship of Mother Earth and the study of metaphysics movement that surfaced in the sixties and seventies has its origin form this philosophy. This religious philosophy became a branch of philosophy concerned with the nature of ultimate reality. The 13th-century philosopher and theologian St. Thomas Aquinas declared that the cognition of God, through a causal study of finite sensible beings, was the aim of metaphysics.

The rise of scientific study in the 16th century soon brought metaphysics and other Greek philosophies into the church. These doctrines have crept in as the new gods of the church but notice that it was in the Roman Catholic Church in which these heresies arose.

There is the Roman Catholic dogma of the immaculate conception, a holding that from the first instant of its creation, the soul of the Virgin Mary was free from original sin. She was given the title the Queen of Heaven, the Mother of God, or that she is the Bride of God. He impregnated her, instead of the Holy Spirit moving upon her, and He activated her eggs in her womb.

This doctrine is not to be confused with that of the virgin birth, which holds that Jesus Christ was born of a mother that was a virgin. The Mother Religion/Revived Catholic Apostolic Church was slowly creeping into the worship of the Church of Our Lord Jesus Christ, which came from Scottish theologian John Duns Scotus, who was a member of the Roman Catholic Church. John Scotus believed and argued that it is better to construct a metaphysical argument for the existence of God.

John Scotus was a **realist** about a given object is the view that this object exists in reality independently of our conceptual scheme. He disliked the hypothesis rather that humanity has an innate nature the more common physical argument from motion favored by Aquinas. He followed many of the philosophers of the past merging theology and philosophy.

The Holy Catholic Apostolic Church would declare in 1833 Edward Irving was condemned and deposed from the ministry of the Church of Scotland because of his teaching concerning "the sinfulness of Christ's humanity." Moreover, the Irvingite's made empty prophecy that never came true. These men started the Catholic Apostolic Church, and they were considered the new apostles of the age.

Their names were: John Bate Cardale, Henry Drummond, Henry King-Church, Spencer Perceval, Nicholas Armstrong, Francis Woodhouse (Francis Valentine Woodhouse), Henry Dalton, John Tudor (John O. Tudor), Thomas Carlyle, Francis Sitwell, William Dow, and Duncan Mackenzie. However, none of these men ever saw God face to face or had a vision of him.

So, the metaphysic view of your perception or perspective of God or theology. Instead of seeing God by the truth of what was written in the Bible, it could be seen in the doctrine of transubstantiation as well as consubstantiation. The Apostles rejected while insisting on the real spiritual presence of the Body and Blood of Christ in the sacrament. Communion was taken in both kinds.[285]

The thing that we, the body of Christ, must understand is that God doesn't need a man to help him with false doctrines of devils and lying wonder. We can believe in Jesus Christ as God wanted without the creation of fables and false doctrine.

Mankind only needs to read the true word to get the real picture of who God is to the world. Beware of false prophets who are masking themselves as Christians. Destroying the testimony of many Christians. They may speak like Christian dress like Christians, and they may live like Christians. But they aren't covered in the blood of Christ Jesus.

CHAPTER 17
CHRISTIAN PSYCHOLOGY, METAPHYSICS, AND SPIRITUALISM

Before we read this chapter, let me make something evident to my non-Christian readers. I believe everyone should use the disciplines of psychology, like any medicine. Only as directed by a doctor or professional, and in moderation. But you need to come to the realization that you are a spiritual being needing God's deliverance through Jesus Christ. A Christian shouldn't use the control of psychology, or the Church will turn into something that Creator never designed for, and that is a religion.

Many unsaved and backslidden people who suffer need help with mental illness. And can't receive relief from the suffering unless they cry out to God. The illness is like any other sickness, like cancer, diabetes, or heart disease—the person born with a chemical imbalance in the brain needs help or healing.

If it is helpful, then the person needs a professional clinician who gives treatment. If it is healing, then it is the Churches mission to pray for the sickness and deliverance the person needs. There is a numeral reason for genetic problems, urethra-cortisol, or person who uses drugs and alcohol caused a psychotic breakdown.

In my case, it was both. Born with Urethra-Cortisol Depression Syndrome (UCDS); because under stress, my biological mother passed on UCDS to me while in her womb. I had the disease, and as a backslider, I became oppressed with a spirit of heaviness. Because of the sin I have done in my past. I am in a forty-year wilderness. I still need help, and medicine is helping me recover.

"The Spirit of the Lord GOD is upon Me, Because the LORD has anointed Me To preach good tidings to the poor; He has sent Me to heal the brokenhearted, To proclaim liberty to the captives, And the opening of the prison to those who are bound; To proclaim the acceptable year of the LORD, And the day of vengeance of our God; To comfort all who mourn, To console those who mourn in Zion, To give them beauty for

> *ashes, The oil of joy for mourning, The garment of praise for the spirit of heaviness; That they may be called trees of righteousness, The planting of the LORD, that He may be glorified. (Isaiah 61:1-3 NKJV)"*

So, can they mix these disciplines to help Christians? It is like oil and water. Who are these wolves and false prophets in the body of Christ? The first one we will look at is the ones who have brought the discipline of Christian Psychology. Now psychology is the study and functioning of the mind, which we know is the soul.

I am not saying that all psychiatrists and psychologists are false prophets. Because while I was in the wilderness. God used some of them while I was in a backslidden state, and for many years God gave special insight on how the mind worked in coherence with the spirit of man. The spirit of man controls the will of a human (desire) that human beings will is linked to the soul. The spirit of man's composition components works with three components of **integrity, intimacy, and intuition**. I knew once I had fallen that my soul and my spirit needed to be under the control of the Holy Spirit. I had to depend on psychology to keep me from hurting myself or others.

The spirit of man's composition is controlled by going through the will of the soul. This same understanding is what the spirit of divination wants to do to humanity. The spirit of divination enslaves the soul by possessing the spirit of man to control the humans three components of integrity, intimacy, and intuition.

God had allowed a spirit of heaviness and bondage to torment me until I cried out to God the Father's forgiveness for temping him. And I have cried out to my Father in Heaven, and he has forgiven me and has filled me with His Spirit.

It was by his mercy that he sent me to *"Lo-Debar"*[76] my time of *"No Word"* would end. And for forty years, I received no word or communication from God. And I would come and sup at the KING'S Table again in the wilderness. So, there is a place for psychology. However, should this discipline be made or forced upon by the secular world? What is Christian Psychology? Who brought it into mainstream Christian denomination?

To prove Christian psychology in the body, Christians won't turn this of psychology in the body of Christ into a witch hunt. Proven factors show the evidence that it is forced well-meaning Christ to use this form of German science of psychology. But what foolish Christians adopted this study to our noted theologians turns into the parable of the taking a pound or a pinch of arsenic. You still die; it just takes longer for the pinch of arsenic! Remember the philosopher Heraclitus, who believes that one could dedicate oneself to a life of reason, virtue, and substance. And he also believes in the form of worship in the fire called *Logos*.

[76] (2 Samuel 9:1-13 KJV)

The philosopher Heraclitus identified with the energy, law, reason, and providence found throughout nature, and was the first philosopher to use the term, logos, in a metaphysical sense. Heraclitus asserted by a fire-like called logos we govern our world. The divine force we produce the order and pattern discernible in the flux of nature. Christian need to remember Christ nor his Apostles ever used psychology to bring healing to the other believers. The power is the Holy Spirit not men.

> *But you shall receive power (ability, efficiency, and might) when the Holy Spirit has come upon you, and you shall be My witnesses in Jerusalem and all Judea and Samaria and to the ends (the very bounds) of the earth. (Acts 1:8 AMPC+)*

In this chapter, we will see what happened to the babies of metaphysics, psychology, and spiritualism. Professor Paul Johannes Tillich (1886-1965) was a German American philosopher (of existentialism[77]) and theologian who was a teacher at Union Theological Seminary in New York City. He main teaching came from Marcus Aurelius philosophies, because he believed that all men are rational being, and appear as brethren and children of *"Zeus."* [78]

Professor Tillich was the leading Ph.D., and Doctor of Divinity at the Divinity School of Harvard University, and the Divinity School of the University of Chicago. [xiii] He wrote many books on and coined the phrase of Christian psychology. Doctor Tillich developed ideas concerning the religious basis of life, including. These disciplines brought about many books on the subject of this form of psychology.

The books were as follows: The Religious Situation (1932), The Interpretation of History (1936), The Protestant Era (1948), The Dynamics of Faith (1957), and The Courage to Be (1952). He discussed the alienation of the individual in society and argued that existence is rooted in God as the ground of all being these books explained existentialism.[79]

Paul Tillich believed that a person must experience the expression that is working against them. This resistance of experience of the expression of the power of being will resist the negative non-existence. It is the will of the universe not God moves us to a mystical state of living.

---

[77] (Editorial department of the Wikimedia Foundation, Inc., 2020) is a tradition of philosophical inquiry associated mainly with certain 19th and 20th-century European philosophers who, despite profound doctrinal differences, shared the belief that philosophical thinking begins with the human subject—not merely the thinking subject, but the acting, feeling, living human individual.
[78] (Aurelius, AD 364 (c.1558 [Public Diminion])
[79] (Wikimedia Foundation, Inc., 2019) Paul Johannes Tillich

Now compare this from several quotes from some Stoics of the time. They only believe that the power comes from either the gods or goddesses. Some force is moving this experience of logos. However, they, as Romans says, being wise have become fools.

The philosopher Zeno of Citium that happiness can only come from the goodness flow of life itself. And when a person has this pursuit of happiness, and not the infilling and received power of the Holy Spirit that strengthens, a person to have joy.

The force comes from man's efforts to build a tower to the sky to the heavens. Not we allow God to come to us like he did in the garden. We develop an altar offer up what we think he wants. Daring him to reject it, and if we do, we shake our fist at God and curse him.

Do we wonder why people in the Church are dying? Why there is no power (authority) in our leaders to stop Satan from shooting up a congregation. Because we have a touchy-feely-kind of seeker-safe-kind of gospel, never being precise in dealing with your sinful nature. Jesus dealt with sin by not exposing, but he would show the sinner they are worth forgiving.

This Christ Jesus redeemed us by his blood, and his purpose destroys the works of the devil in our spirit, soul, and body to make human beings whole. Re-read the blood of the Lamb series for me (Gospel of John, Leviticus Chapters 1-7, the Epistle of Hebrews, and the Epistle of James) He wants a blood sacrifice for our sins. No flesh and blood will do that is sinful. Look at what this Emperor of Rome said:

"Make for yourself a definition or description of the thing which is presented to you, to see distinctly what kind of a thing it is in its substance, in its nudity, in its complete entirety, and tell yourself its proper name, and the names of the things of which it has been compounded, and into which it will be resolved. For nothing is so productive of elevation of mind, as to be able to examine methodically and truly every object that is presented to you in life, and always to look at things to see. At the same time, what kind of universe this is, and what kind of use everything performs in it. And what value everything has concerning the whole."
Marcus Aurelius

Does this sound like the Stoicism? Doctor Tillich believed that Protestant theology might incorporate the critical posture and scientific concepts. To use contemporary philosophy and thought we see the tree in the midst of the garden. Do these philosophical concepts nullify the word of God? He felt the study would never endanger the Christian faith. Jesus said differently, saying, *"Thus you are nullifying and making void and of no effect [the authority of] the Word of God through your tradition, which you [in turn] hand on; many things of this kind you are doing." (Mark 7:18-23 AMP+)*

Our Christian forefathers believed otherwise, because Melito, the Bishop of Sardis, wrote a short treatise on the soul, body, and mind by using the Word of God to correct the soul, and not philosophy. Irenaeus, in his work, Against Heresies II, taught on the subject. From church history about mixing philosophy with Christ, he said, *"A clever imitation in glass casts contempt, as it were, on that precious jewel the emerald (which is most highly esteemed by some), unless it comes under the eye of one able to test and expose the counterfeit."*

The purpose of humanity in Greek philosophy was to appear like their gods, and goddess of silver and gold Irenaeus said, *"... Again, what inexperienced person can with ease detect the presence of brass when it has been mixed up with silver? Lest, therefore, through my neglect, some should be carried off, even as sheep are by wolves."* These strange fires of metaphysics will bring the wrath of God if we don't repent. We also know of the views of Apollinaris of Laodicea (approx. 310-390 AD). It was that we should stay away from the secular philosophers because they believed the man is good by nature. Christ, Jesus felt the same about the traditions of men.

---

*Jesus said again, "Are you, too, so foolish and lacking in understanding? Do you not understand that whatever goes into the man from outside cannot defile and dishonor him, since it does not enter his heart, but **[only]** his stomach, and [from there it] is eliminated?" (By this, He declared all foods N1ceremonially clean.) And He said, "Whatever comes from [the heart of] a man, that is what defiles and dishonors him.*

*For from within, **[that is]** out the heart of men, come base and wicked thoughts and schemes, acts of sexual immorality, thefts, murders, adulteries, deeds of greed and covetousness, wickedness, deceit, unrestrained conduct, envy and jealousy, slander and profanity, arrogance and self-righteousness and foolishness **(poor judgment)**. All these evil things **[schemes and desires]** come from within and defile and dishonor the man.")(Luke 21:36 [Leviticus 10:1] AMP)*

It doesn't matter how you try to package it up with any kind of label. Putting it on t-shirts, selling books, and tapes that makes you millions on the best-seller list. Spiritual actions without the Spirit of God are spiritualism.

The two children of meta-physics seeking the power of the strange fires of *"Logos"* will get you killed. The Body of Christ is never supposed to be worshipped as gods, but we are to do the worshipping towards God. There are some modern-day churches in Dallas, Texas; Redding, California; Tulsa, Oklahoma; Lakeland, Florida, and even around the world, offering these same strange fires. Meta-physics defines what is reality in the cosmos and nature. The worshipping of self can open the door to a person transcendentalism to move in the soulish realm by using Transcendental Meditation to reach the medium spirit of a familiar spirit.

These were some secular writer and other famous people that believed in transcendentalism, which is a form of Hindu spiritualism: Ralph Waldo Emerson, Henry David Thoreau, Margaret Fuller, and Amos Bronson Alcott. Some other prominent transcendentalists included Louisa May Alcott, William Ellery Channing, William Henry Channing, James Freeman Clarke, Christopher Pearse Cranch, John Sullivan Dwight, Convers Francis, William Henry Furness, Frederic Henry Hedge, Sylvester Judd, and Walt Whitman.

Teaching after the Greek Philosophers Plato and Aristotle strongly influenced that. Tillich was quick to formulate a theory of Christian psychology and existential philosophy in his attempts to renew the relevance of theology for a modern secular society. Professor Tillich, Systematic Theology (3 volumes, 1951-63) was the primary instrument of this reformation. Professor Paul Tillich and Augustine of Hippo can both be known as the father of Christian psychology.

The new philosophy in the Church is the belief as a Christian doctrine of metaphysics. This new religion will develop in the 21st century as the new religion of the Church and mate the science of psychology and the theories of philosophy with the traditions of the denominationalism, claiming that mankind must evolve into the new psycho-meta-physics healers of the 21st century to help God. Bring deliverance to humanity without using the Blood of Jesus or the Holy Spirit. I am not saying that some forms of psychotherapy don't support the lost, non-Christians-souls. But once the person acknowledges they need deliverance. The introduction of Christ Jesus as savior must take over, and psychology should move over.

When I was a backslider in Orlando, I got help from a doctor and his wife, who kept the balance of relationship in Christ and the science of the mind, but a born-again Christian only needs to cry out to God the Father and the fruit will produce for itself through the working prayer life.[297]

Never replace God's power and healing from the Holy Spirit with psychotherapy. And instead of keeping the Creator upon your understanding of a new religion. These new levels of new age will develop in the 21st century as the new religion of the Church, and these traditions will mate the science of psychology and the doctrines of philosophy with the traditions. Then an old phantom of the 19th century will return to the United States' shore and will haunt the Pentecostal creators of spiritualism. This movement of metaphysics is the belief that the dead manifest their presence to people, usually through a clairvoyant or a medium.

The spiritualists will say they believe in the Bible, but never quote New Testament scriptures. They will use scripture references from the Gnostic texts, the Apocrypha, or the Dead Sea manuscripts. And if they do quote from the New Testament, it will most of the time be from the four gospels, and not the letters from Paul. When spiritualists try to minister the word, they will only quote from the Old Testament to bring condemnation to their congregation or new converts.

The doctrine and practices of those people who are in spiritualism will have a form of godliness, but they deny the power of the Holy Spirit. So, they will believe in spiritualist camps with their numbers about 400 congregations and a membership of more than 180,000 persons in the United States in the early 1980s. The movement is growing among uneducated whites and blacks in the south.

This movement the now embrace the metaphysical, spiritualism, which the Charismatic Movement, the New Apostolic Revival Movement, and the Latter Rain Revival all are nothing more than spiritualist. The Greek word for charismata means spiritual gifts. These people come with a nicely wrapped gift, and they come with an international world church view. And to blend their world church view with another interdenominational Christian revivalists' movement.

Baptist pastor said it best to me, "I am of a different disciple, and I am not a psychologist."

The Charismatic Movement allows elements of the doctrine and practices of the spiritualist camps, also referred to as Neo-Pentecostalism. The individuals who made up the movement believed in helping the lost. They thought we need the infilled power or to baptize the person with the Holy Spirit through the laying on of hands. To a new impartation of the New Spirit of God but will show no fruit of the Spirit that's vain.

The signs of this baptism's new impartation include such spiritual gifts as speaking in tongues or glossolalia. The term means to practice of speaking in a state of ecstasy and thus in a pattern of speech different from commonly intelligible patterns. The gift of prophecy means to tell the testimony of Christ Jesus, whether through healing to speak in exhortation encouragement or comfort.

To move in the interpretation of tongues means speaking in a language, not your native language, and discernment of spirits means just that see or understand what spirit moves in a person, place, or thing. (1 Corinthians 12:8-10) And the difference from the biblical movement that happens on the day of Pentecost. These movements and revivals lack control of the laymen, and the leaders in walking in the spirit. To walk in the Spirit, and you don't fulfill the lust of the flesh, and by putting to death your actions and works of the flesh draws you closure to Christ.

Many charismatic networks and organizations have risen within the Baptist, Lutheran, Methodist, Presbyterian, and other Protestant denominations since the 1980s. A small element exists within Eastern Orthodoxy, but the most striking recent development is the Roman Catholic. The purpose of the charismatic renewal, which originated in 1967 on university campuses in Pittsburgh, Pennsylvania; South Bend, Indiana; and East Lansing, Michigan.

In 1969 the USA bishops' conference issued a cautiously favorable statement regarding the renewal. In 1975, Pope Paul VI gave an appreciative speech at a unique audience for 10,000 charismatics attending a Rome conference. The purpose is to unite the Church, but not the Body of Christ.

Many essential leaders and lay-people began to raise their unbiblical doctrine of being gods,[300] and not children of God. The Pentecostals have aligned themselves with other Evangelicals and Ecclesiastics denominations in their emphasis on unified effort to evangelize the faith in Christ. But these denominations in their effort to unify are dangerously embracing spirits of error and another Christ. They are ecstatic in worship, although generally more subdued than most conservative Pentecostals, but this doesn't mean that they walk in the royal law of love.

"IF I [can] speak in the tongues of men and [even] of angels, but have not love (that reasoning, intentional, spiritual devotion such as is inspired by God's love for and in us), I am only a noisy gong or a clanging cymbal. And if I have prophetic powers (the gift of interpreting the divine will and purpose), and understand all the secret truths and mysteries and possess all knowledge, and if I have [sufficient] faith so that I can remove mountains, but have not love (God's love in me) I am nothing (a useless nobody). Even if I dole out all that I have [to the poor in providing] food, and if I surrender my body to be burned or so that I may glory, but have not love (God's love in me), I gain nothing. 'Take note: I will throw her on a bed [of anguish], and those who commit adultery with her [her paramours] I will bring down to pressing distress and severe affliction, unless they turn away their minds from conduct [such as] hers and repent of their doings.' (This kind of behavior is what brings God Wrath on a soul who is a hypocrite)" (Revelation 2:22 [1 Corinthians 13:1-3:]AMPC+)

There will be two spirits joining in making this baby from the Mother Earth Religion, and they need to repent from their sin. The first spirit is the spiritualist who will be headed by the false prophet (spirit of error), and the other is the charismatic movement (the spirit of whoredom), which has to fall prey to the Beast. Be careful not to fall into denominationalism. Paul the Apostle warned that because of these multiple-denominational splits, God would use the Seven seals to send them strong delusion, that they should believe a lie. *"The watchmen that went about the city found me, they smote me, they wounded me; the keepers of the walls took away my veil from me—"* *(Song of Solomon 5:7 Webster)*

CHAPTER 18
THE LAW OF RIGHTEOUSNESS

But Israel, which followed after the law of righteousness, hath not attained to the law of righteousness. In the last chapter, we saw the result of not operating in faith, true faith. Not working in love, the unconditional love.

Our passion has become conditional, and we have conditional love. We judge those who don't meet our requirements for our religion. Jesus never taught these types of actions to his disciples. This hidden mana or the veil that Israel didn't have because they couldn't see who God was in the temple in the Holies of Holies. A cloud separated God from Israel until the Messiah had come. The natural laws are the veil that blinds us!

The veil taken away is righteousness—the definition of this word for faith and love. The combination of these two elements came from Jesus Christ. Moreover, it is Jesus Christ righteousness that covers the believer only by the blood of our savior. The spiritualist and the false prophets of Christian psychology begin to strip away that if the believer trust in the traditions of philosophy and the doctrine of self-control, then they will be whole.

The watchmen that went about the city found me, and they smote me, they wounded me; the keepers of the walls took away my veil from me. (Song of Solomon 5:7 Webster)

What happens every time someone in the Body of Christ when a legalistic or spiritualistic comes into a church? The preachers, elders, or anyone actions in a medium for the Devil. They start acting like an intercessor will do to a newcomer to their church. They change them to move in the laws of Moses that keeping is impossible. Instead of helping the believer to walk in grace and truth.

These actions are not righteous. They don't let the person worship the Holy Spirit; however, it is not our worship that covers our sin. It is the Blood of Christ and our testimony and standing firm in the faith even if it cost us our lives.

Finally, we must refer to what I call the true meaning of the Tree of Life, and how humanity and mankind can live under the peace of God that passes all understanding. The factor found in Christ for the Christian is righteousness with God the Father. These factors of living under God's peace are the seed of the law of righteousness.

The root of this law is faith and love, according to Romans 3:27 and James 2:8, and the tree is life, or justification to live for God the Father for all eternity. All of these come by seeking the kingdom principles.

But first and most importantly seek (aim at, strive after) His kingdom and His righteousness [His way of doing and being right–the attitude and character of God], and all these things will be given to you also... for the kingdom of God is not a matter of eating and drinking [what one likes], but of righteousness and peace and joy in the Holy Spirit.— 1 Thessalonians 5:8 KJV

Notice that this is the fruit of the Spirit, in which this fruit comes from the tree of life. Yet all humanity can receive the benefits of this fruit if you come to the one that planted the tree. If you are a denominationalist, charismatic, spiritualist, or sinner, we need Christ Jesus saving grace and truth. It doesn't matter all can come to the tree.

We can come to know God for what his word stated, and not by what we can get from God to make ourselves gods like in the garden. We aren't God's, but his creation. We as believers don't believe, or make other things, nor people into God's by supporting them by sending money because we were all made in the image of the Creator.

He alone deserves our worship, and that worship is the fruit of righteousness. A fact of us producing the fruit of the Spirit. When we inject the fruit of righteousness that comes from the tree of life working with the Holy Spirit.

God gave when he gave the Holy Spirit through the fruit of the Spirit. One part of the fruit of the Spirit is peace. However, you must be willing to operate in harmony to have the covenant of peace to make peace with God and humanity. (James 3:18) So, who are we to force God to make peace with us if we refuse to obey him *"Kiss the Son, lest he be angry, and you perish in the way, for his wrath is quickly kindled. Blessed are all who take refuge in him."—Psalms 2:12 ESV*

The law of righteousness works only when the blood of Jesus is applied, and the person moves into true faith toward God—working in faith a person to accept the truth of Christ. Recognizing this truth will bring the power of sanctification. Once the Spirit of grace and supplication is put into motion in the person's life. The love of God by the Holy Ghost is put into the person's soulish will to begin to change the sensual nature of the person into the supernatural mind toward Christ.

The spirit of man is then born anew from that moment on, and the Spirit of Christ (which is the Holy Ghost) now begins his new reign over the living sacrifice of his new creature in the kingdom of God. So, the more the person seeks the kingdom of God in righteousness (faith and love), the more God pours out both his supernatural (spiritual) first, and then the nature things needed to stay alive. That is how this law works, and now let me conclude for those of you trapped by the bondage of religion, lust, and those just plain having a taste for the sinful nature.

To the carnal Christian, I say to you, quite backsliding and repent! The religious person filled with the Holy Ghost removes the emptiness of spiritual bondage and performance. We get delivered by Christ Jesus. Stop having a form of godliness but denying the power of God.

Finally, to the sinner who reads this book, receive Jesus Christ as Lord and Savior of your life, and be filled with the Holy Ghost. Now, if all of you are ready, let us who have heard and are convicted begin by repenting and coming back to Christ! We must learn how to work in the power of God through praise.

CHAPTER 19
THE POWER OF WORSHIP
(HEARING THE VOICE OF GOD)

When we hear the words Thanksgiving, praise, or worship, what pictures come to mind? Well, I never understood these words that came to my mind. Because these words were always foggy, very misused, and not clear in their meaning. The words of God spoken or defined by ministers of God. In the times of praise service, we were told in the Catholic Church to be very respectful and quiet in worship. Even smoother when the priest was giving his dissertation. Well, excuse me. I thought this was God's house! When am I going to hear from him?

Moreover, in the Protestant churches, you would hear a plethora of over and over, saying, *"Thank you, Jesus, Thank you, Lord!"* The preachers asked the laity in the Pentecostal Churches to praise the Lord. And the parish would respond to clap their hands while others would shout, *"Shout thank-you Jesus."* When the preacher would tell the congregation to praise him louder, they would clap harder and shout louder.

The more the preacher would shout to the congregation to praise the Lord, the more the shark fed frenzy of noise would drown out the voice of God. These actions of pendulum swings by the Orthodoxy and the Protestant denomination often silenced the real purpose of Thanksgiving, praise, or worship. We didn't come to see the three-ring circus of religious chum. We came to see Jesus.

If you came to see Jesus in his church and not meeting Jesus, I will give this example. You were in 1999, and you pay $200.00 apiece to go to a Michael Jackson concert. You get your tickets, and you find your seat. When the show starts, the only entrainment you see is a dog scratching in the middle of the stage as the dog runs off the stage. The announcer tells everyone, *"That's it, folks. Thank you for coming."*

You and I both know that the announcer would be tarred and feathered, and the burnt down concert hall by nightfall, and the promoter is tarred and feathered. If everyone's money isn't refunded that same night, then I must ask the same question to the body of Christ. Why are we going to churches across America? Why are we paying our tithes? Only to see a man scream and yell fire and brimstone, or they give us a profound philosophical sermon that these words are empty and meaningless.

We give them our time and money only for them to cheat us out of seeing the power of God demonstrated. For this reason, many people leave the church not seeing his power, and seek out Wicca, Eastern religions, or become agnostic. It's God we want to hear from and healed in our soul and body.

I don't understand that the tithe is a form of Thanksgiving for the pastor. The staff, and the care of the church, but like when after the resurrection Jesus. He commissioned Peter to feed his sheep and lambs, which the lambs being fed can be the sacrifice of peace. However, the haunting question still comes to my mind every-time I come to the church.

Where is God? I came to church to see the power of God's Spirit and to hear his voice. Not some man who did a terrible job of explaining who or what God is with theology. So, in this chapter, I am going to tell these three elements of hearing the voice of God using the scripture. The study of using Psalms 51 showing what Thanksgiving is asking God for forgiveness. Using thanksgiving is done by the acronym ASK (You keep Asking, you keep Seeking, and you keep Knocking until you hear his voice), and not in vain repetition. Then we study the book of Psalms 61, teaching how to move in praise. And Psalms 91 showing what is true worship. I will try to make clear our part in working in these three actions, so let's begin.

In the Fifty-First Psalms: David had written this melodic tune after Nathan, the prophet, told him of his adultery with Bathsheba and the murder of Uriah the Hittite. In **verses 1-3,** David is asking God for mercy and loving-kindness. He prays for God to cleanse him from his transgression.

In **verses 4-5,** David acknowledges that his sins were against God and that although God should judge him according to the law. He asked God to forgive him through mercy, but David didn't know if he would pardon him. David recognizes that from the moment he was conceived. He was shaped in iniquity. David admits that he has inherited the curse of Adam.

In **verses 6-11,** David asked God to give him wisdom and the truth beyond the natural laws. David asks God to purge, wash, and restore him. King David prayed for healing from the damaged he caused by sin, and he knows he needs to be filled with God's Holy Spirit. The infilling of the Holy Spirit real purpose is the gift of Thanksgiving. And Something we celebrate as a vacation in November, we need to dig deeper into our working on Thanksgiving. Thanksgiving is more than just an act of being thankful; it is a prayer.

The Prayer of Thanksgiving came from the Thanksgiving offering, or the Peace offering from the book of Leviticus chapter three. This type of offering was mentioned as offered with Burnt Offerings, at a time of national sorrow and fasting. Moreover, it was also necessary that the person is praying. So, Thanksgiving prayers often had the mentioning of the people must wash [redeemed] through redeemer, and restoration happens.

In **verses 12-16,** David asked again for restoration to move in the joy of salvation. Then he can to teach others about the lesson he learned. To be delivered from the bloody hands and darken the heart of iniquity. It is here that freedom comes, for the person to say or sing what they're thankful for in their deliverance. Like the African American Slaves of the South singing when they were working in the fields. And after they free us. They would sing aloud the old Spiritual that they would one day be free

In these final verses of his prayer of Thanksgiving, David realizes that he needs a broken spirit, and his heart needs to be contrite. However, he realizes that the sacrifice of the Old Testament law will not deliver him. Moreover, David must go beyond the natural and receive the spiritual acts of God's deliverance. He asks for God to build Zion and be pleased with the sacrifice of righteousness that is the principles of faith and love.

In Psalms 61, this is a prayer of praise. The Psalm was written by David as well. In **verses 1-4,** David shouts that God will hear his cry. The Hebrew word used for cheer is (rinnâh [רִנָּה] properly meaning a creaking [or shrill sound], that is, shouts of joy or grief:- crying of gladness, in the pleasure of proclamation, rejoicing, shouting, singing, or triumph.)

In these verses, we hear the psalmist say Selah (Meaning for us to pause, think, or meditate). We should proclaim that God is three truths. Our strength, our protection, and our source of abiding!

In **verses 5-8,** David promises to remember the vows of his previous years, and the promise to keep the kingdom of Israel, and his royal seed forever. He proclaims that he will daily sing the praises of the Lord all the days of his life. In tribute, only a liberated soul can shout for joy and sing the promises of God. The law of liberty's execution happens in the operation of approval.

Now to worship, that is the process of hearing the voice of God in **Psalms 91**. This Psalm is supposed by some to have been composed by Moses on the same occasion as the preceding, but others think David wrote it after he advised his son Solomon.

In verses **1-4,** It's the purpose of the believer to put themselves in the dwelling place of the secret residence of God, which this mysterious place is the holy of holies. By being in this place, God is the protector of the saint, and truth covers us in the power of the Holy Spirit. But we must hear from God to do the works of Christ.

In verses 5-7, Hearing Gods voice will comfort the believer from every terror and stop the pestilence. Destruction of Satan and the world [evil rulers, war, diseases, scarcity, and even oppression.] A thousand will fall on either side of you, but you, the believer, will be protected.

In verses 8-13, The wicked will see destruction, but as we keep our feet in the habitation of God's presence. It is the Lord will to protect you. God the Father will bear you up and keep you in charge of the angels. The Lord will stop the roaring lion of the devil and make you to conquer all the realms of darkness. We must never tempt God over our death, but we are to remember his angels will protect us.

Here is the key. **In verses 14-16,** we must set our love upon Christ; therefore, he will deliver us. Moreover, he will set us on high, and we will know his name. This action of unconditional love acting as we worship Jesus.

When we call upon Christ, he will answer. In hearing Gods voice. When the voice God speaks, deliverance comes in times of trouble. In salvation, we will be blessed with long life, and our lives will be satisfied.

I must have concluded by saying that when we are born again, children of God our Father. Allow him to take over the service of the congregation of the righteous. We can genuinely have church service in the way God intended purpose, for the congregation of the righteous is to work in the power of the Holy Spirit.

And we aren't to stop or hinder the flow of the Spirit in our church service. When we follow these patterns of Thanksgiving, praise, and worship, as seen in these psalms, we all can speak, adore, and hear the voice of the Lord. Even in a cloud of witnesses of this love feast. We must give in to the will of the Father, which I gave in the pattern that I showed my readers from the Bible.

Only then can we get the true glory of God, and not the smoke and mirrors that are being shown in some modern church with barking like a dog or being out of control by performing false signs and wonders. Calling these actions from the Holy Spirit, "… for God is not the author of confusion, but peace, as in all churches of the saints. Let all things be done decently and in order." We must let the living water of the Holy Spirit flow in celebration in our services toward God.

CHAPTER 20
THE UNITY OF THE FAITH AND THE BODY OF CHRIST

The Body of Christ Using of the Spiritual Laws of Christ. In this chapter, I would like to show the body of Christ is liberty in being unified, and I will give an example in the form of a story. There was a man of God that lived in a foreign land. He came from a kingdom that rose from twelve castles, and each of those castles was strong in its strength.

The man of God came and told them of a vast, massive army that would come from afar. Knowing the high strength of the massive army, he tried to warn the people in the other castles and make them band together in unity, but the other lords laughed him to scorn. They felt he was weak and foolish in his prophecy, though he had no power from God.

Henceforth, as time moved on, the massive army moved against the land, and when they landed, each of the other castles, though valiant in their weak efforts, were overthrown and destroyed, each only leaving a small remnant of refugees that were children in hiding. The man of God came up with a plan to gather the little piece of refugees that were children in hiding.

The man of God came up with an idea to collect the small bands of child refugees and put them into one group, and he repelled the massive army, as the children who were refugees outnumbered the great army that was defeated and pushed away from the kingdom.

In this story, we, as the body of Christ, are very much divided, like this vast kingdom. We find our part fragmented into 1,052 different denominations. That was Satan's plan, and as long as Satan divided the church by sowing confusion by infecting us with Urethra-Cortisol Depression Syndrome (UCDS) by affecting us racial, gender, and doctrinal beliefs. We, too, will come to that same fate. As Paul wrote: For ye are yet carnal: for whereas there is among you envying, and strife, and divisions, are ye not carnal, and walk as men? For a while, one said, I am of Paul; and another, I am of Apollos; are ye not carnal?

They have even affected our worship toward God the Father, because they can't come into a divided house that won't let Christ or the Holy Spirit move the service to bring deliverance. If the church of God is nothing more than a money-marketing den of thieves, then we can no longer call God's house a house of prayer.

We have even turned the words "house of prayer" into a denomination doctrinal argument that this word has become an idolatrous word of the spirit of whoredom. This worship is much like the children of Israel turned an item that brought healing to Israel, which the issue was the "Brazen Serpent" of Moses.

The symbol that was created by Moses because the Israelis were murmuring against the leadership of God. Vipers there when they bit the people would cause grievous burning and then death. The Children of Israel cried out to God, and God gave Moses and answer to heal them. He told Moses to make a "Braze Serpent" and hang it on a pole.

When the Children of Israel looked at the pole, they rod healed them if they looked at it. The priest put the Item in the Tabernacle, and then it was put into the Temple of Solomon. The Children of Israel called it the Nehushtan נְחֻשְׁתָּן (pronounced in Nehōōshtān) means bronze thing. Later King Hezekiah destroyed it because many people were sacrificing to it in the temple.

Satan has successfully attacked and crippled the Body of Christ in three areas of coming closer to God and praising the Lord. Happens every time we have a revival, and from that revival, we create another denomination. These areas the world will judge us, and God will deliver us through fasting, weeping, and prayers. Then we will become the bright and morning star before his return with the trumpet sound.

First, in the power of thanksgiving, we have to find out what God's word says about praise. The states in Psalms 100:4 from the Modern King James Version: *"Enter into his gates with thanksgiving, and into his courts with praise."* The door of the Tabernacle of God is through the gates of Thanksgiving by way of Psalms 51, and a plying of the Blood of Jesus, which when we become saved will take your ashes of a destroyed life, and bring you the beauty of a meek and restored life in Christ Jesus.

Then we must be washed by the word of God that we might be cleansed and sanctified. At the gate of Thanksgiving, the word of God's used as a point of contact. We confess and mortifying the members of the flesh. This washing will bring peace to the spirit of man and wisdom to the soul. Thanksgiving is the admonishment of the body of Christ throughout the psalms, hymns, and spiritual songs to one another.

When singing these songs, we bring the presence of the Holy Spirit by the anointing of Jesus Christ. Jesus was always a shadow of the anointing called the Holy Spirit, and the Holy Spirit gives us the ability to operate in action like Christ Jesus to remove burdens and destroy yokes.

Then second, through praise, which is the soul's time to rejoice in its liberty and freedom from the carnal nature, praise is the body is being allowed to party with God. First is the oil of joy upon the head the feast of the bread of life and new wine, and then comes the audience of the king at the altar.

However, doing miracles isn't enough, but we need to act like Jesus Christ did when he operated in the fruit of the Spirit as we with the wonders and healings he did in the body of Christ. In turn, it gives the receiver of the gift of those miracles to provide Jesus with Christ, Thanksgiving, praise, and worship.

In the humble human being, these acts of adoration toward God the Father. We see that worship is the end, much like an exclamation, question mark, or period in a sentence. The declaration of the master's arrival will be expressed in praise and speaking the testimony of the name of Jesus Christ in worship. This worship of revival produces the Spirit of prophecy.

The name of Christ Jesus is always spoken. The altars of God resemble every characteristic of who God is, so for more information, go to chapter nine, page seventy. So, faith is the slow-burning fire in the altar, and the smoke is the Biblical words of God from the prayers of both Christ Jesus and the Saints of God. However, the incense coals are the aroma of peace.

The altars of God Almighty represent the thrown of God Almighty (which is interpreted in Hebrew as El Shaddai, and it means the mighty one that satisfies). God set a pattern of the first Thanksgiving to clean the soul and body from sin before they can enter into the presence of God.

You are bringing your gifts of thanksgivings, oblations, supplications, intercessions, and prayers, and then unto the mercy seat and before the Father to hear his voice. We see in this graphic illustration of the Holy place and then coming in the presence of God the Father that to go to God, it must be through the blood of Jesus and the cross of Calvary. But we must speak in our neighborhood, in our churches, on the street, and where we work the testimony of Jesus.

Finally, we deal with hearing the voice of God the Father. That is what worship is to the believer. There is no condemnation, and you are considered to God the Father by the blood of Jesus Christ, made holy, acceptable, and ready to serve. In the place of worship, we see and hear God for the first time as the Father, and no longer as the judge, because we have judged ourselves.

Then God can see man as children of Christ and heirs of the throne, but we have cut the process because the flesh has come into the church. God doesn't have a problem with the style of music, but if the anointed word isn't coming out of the anointed body, then the Anointed One will not show up, releasing the Holy Ghost to move in the spirit of man and on the soul of others around the assembly. So, what is the problem?

The pastor conducting the service doesn't allow the Holy Ghost to move through the people. Even when they invite the Spirit of God into the church, they run him back out, allowing Him to operate according to the word, which reads:

"Now, you are the body of Christ and members individually. And God has appointed these in the church: first apostles, second prophets, third teachers, after that miracles, then gifts of healings, helps, administrations, varieties of tongues. Are all apostles? Are all prophets? Are all teachers? Are all workers of miracles? Do all have gifts of headings? Do all speak with tongues? Do all interpret? But earnestly desire the best gifts.

And yet I show you an excellent way. But now, brethren, if I come to you speaking with tongues, what shall I profit you unless I speak to you either by revelation, by knowledge, by prophesying, or by teaching? What is the conclusion then? I will pray with the spirit, and I will pray with the understanding. I will sing with the spirit, and I will sing with the understanding. How is it then, brethren? Whenever you come together, each of you has a psalm, has a teaching, has a tongue, has a revelation, and has an interpretation. Let all things be done for edification." (1 Corinthians 12:28-31; 1 Corinthians 14:6, 26)

Now, if these are the principles of how to operate in Thanksgiving, praise, and worship, then why no bring out the tradition of men and allow the Holy Spirit to use the people. Instead of making our pastor and musicians idols and stars? Or worst, the spiritualist has people laughing or barking like dogs. My brothers and sisters are how the spirit of whoredom divination crept in and defiled the people. As the Apostle Paul wrote, *"The people sat down to eat and drink, and rose to play." (1 Corinthians 10:7 ESV)*

Furthermore, with this factor in the church, we as the leaders of the body of Christ must divine out, and it only comes out by praying and fasting, yet we distinguish first, naturally, then a spiritual fast. Secondly, in the power of praying and fasting, which opens the heart of God's people and leaders, we are to walk in the spirit and stop the works of the flesh. But you are asking what I meant by a natural and spiritual fast. To understand this, we must read Isaiah chapter fifty-eight verses three through twelve:

"Why have we fasted," they say, "and You have not seen? Why have we afflicted our souls, and you take no notice?" In fact, on the day of your fast, you find pleasure And exploit all your laborers. Indeed, you fast for

strife and debate, And to strike with the fist of wicked You will not fast as you do this day, To make your voice heard on high. Is it a fast that I have chosen, A day for a man to afflict his soul? Is it to bow down his head like a bulrush, And to spread out sackcloth and ashes?

Would you call this a fast, And an acceptable day to the lord? Is this not the fast that I have chosen: To loose the bonds of wickedness, To undo the heavy burdens, To let the oppressed go free, And that you break every yoke? Is it not to share your bread with the hungry, And that you bring to your house the poor who are cast out; When you see the naked, that you cover him, And not hide yourself from your flesh?

Then your light shall break forth like the morning, Your healing shall spring forth speedily, And your righteousness shall go before you; The glory of the Lord shall be your rear guard. Then you shall call, and the Lord will answer; You shall cry, and He will say, "Here I am." If you take away the yoke from your midst, The pointing of the finger, and speaking wickedness, If you extend your soul to the hungry And satisfy the afflicted soul, Then your light shall dawn in the darkness, And your darkness shall be as the noonday. The Lord will guide you garden, and like a spring of water, whose waters do not fail. Those from among you Shall build the old waste places; You shall raise the foundations of many generations; And you shall be called the Repairer of the Breach, The Restorer of Streets to Dwell In..." (Isaiah 58:3-12 ESV)

Simply put in layman's terms, the fast is an entire event and not a wasteful (hypocritical part) of religious play-acting. You will be the hands and feet of Jesus. Having his power and authority never means to misuses it instead of being philosophical. Making the soul submit to the will of God may prove difficult.

When fasting, you need to see a change. Fasting will break the flesh and soulish nature, not to be righteous or get closer to God. It is the steel of the sledgehammer, and the Word of God is the handle. The Blood of Jesus has gotten you as close to God Almighty as you will ever need to be, nor your flesh will allow you to get closer. *"... Is this not the fast that I have chosen: to loose the bonds of wickedness, to undo the heavy burdens, to let the oppressed go free, and that you break every yoke?" (Isaiah 58:8 ESV)* Fasting only puts the body and soul in check while the spirit rejuvenates.

Now fasting is empty without the partner known as prayer and speaking the word of God, which helps in breaking the darkness hidden in the chamber of the soul's mind, will, and emotion, as it is written, This kind can come out by nothing but prayer and fasting. Finally, in the power of confessing and understanding the word of God to beat us into the image of Christ as the body of Christ, we must use the word of God as a weapon of the will by casting down the image of the enemy of both you and others that are using carnal weapons of mass destruction.

Therefore, if the house of God isn't confessing the word of God, then they have lost their flavor. *"Salt is good, but if the salt has lost its flavor, how shall it be season? It is neither fit for the land (to help fruit trees to produce fruit), nor for the dunghill, but men will throw it out. He who has an ear to hear let him hear!" (Matthew 5:13 KJV)* Confessing the word brings unity and boldness, as you see in the **book of Acts, chapter four verses twenty-six through thirty-one under the King James Version**:

"And when they heard that, they lifted their voice to God with one accord, and said, Lord, thou art God, which hast made heaven, and earth, and the sea, and all that in them is: Who by the mouth of thy servant David hast said, Why did the heathen rage, and the people imagine vain things? The kings of the earth stood up, and the rulers were gathered together against the Lord and his Christ. For of a truth against thy holy child Jesus, whom thou hast anointed, both Herod, and Pontius Pilate, with the Gentiles, and the people of Israel, were gathered together, For to do whatsoever thy hand and thy counsel determined before to be done. And now, Lord, behold their threatening's: and grant unto thy servants, that with all boldness they may speak thy word, By stretching forth thine hand to heal; and that signs and wonders may be done by the name of thy holy child Jesus. And when they had prayed, the place was shaken where they were assembled, and they were all filled with the Holy Ghost, and they spake the word of God with boldness..."

We put confessing the word into use by first studying the word from the pastor of our congregations. You can take the notes of his outline, study them, then make prayers and confession of faith from the very subject he or she taught on. Understanding the word of God is the final point. The Holy Spirit gives an understanding of how the word of God plays. An essential part of the unification of the faith and the Body of Christ. To understand this point, we need to read **Ephesians chapter four, verses three through thirteen with King James Version**:

"Endeavoring to keep the unity of the Spirit in the bond of peace. There is one body, and one Spirit, even as ye are called in one hope of your

calling; One Lord, one faith, one baptism, One God and Father of all, who is above all, and through all, and in you all. But unto every one of us is given grace according to the measure of the gift of Christ. Wherefore he saith, "When he ascended on high, he led captivity captive, and gave gifts unto men. (Now that he ascended, what is it but that he also descended first into the lower parts of the earth?" He that descended is the same also that ascended far above all heavens, that he might fill all things.) And he gave some, apostles; and some, prophets; and some, evangelists; and some, pastors and teachers; For the perfecting of the saints, for the work of the ministry, for the edifying of the body of Christ: Till we all come in the unity of the faith, and the knowledge of the Son of God, unto a perfect man, unto the measure of the stature of the fulness of Christ..."

Christ Jesus called us to be both peacekeepers and makers. The makers of peace called the Children of God to move in His authority, while we keep the order are to execute judgment over the lawless demon. We use the law of sin and death to expose the nature of sin and allow the Holy Spirit to show the person their sin through conviction. While we show love to the sinner as Jesus did throughout his earthly ministry.

When we are one in faith, belief in the lord, and one in Christ Baptism, the Body of Christ walks in perfection with the saints in the word. We work in the ministry of reconciliation. The word edify means to teach one another each other by the Spirit of wisdom and understanding, the Spirit of prophecy, and the Spirit of knowledge and the fear of the lord.

The Body of Christ must speak using the law of kindness. Notice the three characteristics of the Holy Spirit our speaking distinctions; King Solomon wrote, *"She opens her mouth in skillful and godly Wisdom, and on her tongue is the law of kindness [giving counsel and instruction]." (Proverbs 31:26 AMPC+)*

Understanding the word of God is my final point. *Wisdom is the principal thing; therefore, get wisdom. And in all your getting, get understanding." (Proverbs 4:7 KJV)* Many people in the United States of America have idolized wisdom as the principal key to knowledge and to getting to understand the true nature of one's self. The ecclesiastical and academic disciplines embrace that you can only get of wisdom through education.

This belief is partially true, and the reason I say this is simple. A person's education can only give them knowledge, but you must apply the experience to get wisdom. So, is it with the Word of God? If you only know the Bible and can never use it like Christ and his Apostles did daily by the heard orders of God, the Father. Then the knowledge isn't worth having. The confusion presenting the word in unity proves why the world mocks us!

They read about the miracles Christ did the healings, the dead from the tombs, and the deliverance of the demon-possessed. And we can't even feed fifty people in a park. We have become Luke-warm and our churches a den of thieves. The essential that we need to…

"… Speak in the tongues of men and [even] of angels, but have not love (that reasoning, intentional, spiritual devotion such as is inspired by God's love for and in us), I am [we are] only a noisy gong or a clanging cymbal.

And if I [we] have prophetic powers (the gift of interpreting the divine will and purpose), and understand all the secret truths and mysteries and possess all knowledge, and if I [we] have [sufficient] faith so that I [we] can remove mountains, but have not love (God's love in me) I am [we are] nothing (a useless nobody).

Even if I [we] dole out all that I have [to the poor in providing] food, and if I [we] surrender my body to be burned or so that I[we] may glory, but have not love (God's love in me), I [we]gain nothing."(1 Corinthians 13:1-3 AMPC+)

So, to prove the above scripture and my statement, we can't get of wisdom through education only. I am going to employ a thesis. We will take two people from one family, and we will give them five thousand dollars. Both persons will have the wisdom of banking financially and capitalizing. One will go to college for four years and get a degree in business, and the other person will start a business learning on his own.

After four years, the college graduate will look for a job at a banking and financial institution. Keeping the money in a savings account while he works his way up the corporate ladder. Meanwhile, the other person will already in the four years increase by quadrupling his assets. The second person gave four times the amount given to him by the master.

Now the question I have to you is, which person will do better after the next four years? The answer is the one that has his own business. This style of giving shows how the law of kindness and the royal law of love works. Love and kindness are applied application, and not just studied to have a mental acceptance.

A person educated in school which using theology, and they never apply the Bible. They are one person that has a bunch of head knowledge. The person with all the understanding, but they're afraid to apply their knowledge is foolish, and untrustworthy with God's power. Because they bury it for the lack of faith, they have in that God has the action of forgiving them indeed, so they bury it in the ground of their soul.

They are afraid because they are not famous in humanity, but the heart of the will of God. The reward to humanity comes as they submit to the Holy Spirit and God the Father's will by bearing their cross (purposes).

What the person with excellent knowledge is looking for isn't to do what the word of God emphasizes. They will only look for a pulpit to preach from, never walking in the promises. Sure, everyone needs to a mentor, but look at God's school versus man's traditional institutional way of doing things.

Understanding the word also comes by studying and receiving the wisdom of God by revelation through the Holy Spirit. However, it doesn't bring faith. Faith comes by hearing (understanding) and hearing by the word of God. Just studying the word brings carnal and natural results. Still, if put into a pity practice of meditation, this form of worship will put the carnal nature under subjection. Be submissive to the lord's call, and doing his will open the door for deliverance.

It will allow for your intercession group at your local body to share the wisdom of the truth. Bidding the oppressing spirit that is attacking believers or deliver the possessing demonic spirit controlling the person. Being opened to receive a punishment from one another brings the Spirit of [meekness] humility through the Holy Spirit to speak to the people by a word of wisdom, word of knowledge, or prophesy.

The mission of ministering the word always meant to teach the parish by the elders. And the pastor keeps the Biblical order in the sanctuary while feeding and caring for the flock. Moreover, neither are they to lord their authority over the people with standards of moral codes or religious morality, nor are they to make the house of God a place of commerce.

"He made a whip of cords, and drove them all out of the temple, with the sheep and the oxen; and He scattered the coins of the money-changers and overturned their tables; then to those who sold the doves, He said, 'Take these things away! Stop making My Father's house a place of commerce!'" [Your precepts are fully confirmed and completely reliable; Holiness adorns Your house, O LORD, forever. [Psalms_93:5] (John 2:15-16 AMP,)

I will not be the one standing in the courtyard of the church—anyone sanctuary with a bullwhip driving anyone into the submission of the word of God. And I will not be overturning any tables of the multitude of par-ministries across the world in stadiums and concert halls.

Christ, Jesus will do that all by himself. I did build the church. He promised much like he did with Israel when he told Jeremiah to remind the children of Israel about their religious rituals that have now become idolatrous.

"Say this to him, The LORD speaks in this way, 'Behold, what I have built I will break down, and that which I have planted I will uproot, that is, the whole land!'." (Jeremiah 45:4 AMP) Remember when you're setting up that display table, for that religious function, or buy and sell your items.

I'm not saying that anyone working in giving honor to a teacher of the gospel means to honor them with offerings, or special tribunes. As I note did in chapter four on page forty-one: You shouldn't rob a person of the gospel of what they've worked for in the ministry.

We need to stop being a non-profit and change to a for-profit origination if we are going to buy and sell the gospel because "Big Brother is always watching with cameras everywhere, and even invading our privacy peering into companies like Yahoo™, and Microsoft™.

My question is, will morality in the coming centuries be able to uphold the question of right and wrong if the clogging up of the church. We become compromised in the preaching of the word of God. I can personally say, no, because when humanity has no belief in absolute truth, moral code, or compass.

And humanity starts judging others on what they think is right or wrong instead of believing what the word of God is righteous. Then the answer will always be no, but God doesn't judge us based on a moral code he decides us based on righteousness.

So, what do we as the Body of Christ do? When our flesh, the world, and the Devil are beginning to label us as prey. When scientists tell us we came from monkey-slime? The academic world tells us there is no absolute truth. Moreover, politicians silence us, saying we can't speak our reality in the political arena. Simple, we roar!

I have been silent based on other people versions of morality. They taught me to think about what was right and wrong, judging everyone, including God. However, God judges based on the truth of righteousness, which, in my opinion, is an absolute truth, although many philosophers and education disciplines make my beliefs foolish.

Then tell that to scientists who have come up with a theory to cure cancer even though they wouldn't accept the belief in a higher power or Supreme being. They allow one's faith in God to bring healing. If scientists didn't believe in a no absolute truth, then how do they know their formula will work. Simple, they know and see the proof of a Creator in nature through the natural laws of the laws of physics and nature.

The factor that the Bible is absolute truth shouldn't be argued, but understood, which Biblical truth will always be pure! Because it has formulas that work as well and works of the same principles/laws as natural laws of physics and nature.

Two plus two will always equal four. We can wish the arithmetic problem to equal 6, 7, or 1! Two apples and two oranges (thought objects are different) will always equal four pieces of fruit. The fact forever remains that there are absolute truths in life, and in the world to come. This factor of truth used by the elders to keep the order by using the Bible, which this truth is the absolute truth.

We never use the Bible as a rod of correction on the world uses less God is doing the correction. When applied correctly, it will bring grace and truth to the Body of Christ. When a word of wisdom, word of knowledge, or prophecy comes, the absolute truth of the Bible will help the congregation grow. Keep the spirits of divination and whoredom out of the congregational governing body of Christ.

However, you must allow the people to be led by the Holy Spirit, which the Holy Spirit is also known as the Spirit of Truth, and reframe from the leaders just amusing the congregation into a false sense of slumber with the meaningless program. These programs only create a battle of the preachers and the fleecing of the sheep. Bringing the congregation into whoredom (idolatry) and rebelling (divination) with the pastor like one church in Redding, California is guilty of using magic trick and allusion to fool the congregation. *"Let him that thinks he stands take heed lest he fall." (1 Corinthians 10:12 KJV)*

The Body of Christ will need to realize one thing, and that is, either we will fall on the rock of the Word of God, and we become broken, or the stone will fall on us and crush us to powder. [80] The power of praise brings in components of the power of prayer and fasting.

And the power of confessing the word, which brings understanding to the word of God. Brings the anointing of God that is the Holy Spirit. The power of the Holy Spirit is the burden of removing yokes, can destroy all oppositions against God's real power (the duomos), which only God the Father, Jesus the Son, and God the Holy Spirit have in their sovereignty purpose as the only true God of God's.

Now in the church if the anointing, this anointing is only found in God the Father, Christ Jesus, and the Holy Spirit. Isn't present in a local church body. Then no longer will the Body function, and the Body of Christ will suffer from AIDES (Acquired Infected Demonic Events of Satan). Look at what Christ Jesus spoke about the Church of

---

[80] Luke 20:18 ESV

Laodicea in Revelation, chapter three, verses fourteen through twenty in the Amplified version:

"To the angel (divine messenger) of the church in Laodicea write: "These are the words of the Amen, the trusted and faithful and true Witness, the Beginning and Origin of God's creation: 'I know your deeds, that you are neither cold (invigorating, refreshing) nor hot (healing, therapeutic); I wish that you were cold or hot. So because you are lukewarm (spiritually useless), and neither hot nor cold, I will vomit you out of My mouth [rejecting you with disgust]. Because you say, "I am rich, and have prospered and grown wealthy, and require nothing." You do not know that you are wretched and miserable and poor and blind and naked [without hope and in great need], [Hos_12:8] I counsel you to buy from Me gold that has been heated red hot and refined by fire so that you may become wealthy; and white clothes [representing righteousness] to clothe yourself so that the shame of your nakedness will not see it, and healing salve to put on your eyes so that you may see. Those whom I [dearly and tenderly] love, I rebuke and discipline [showing them their faults and instructing them]; so be enthusiastic and repent [change your inner self–your old way of thinking, your sinful behavior–seek God's will]. [Pro_3:11-12; Heb_5:8; Heb_12:5-7] Behold, I stand at the door [of the church] and continually knock. If anyone hears My voice and opens the door, I will come in and eat with him (restore him), and he with Me."

Is this the actual state of the body of Christ in the 20th and 21st centuries? Because the Holy Spirit isn't being allowed to move in the church today freely. Programs of legalism, or spiritualism with a magic show of false signs and wonders. (people throwing coins on the grown saying came from heaven, or sprinkling gold dust on a person hands while their eyes are closed saying it's angel dust)

Soon spiritualism will replace God's word, and this spiritualism will bring open action of divination, that, as we have discussed before. And if the congregation doesn't believe it from God, then they will be told they have blasphemed against the Holy Spirit, which will create fear in the church. When the spirit of divination comes, then it will move its works toward the pastoral staff to present strange fire before God in the acts of coveting and idolatry, and the spirit of whoredom will control the people as it is doing now!

I saw the early stages of this while I was in Little Rock, Arkansas. The church was operating his magic, and had the church moving in a three-ring-circus-church syndrome, with the pastor insanely being out of control.

It was as if he was trying to offend me while was trying to worship God. Moreover, when I would confront him about his action. I began to notice that the pastor of the local church would be rudely joking with me. Every time I would call him on it, he would say he was only kidding, and that I could take a joke.

Sometimes he would stop his behavior for a while, but then he would start up again when I would try to enter into worship toward God. It was as if he knew that if he could offend me that I would be able to worship God. He wanted to be a god.

One day, I was talking with one of the elders of the church about his behavior issues, and he said, "Oh, that, he does that with everybody that he feels is getting more attention than him!" He later told me if I would just bind the spirit of whoredom before getting into a discussion with him. I would notice a change in the conversation and his behavior.

Later the elder who confessed that he was his Father told me that when the pastor was a child, he used to alone always. Instead of the church, go out to make friends to invite people to visit the house of God. He would be in his room, crying. Both of his parents would try to make him go out because the Father had a job that kept him away.

The spirit of whoredom would feed off his starvation for attention. He grew covetous of other's relationships with other people or even their relationship toward God. Thinking he should be the center of attention of those around him, he would continuously work or talk to people rudely. This behavior would cause him to get that attention and would make the pastor feel secure and essential.

I am not saying the parents were right or wrong in how they raised their child, because maybe it wasn't an issue of morality, but the son using good common sense. He needs his Father's attention, and perhaps the Father could have done more by taking time for his son's need.

However, it's a simple fact that if you can't change your circumstanced. Then change your surroundings, and then change will come if not for others. It will go for you in your life. Studies have shown that 20% of people mood change just by them moving to another location of the country.

The spirit of whoredom draws its strength from lust. The three components of worldliness made up as the lust of the eye, the lust of the flesh, and the pride of life. The person working in this spirit will drink from the chalice of the spirit of divination. People who are influenced by these spirits will bind up the work of the Holy Spirit. Both of these spirits are working together to stop the flow of worship toward God. And God allows it because of freedom of choice.

The only goal of any hindrance is to stop someone from getting to their goal, which the intention of the spirit is controlling the other person for their benefit for payment (that is what whoredom or prostitution goal), and this is the goal of a spiritual, soulish, or physical hindrance.

These hindrances are called Satanic Traditions and Doctrines of men that I call STD's, which these demonic influences put people in bondage. Moreover, only crying out to God's and confessing his word can bring rescue and deliverance for people from these STD's. We must bow to the throne of God, our Father. Instead of burning in the lust of the flesh, the lust of the eyes, and the pride of life.

If we begin to use the power of praise, the power of prayer and fasting, and the power of confessing and understanding the Word of God, only then will the people of God be freed from the wilderness using these factors, and these factors used brings true brokenness and humility. This type of break-through will bring wealth (not so much financial but health and spiritual), healing, and you shall be a repairer of the emptiness of other's lives. You will do the work of the Kingdom of God.

And you will open doors of the supernatural using the spiritual laws of Christ to work freely as God the Father intended man to work among all believers, both Jew and Gentile. Using entertainment in the church can only bring the coveting of other's belongings, lifestyle, and beauty, which coveting is only idolatry, and that idolatry is the spirit of whoredom.

In chapter four, we discussed that the divine laws are above the natural thinking of man, and only spiritually re-born humans of the Spirit of God can only use and understand these principles. We can only, through God, use these laws if we have the character of God, which this character is the Holy Spirit. Only a born-again believer will possess the supernatural power of God.

"Adultery, fornication, uncleanness, lasciviousness, idolatry, witchcraft, hatred, variance, emulations, wrath, strife, seditions, heresies, Envying's, murders, drunkenness, reveling, and such like: of the which I tell you before, as I have also told you in time past, that they which do such things shall not inherit the kingdom of God." (Luke 12:32 paraphrased)

On the other hand, *"... it is your Father's good pleasure to give you the kingdom..."* *(Galatians 5:19-21 ISV)* Then, why is it that we don't have the promises that we should have? Is it because we don't confess the word enough? Is it because we don't pray enough? Is it because we haven't loved ourselves enough? The answer to these questions is no!

Then why do we fall into temptation, sin, and then destroy ourselves? Why do we find ourselves in the destructive tornado of loneliness, grief, and shame? To find the answer, let us read this next passage to get a better understanding.

Moses, my servant, is dead; now, therefore, arise, go over this Jordan, thou, and all this people, unto the land which I do give to them, even to the children of Israel. Every place that the sole of your foot shall tread upon that have I given unto you, as I said unto Moses. From the wilderness and this Lebanon even unto the great river, the river Euphrates, all the land of the Hittites, and unto the great sea toward the going down of the sun, shall be your coast. There shall not any man be able to stand before thee all the days of thy life: as I was with Moses, so I will be with thee: I will not fail thee, nor forsake thee. (Joshua 1:2-5 NASB paraphrased)

So, what happened? The orders where clear. Possess the land from the West of the Mediterranean Sea to the East of the River Euphrates. The Northern border of the country of Lebanon and all the area of the Hittites. Even the Southern edge of the Saudi Desert. Why didn't this happen? *"God isn't a man that he should lie, nor the Son of man that he should repent." (Numbers 23:19 ESV)*

Who failed? They did, and it was because of fear that humankind failed, not a lack of faith. The same reason the church didn't conqueror the world and hold it down in the "Great Commission." The same mission he gave the Children of Israel. Jesus gave the adopted Children of Christ.

And Jesus came and spake unto them, saying, all power is given unto me in heaven and earth. Go ye therefore, and teach all nations, baptizing them in the name of the Father, and the Son, and the Holy Ghost: Teaching them to observe all things whatsoever I have commanded you: and, lo, I am with you always, even unto the end of the world. Amen (Matthew 28:18-20 KJV)

It was fear that stopped the power of God in the Holy Ghost. Reading in the King James Version, the parable of the sower **Matthew, chapter thirteen, verses three through nine and then verses eighteen through twenty-three:**

"And he spake many things unto them in parables, saying, Behold, a sower went forth to sow; And when he sowed, some seeds fell by the

wayside, and the fowls came and devoured them up: Some fell upon stony places, where they had not much earth: and forthwith they sprung up, because they had no deepness of earth: And when the sun was up, they were scorched by the sun. And because they had no root, they withered away. And some fell among thorns; and the thorns sprung up, and choked them: But other fell into good ground, and brought forth fruit, some an hundredfold, some sixtyfold, some thirtyfold. Who hath ears to hear, let him hear. Hear ye, therefore, the parable of the sower. When anyone heareth the word of the kingdom, and understandeth it not, then cometh the wicked one, and catcheth away that which was sown in his heart. This is he which received seed by the wayside. But he that received the seed into stony places, the same is he that heareth the word, and anon with joy receiveth it; Yet hath he not root in himself, but dureth for a while: for when tribulation or persecution ariseth because of the word, by and by he is offended. He also that received seed among the thorns is he that heareth the word; and the care of this world, and the deceitfulness of riches, choke the word, and he becometh unfruitful. But he that received seed into the good ground is he that heareth the word, and understandeth it; which also beareth fruit, and bringeth forth, some a hundredfold, some sixty, some thirty."

We all, as believers, have a seed (measure) of faith planted in our spirit. When we were baptized in the Holy Spirit (Christ baptism). This is a two-fold type of baptism. One is for salvation, and one is burning away and overcoming sin. The other baptism is to bring repentance and power toward others through healing, deliverance, wisdom and understanding, and the love of God's presence.

Fear causes man to fail, and not the lack of faith. We fear what we can't control, and that thing we can't control is the fire of the Holy Spirit. Jesus' Baptism burns all sin and iniquity uncontrollably out of the soul of humanity, and humanity fears that kind of power.

For God hath not given us the spirit of fear, but of power[faith], and of love, and a sound mind (2 Timothy 1:7 KJV)

Like Peter did when he asks the Lord Jesus to summon him out of the boat. He had the faith to believe, and as long as he fixed his sights on the virtue of Christ Jesus' power, he could walk on water, but it was the knowledge of his thinking that got Peter in trouble. Instead of Peter believing that Christ, Jesus could do all things in Christ, Jesus. He doubted (I can't walk on this windy, stormy sea), and he sunk.

So, it is with the Body of Christ we fear what we can't control. We fear we may fail him instead of just walking toward Christ, and that is why we sink. I hope we have the sense to cry out to God. "Lord, Save Me!" We are the beginning of a new revival, not one lead by a man or woman. One appointed by Jesus Christ, and it will be him that leads us back to the boat.

Only be strong and very courageous that you may observe to do according to all the law, which Moses my servant commanded you; do not turn from it to the right hand or to the left that you may prosper wherever you go (Joshua 1:7 KJV paraphrased)

Prosperity brings the believer into the place of more than people just having enough. However, we, as the church and the Body of Christ are to have wealth in the flesh, soul, and spirit.

"'Gather up the fragments that remain, so that nothing is lost.' Therefore, they gathered them up and filled twelve baskets with the fragments of the five barley loaves, which leftover by those had eaten." (John 6:16-17 KJV)

The master didn't take the opportunity by buying the love of the children of Israel. But he earned their love at the end of his life. When he laid down his love for them, we can't be in bondage to people and buy their love, but we must gather the fragments of the broken that nothing may be lost. They are valued in God's kingdom, no matter what condition humanity they are in a while on earth. This hasn't been our history throughout the different denominations that de-valuation was the reason for the many separate revival. The problem wasn't human, but us!

"For [the Spirit which] you have now received [is] not a spirit of slavery to put you once more in bondage to fear, but you have received the Spirit of adoption [the Spirit is producing sonship] in [the bliss of] which we cry, Abba (Father)! Father" (Romans 8:15 AMPC)

Whether prosperity, gifts of the Spirit, or talents, all must use their solutions of gifts from God Almighty, not to try and make themselves gods. However, God wrote in the King James Version of Psalms chapter eighty-two and verse seven, *"Ye shall die like men, and fall like one of the princes."* The word used for a prince in Hebrew is רַשׂ [pronounced śār] that means *a* head *person (of any rank or class like a captain or even a governor.* [81]

AND AT that time [of the end] Michael shall arise, the great [angelic] prince who defends and *has charge of your [Daniel's] people. And there shall be a time of trouble, straightness,* and *distress such as never was since there was a nation till that time. But at that time your people shall be delivered, everyone whose name shall be found written in the Book [of God's plan for His own]. (Daniel 12:1 AMP+ paraphrased)*

I thought I was this angel, and that I had fallen from God's grace; because, I fused to accept what Christ did on the cross of Calvary. So, I sent to earth to understand salvation through being human. I would have dreams about the day Christ Jesus died and that I was up in heaven. I asked myself in my soul, and when I stood before God the Father. In the dreams, I asked the question,

---

"What is man, that thou art mindful of him, or the son of man, that you visited him?" *(Hebrews 2:6 [Psalms 8:4] paraphrased)*

I believed for many years until and was told by the Watcher's I was a fallen angel. I had the same delusion because when I was a child, the Watcher's would come into my room, and throughout my life, they would appear to me saying they were the Watchmen. A secret society that were all killed during the Civil War. When they were in the South, helping to keep slavery active. I asked, "Then why are you asking me to revive institution?"

One of them told me, named Watchmen Lafayette, *"We saw the error of our ways, and we know that this is the feet of clay that must bring him."* I asked, "Who?" Lafayette replied, *"Our true king."* I later realized that the king the Watchers were talking about was the Antichrist. Christ earned his Kingship through his death. So, what makes us think we can run out, and we just act like a god without paying his price of blood?

"Then they will deliver you up to tribulation and kill you, and all nations will hate you for My name's sake. And then many will be offended, will betray one another, and will hate one another. And when he had opened

---

[81] (Strong, 1890 [Public Domain]) H8269

*the fifth seal, I saw under the altar the souls of them that were slain for the word of God, and for the testimony which they held: And they cried with a loud voice, saying, How long, O Lord, holy and true, dost thou not judge and avenge our blood on them that dwell on the earth? And white robes were given unto every one of them, and it was said unto them, that they should rest yet for a little season, until their fellow-servants also and their brethren, that should be killed as they **were,** should be fulfilled."* (Jeremiah 45:4-5 NKJV [Matthew 24:9 NKJV; Revelation 6:9-11])

We must be like Jesus to reign like him; because both the secular and religious world is wondering if they can help there with storming the gates of the kingdom of heaven the same way Satan tried to do. However, their fate will be as his... *"I saw Satan fall like lightning from heaven." (Luke 10:18 ESV [Isaiah 10:27 NKJV])* We must remember that Christ Jesus has taken Satan control by the blood of Jesus, and he removed our anxieties and destroyed our constrains in our thinking. [352]

The only way the body of Christ is going to get the crown of life, victory, and righteousness is to do it the way Jesus did it while he was on earth. The mind of Christ is giving, and we shouldn't be running around after the vainglory of success. *"Let nothing be done through strife or vainglory; but in lowliness of mind let each esteem other better than themselves." (Philippians 2:2-4, 5-8 NKJV)*

Doing the will of God will crucify the flesh by killing the pride of life. The reason Christ Jesus walked in the supernatural and the natural wasn't to control the Roman government or the Sanhedrin. His purpose was for what he said, proving and fulfilling prophesy. He walked in the power of the spiritual laws, not only for what he said, but by what he did, but why?

It was the Father will that Jesus of Nazareth was doing, and not him being seen. Sometimes Jesus Christ would allow people to worship him, but in secret. He would allow the demon to say who he was in front of his disciples, but never in front of the Jewish people or the governmental official.

We, as the body of Christ, must stop looking for our interests but also for the interest of others. Compassion moves out toward others to help others. Where passion is like a fire that consumes others for their purposes and not to help others. The reason we don't see the supernatural power of God in the church today isn't that God doesn't want to bless his children, for it is written:

"Beloved I pray that you may prosper in all things and be in health, just as your soul prospers." (3 John 1:2 NKJV)

Instead, we make God's prosperity a hustle, a three-ring circus, or a magic show. We would rather have a program after program depicting the life of Jesus healing the brokenhearted, bringing sight to the blind, opening the ears of the deaf, and setting at liberty those who are demonically oppressed. Meanwhile, we sign to the deaf, pay money to surgeons to fix the diseased or give seeing-eye dogs, and red and white blind canes to the blind. Holding mass-healing prep-rallies and pre-paid seminars to teach men and women how to cast out devils. We are always learning and never able to come to the knowledge of the truth.

The truth doesn't set a person free, but real fact that comes from our Messiah makes us free. Imagine a bird in a cage that sees in a marketplace. You buy the bird in the cage, and no matter how hard you try to set the bird free. The bird will fly around the cage, fearing freedom. You stick your hands in the cage to grab the bird, and it just pecks at your sides.

However, take that same cage and some wire-cutters and cutting the top of the cage removing the wired portion of the cage. Now you have made the bird free. Christ Jesus will set the bird free as it is written.

"Behold, what I have built I am breaking down, and what I have planted I am plucking up—that is, the whole land. And do you seek great things for yourself? Seek them not, for behold, I am bringing disaster upon all flesh, declares the LORD. It is not by force nor by strength, (the hands of the wirer-cutters removing the bondage), but by my Spirit, says the LORD of Heaven's Armies." (Jeremiah 45:4-5 NKJV [Zechariah 4:6 NLT])

My friend, it will be the same way when we become doers of the truth, and not just hearers of the word. I struggle these days with bitterness in seeing what the church of God and the tradition in the body of Christ. I find myself almost being like Jonah under that gourd tree, waiting for the judgment of the church that has disunited us, but God has warned me not to beat his sheep, nor to strike the Rock of Christ Jesus to give his chosen the water of the word. I am only called to warn the body of Christ about what has come in the church.

That is why he told me, *"Michael, my word is in you. Go tell my people that they have forgotten me and my covenant."* We have forgotten him by not allowing him to be the head of his body. *"But to all who believed him, and accepted him, he gave the right to become the children of God."—John 1:12 NLT.* If I just believing he is a good man, but I don't either believe he, my savior. Because there are many to reach heaven or God. Neither accepting his Lordship and I take matters into my hand makes me a judge or a god of my own life.

I must accept him as savior and Lord. I must always trust the power of God's word (the power of his divine expression, which is Jesus Christ) that he bought and paid for us with his blood. We are like a wife who goes ahead of the husband in a distrust in his authority. Whether she speaks for him, or doing his business without his permission, or misrepresenting him in his affairs.

The church has done the same thing by putting the name Christians like it's a product. The name Christian was a mockery of who we were at first; because this word meant that those who represent this word should manifest the qualities or the very Spirit of Christ Jesus or Christlikeness.

Christ Jesus, who is the Anointed King-Priest-Prophet, which he embodies the Son of God, is the Messiah, and the Son of David, the rod of Jesse. He is the Lord's Anointed, or the Anointed One. Christ Jesus never intended for his children to be named with the thinking of the world.

Instead, what he wants us in the world, putting on Christ by doing his work, and not to these occupations with the title of Christian. See if these professions and entities are an oxymoron: Christian psychology and counseling, Christian radio and television, Christian artist, Christian musicians, Christians scientist, Christian dancers, Christian actor, Christian comedians, Christian plays, Christians magicians, Christians movies, Christian writers, Christian wrestler, Christian boxers, Christian clowns, etc. Are these things evil without the word Christian? No, but they aren't anointed we have put Christ at the beginning of the occupations.

I am not a Christian writer or artist. Just like me being an African American, so I am not Michael Tsaphah, Christian African American, artist, or writer. I am a Christian and an African American who is a writer and an artist. In reality, I have the anointing of God to uses my talents and gifts for the glory of God, but not to put them in a title. The anointing of a title theirs no power. I learned that the hard way, but Jesus Christ is the anointed one in me.

In the genuine sincerity, people wanting to minister to the lost without the involvement of Christ that's wrong, when they leave Christ out of their ministry. Because if Christ is not involved, he will not have the Holy Spirit operate in the burden removing and yoke destroying power of God.

Without Christ, Jesus as the head and the Holy Spirit moving on your behalf. We could even put the title of Christian on otherworldly occupations saying: "I am a Christian prostitute, Christian drug dealer, Christian thug/gangster, Christian bank robber... etc." While Israel was a nation in the Davidic Kingdom, they had prostitutes, soothsayers, and false prophets in the temple of Solomon.

Now the anointing is even for sale in the church. Just send $19.95 plus shipping and handling, and you can learn how to be anointed just like your favorite televangelist, or send your best offering, and they will send you the newest holy trinket of the month to heal, bring wealth, or save a lost love one. You can go to your local spiritualist, Shaman, or witchdoctor to get the same results.

Forgetting who Christ is and not doing what Christ did, we do two things. First, we have separated the body into functions that look like a worldly corporation and not an institution (God isn't a capitalist, Democrat, Republican, nor is he a Communist). Second, God isn't divided into 485 now 2018: 1,052 sects, doctrines, denominations, and traditions.

He is three in one, and that trinity is what the body of Christ was like on the day of Pentecost. When the Day of Pentecost had fully come, they were all in one accord in one place. Like Christ, Jesus whipping out the money-changers out of the temple. Christ Jesus will whip the Body of Christ out of the Church world!

If we don't put away our toys through breaking our hearts prayer and fasting, Father God will do it for us, *"... but when I became a man, I put away childish things."(Joel 2:12 NASB ([1 Corinthians 13:11 (Webster, 1833 [Public Domain])* Christ will break down all plants.

Whether he planted them or not, he will bring everything under his feet. So, you may be asking what we should do to come out of the wilderness we created? The answer is in the book of Joel, which reads:

"Now, therefore," says the LORD, "Turn to Me with all your heart, With fasting, with weeping, and with mourning." So, rend your heart and not your garments; Return to the LORD your God, For He is gracious and merciful, slow to anger, and of great kindness; And He relents from harm." (Joel 2:12-13 NKJV)

We have our mission, and Christ has shown you the clear and present path we have fallen from in Christ Jesus. Let us repent. Now let us summarize the entire book so you can understand my core beliefs and my vision of why I do what I do. What is the meaning of the tree called morality?

CHAPTER 21
A TREE CALLED MORALITY
(THE MEANING OF THE TREE OF THE KNOWLEDGE OF GOOD AND EVIL)

The meaning of traditional values based on what we have studied, in my opinion. I define this word as the principles or standards a person follows and revered by a people continuously from generation to generation. Therefore, I believe that all humanity sees the world as principles or theories that they can alter by the person will of their soul. Like Tony Shalhoub as Jack Jeebs yelled, *"Let's make it happen Cap'n!"* [82] Humanity refuses to bend their thinking to allow it to be godly in righteous (remember what I said righteousness is faith + love = righteousness *[1 Thessalonians 5:28 KJV]*)

In my opinion, this kind of thinking of being familiar, sensual, and natural deals with behavior. Anything dealing with our behavior comes from the will of the soul. And when we see human beings reacting or responding to an action. It is always based on our environment. What raised us to do the will significantly influence our responses or reaction to the Holy Spirit allows us to happen.

Whether it is mob rules or being moral, do a study in behavioral psychology and see if I am right. Jesus, dealt with the mobs, showed that crowds can't be trusted; because, on a Palm Sunday, the mob was worshipping him. And on Wednesday, they yelled for his death. I said the religion of Christianity and the discipline of Psychology don't mix doesn't mean the science and philosophy of the soul is false.

We become ignorant of the fact that Satan had studied man (used the very study of psychology) and deceived Eve. He knew that if he would have a better chance of success if he could get the weaker of the two, that was one in the flesh. The woman observed the fruit looked delicious and pleasing to the eyes. As the one more emotional and more in tune with her senses. The prince of darkness had to test his theory of whether Adam had given Eve the rules or moral code of the garden. So, Satan used his test subject Eve as a psychological cadaver.

---

[82] (Sonnenfeld, 2002) Men in Black

Do not love the world or the things in the world. If anyone loves the world, the love of the Father is not in him. For all that is in the world—the lust of the flesh, the lust of the eyes, and the pride of life—is not of the Father but is of the world.

Test number one, the lust of the flesh: *'Satan asked the woman, "Did God say you must not eat the fruit from any of the trees in the garden?" The woman said, "Of course, we may eat fruit from the trees in the garden, but It's only the fruit from the tree in the middle of the garden that we are not allowed to eat. God said, 'You must not eat it or even touch it; if you do, you will die.'" "You won't die!" the serpent replied to the woman. "God knows that your eyes will be opened as soon as you eat it, and you will be like God, knowing both good and evil."'* (Genesis 3:1b-5 NLT)

Test number two, the lust of the eyes: *"The woman was convinced. She saw that the tree was beautiful, and its fruit looked delicious..."* (Genesis 3:6a NLT) **Test number three, the pride of life:** *"...and she wanted the wisdom it would give her..."*(Genesis 3:6b NLT) And you know the rest of the story, but I have a question. When did Eve find out about this information about the fruit is good for food and pleasant to the eyes, or the tree was too desirable to make one wise? Where did she get this information?

Because the only conversation that was recorded was in the first five verses, in my opinion, Satan caused Eve to have psychosis of an audible hallucination, or he possessed her soul, and spoke to her imagination. She should have cast down the thoughts. Even Adam should have helped her, so where was he at during this event? Why didn't she call out to Adam? Was he right their right? He wasn't paying attention like all of us men tend to do with our wives.

Maybe he was looking at Eve's beauty, which her beauty entranced him to the point that whatever she did (because she did say anything) wasn't wrong. The foolish man! Eve was the queen/pawn to attack the seed of man, because only through his bloodline could the curse continue.

Man was the target of the devil's attack. He knew if man partook of the tree of the knowledge of good and evil. Then humanity would always be in bondage into the thinking by good and evil. My question is, what is the judging of good and evil?

The judging of good and evil is based on a sense of duty, such as religion. Religion is defined as a specific system of belief, work, and belief in the worship of a deity. These religious beliefs will follow natural laws or moral codes of ethics.

The definition of morality I believe that like Edward Cooney and in my opinion, *"Mankind both male and female have the God-given freedom to have their moral compass to make rational life decisions. Humanity beings to think they have the eternal law by making it become the natural moral law.*

Man must come to God for the eternal wisdom and worship of the Lord (the fear of the Lord God), which God will give them the Spirit of knowledge who the Lord is in Christ Jesus.'—Isaiah 11:2KJV.

Instead, the consciously choose the wrong tree of the knowledge of good and evil that makes them believe all pragmatic theories that supposed to bring them closer to becoming **"you are gods..."**. *Psalms 82:6-7 NASB paraphrased*

Because the pragmatic people who refuse the believe there is a God or universal higher power or find that the ideas of the Bible are the absolute truth. They take theories and ideals about absolute truth tested them in a practiced controlled environment, by assessing whether they are correct. And when the ideal or philosophy produces the desired result. The scientists take their thesis and make it into a law.

According to the pragmatist, all claims about truth, knowledge, morality, and politics must all be tested (judged) in this same way. Now the fact of the thinking of humanity brings me to this conclusion. Morality is the tree.

We have learned in conclusion is that the first two trees were in the midst of the Garden of Eden. The first tree was the tree of the knowledge of good and evil, and the second tree was the tree of life. The fruit of the tree of life was holiness, which this fruit is was we are (when we work in the fruit of the Spirit) according to the word *"...a living sacrifice, holy, and acceptable unto God." (Romans 12:1b MKJV)*

Then second, to live in the law of the Spirit of life in Christ Jesus makes you separated toward deliverance and sanctified unto life. To have anything else would be sin, death, and the will brings judgment to all that don't operate by this principle in Christ Jesus, and none can be absolutely free.

Humanity brings deceived understandings that he could judge God, as he is dead by using the basic concepts and principles of many of the theoretical sciences such as: logic, biology, physics, metaphysics, and psychology.

Many of these real sciences God used to create the universe, and he used the natural law of the laws of physics and nature was founded by these sciences, and not based on logic and philosophy. As **the King James Version read Romans chapter one, verses twenty-one through twenty-five reads:**

"They know the truth about God because he has made it evident to them. Forever since the world was created, people have seen the earth and sky. Through everything God made, they can see his invisible qualities—his eternal power and divine nature. So, they have no excuse for not knowing God. Yes, they knew God, but they wouldn't worship him as God or even give him thanks. And they began to think up foolish ideas of what God was like. As a result, their minds became dark and confused. Claiming

> *to be wise, they instead became utter fools. And instead of worshiping the glorious, ever-living God, they worshiped idols made to look like mere people and birds and animals and reptiles. So, God abandoned them to do whatever shameful things their hearts desired. As a result, they did vile and degrading things with each other's bodies. They traded the truth about God for a lie. So, they worshiped and served the things God created instead of the Creator himself, who is worthy of eternal Praise! Amen."*

The foolish wise people of humanity though they could wish God away. But his signs and wonders. His power in heaven shows his presence! I raise a hallelujah for my Lord! Humankind has created their religion of modern-day morality.

They define it as a sense of duty through which one-self offering payment and honor by following the natural laws or a moral code. This law, whether religious, governmental, or self-rule, will do one thing always. Working in these natural laws will cause you to judge all, including God. We can see this more and more today in our religious leadership.

This kind of behavior is like what I told a person who was thinking of abandoning the teaching I was trying to show him. I said to him, *"You have two choices, think of two suits, one suit is made of valuable jewels and is expensive. While the other suit is made of sackcloth, and this suit is free."* Instead of the church teaching and creating an atmosphere of being in a place where healing, restoration, and teaching humanity with a better knowledge of God's love toward mankind.

The religious of mankind have made it a three-ring-circus, and the pulpit is a sideshow-magic exhibition, for the new freak in town. The people of God never use the gifts of God to find out who they are in Christ, and they end up dying of no spiritual growth. Having a form of godliness, they deny the power.

Consider the fundamentally unchanging and universally applicability, because of the ambiguity of the word "nature," the meaning of "natural" may also vary. The natural are, therefore, interwoven with the traditions of men. Because the traditions of men make the word of God of no effect, now we find God moved out of the way of the picture, and humanity makes his religion, and it will be spiritualism. It, like the people of God, have forgotten that we are Forever Under the Christ Kingdom.

Instead, we want to disobey God's Commander and Chief, who is Christ. Moreover, we want a rapture to happen before the judgment comes to shakes the church. I'm not talking about Jacobs trouble Read Revelations chapter fourteen verses fourteen thru eighteen. The consequences and repercussions of our rebellious and disobedience works. Concerning my views, the rapture, and the Second Coming of Christ. Here it is in blue and white.

Again, I looked, and behold, [I saw] a white cloud, and sitting on the cloud One resembling a Son of Man, with a crown of gold on His head and a sharp scythe (sickle) in His hand. [Dan 7:13] And another angel came out of the temple sanctuary, calling with a mighty voice to Him Who was sitting upon the cloud, Put in Your scythe and reap, for the hour has arrived to gather the harvest, for the earth's crop is fully ripened. [Joe 3:13] So He Who was sitting upon the cloud swung His scythe (sickle) on the earth, and the earth's crop was harvested. Then another angel came out of the temple [sanctuary] in heaven, and he also carried a sharp scythe (sickle). And another angel came forth from the altar, [the angel] who has authority and power over fire, and he called with a loud cry to him who had the sharp scythe (sickle), Put forth your scythe and reap the fruitage of the vine of the earth, for its grapes are entirely ripe. (John 5:39 [2 Peter 1:3] AMPC+)

The doctrine of this is a real subject of what is going to happen to me. I don't have one! Leave that to the theologians! Let them study God under their morality microscope! They will continue to be the fools that they are.

"You search and investigate and pore over the Scriptures diligently because you suppose and trust that you have eternal life through them. And these [very Scriptures] testify about Me! His divine power has bestowed upon us all things that [are requisite and suited] to life and godliness, through the [full, personal] knowledge of Him Who called us by and to His glory and excellence [virtue]." (Proverb 18:2 AMPC+)

Get out of the church of Laodicea by stop being lukewarm, not allowing the Holy Spirit to move freely in the church) before Christ Jesus. Christ, Jesus promises to vomit your church out of his mouth. How do we get out of being involved in the Laodicean Era?

First, move the pastor out of the forefront as the lone wolf dictator and put them back in the pulpit as a conductor, by serving the word of God, and washing the feet of saints. Becoming a conductor in the body of Christ would mean you would spend more time before God in word and prayer.

We need to let the elders of the church take on more responsibility for the sheep. Praying and healing the sick, the oppressed, and hurting in the congregation. They would run all home Bible Studies. Instead of possibly trying to compete for the next runner up to preach.

Second, begin to move the other ministers of the church to start home Bible studies in their neighborhood, cutting out the Program Traditional Syndrome and Doctrinal operations. These programs only have a prayer (Thanksgiving), Praise (two or three songs in Praise), preaching the word of God (the worship, but God himself doesn't speak man does) sometimes, God will get the glory.

The three-ring-circus-church I am talking about, which this type of PTSD makes the parishioner empty. Because the movement burdens don't happen, and the destructive spirit of mental yoke stays the same. Making them ask, "Where's God?" Cut out or limit the TV and radio broadcasting, and the media ministry will assist the Home Cell groups in making special tapes and videos for the pastor and the other ministers.

Finally, teach more to the congregation as a whole to operate in the spiritual gifts of God, and begin to study more on the fruit of the Spirit in Home Cell—Groups that will bring unity to the faith rather than confusion and strife.

This last statement brings me to mankind's and humanity's understanding of what is spiritual gifts of God, and how do we believers operate in the basic principles of Christ. And does our diverse congregation of Christianity teach the doctrines of Christ, which these doctrines of Christ are found in Hebrews chapter six verses one and two? Learning to walk in the spiritual laws of Christ, and how we can operate as Christ did on the earth.

The spiritual (supernatural) laws of Christ is above the natural laws of mankind, and the logical thinking of humanity. God can only use the spiritual laws of Christ through the Holy Spirit in his people. These days unless the person is holding the very character of God, this character is the promise of the Holy Ghost. Moreover, we need to remember that only born-again believers can possess the power of the supernatural works of God. God gives them to whom he chooses.

Finally, remember, once the Spirit of grace and supplication is put into motion in the person's life. The love of God by the Holy Ghost is put into the soulish will to begin to change the sensual nature of the people they pray for in society. God wants all believers, but especially those with his character of prayer in grace and supplication, to break spiritual or soulish oppression.

The true believer is to function by first reading and studying the Word of God. Then we are to pray about the scriptures we read to get an answer. This kind of prayer is the true meaning of praying in the Spirit. Next, the believer is to stay in fellowship and witness to others in humanity to get the body of Christ to grow.

By doing this action, the preacher expounding great sermons, now don't get me wrong, a right pep rally is nice, but it the player going into the game that wins the championship. We are the team! The pastors, teachers, evangelists, and the prophets are the cheerleaders, while Jesus Christ and the Holy Spirit are the coaches.

The spirit of man is then born anew from that moment on, and the Spirit of Christ (which is the Holy Ghost) now begins his new reign over the living sacrifice of his new creature in the kingdom of God. So, the more the person seeks the kingdom of God in righteousness (faith and love), joy, and peace in the Holy Ghost, the more we are united in Christ.

It is Satan that wants us divided. Why? Because the seeds are the lust of the flesh, the desire of the eye, and the pride of life. Those religious arguments that you have about theology will only lead you into bondage, and fear of death. We must take control of the soul nature or die trying, through salvation!

Wherefore, the law was our schoolmaster to bring us unto Christ that we might be justified by faith, but after that faith has come, we are no longer under a schoolmaster. According to the scriptures, the schoolmaster is the Mosaic Law, and these laws put mankind under bondage.

Now we have received, not the spirit of the world, but the spirit, which is of God; that we might know the things that are freely given to us of God. The power that Satan uses is the fact that he knows your power (authority) that was given by God Almighty, which is the power of our words that give life or death to others.

We, as the body of Christ, will need to make our own decision on what tree we will eat from. I have decided to eat from the second tree of life. Thirty-seven years ago, I chose to eat like all my ancestors did to eat from the tree of the knowledge of good and evil. I wondered around the wilderness both stylishly and physically. I was back to Reno, the place of my birth, to redeem my life again and be tried in my soul by the enemy Satan.

I have studied the principles of the seven spiritual laws, and I have defined **my core values** as these five things I must never compromise, and they are the following:

1. Don't Fence me in—Don't control my life or what I believe as long as I am operating under the leading of the Word of God and the Holy Spirit [But I respect others choice in life.]
2. Don't Control my way of expressing my belief toward or mock what I believe in who God is and respecting his house as a house of prayer and not a house of merchandise.
3. Don't control how I feel in my soul [Unless you can bring deliverance and comfort]—don't control my thinking of my mind [if it's based on truth]. Don't control the feelings of my emotion [let me own them and repent when they are

out of control]. Don't control the action of my will in me working for God's purpose for my life. [I will always respect other vision and their will to either serve God or themselves]. Don't think I won't give someone a second chance.

4. Honor the spiritual laws of Christ.
5. I acknowledge powerlessness to keep the Ten Commandments. Knowing that none of humanity or mankind is perfect.

Because of these weaknesses in my life are there. I have decided to finally take up my cross and obey the Call given to me these thirty-seven some plus years ago. I welcome all of you, my brother and sister, to join me go up to the mountains of the Sierra's. And let us go before the Lord in Thanksgiving, Praise, and Worship by humbling our soul to repent for being Lukewarm. Let us stop saying what that church of the Laodicean spoke in their hearts to Christ Jesus:

I know your [record of] works and what you are doing; you are neither cold nor hot. Would that you were cold or hot! So, because you are lukewarm and neither cold nor hot, I will spew you out of My mouth! For you say, I am rich; I have prospered and grown wealthy, and I require nothing; and you do not realize and understand that you are wretched, pitiable, poor, blind, and naked. [Hosea 12:8] Therefore I counsel you to purchase from Me gold refined and tested by fire, that you may be [indeed] wealthy, and white clothes to clothe you and to keep the shame of your nudity from being seen, and salve to put on your eyes, that you may see.

Christ Jesus let me know several times that he would continue to chasten me with his word, and Christ Jesus was allowing Satan to buffet my soul and body with pain, mental illness, and oppression until I would cry out! Not just in pain, but in repentance for my iniquities and sins.

Those whom I [**dearly and tenderly**] love, I tell their faults and convict and convince and reprove and chasten [**I discipline and instruct them**]. So be enthusiastic and in earnest and burning with zeal and repent [**changing your mind and attitude**]. [Proverbs 3:12] Behold, I stand at the door and knock; if anyone hears and listens to and heeds My voice and opens the door, I will come into him and will eat with him, and he [**will eat**] with Me. He who overcomes (**is victorious**), I will grant him to sit beside Me on My throne, as I overcame (**was victorious**) and sat down beside My Father on His throne.

Because Satan knows about those factors, he will use our soul by planting thoughts in our imagination. When he does that, our soul begins to order our emotions, and our will to speak to our flesh to move out of fear and not by faith. Through death he (Jesus Christ) might destroy him that had the power of death, which is the devil, and deliver them (mankind) who, through fear of death, were all their lifetime subject to bondage.

It was by the misuse of the law of sin and death that Satan launched his plot to take dominion over man's world. Satan's weapons are fear, bondage, and death. What is the fruit of this tree? The fruit will be in the years to come in the form of a man called the Beast, the very son of Satan, or should I say Lucifer in the flesh, and he will have a man to worship in witchcraft and spiritualism.

God can't deal with the natural thinking of man in a holy place, better known as the temple, or the body of Christ, which you are, so you must ask yourself this truthful question. If being in the shape of Christ means to become born again by being Holy Ghost filled, led, and productive (involving producing the fruit of the Spirit and not just works of the flesh). Then you must ask, am I? Or state I am!

If it is, "I am," then you will be called home when the Lord Jesus Christ returns. But if you're asking, am I just an ethical and moral person? Am I righteous? Am I good enough to come into the kingdom of God? Remember now that you have reviewed the truth.

Only you can ask these questions because they are not based anymore on just a tree called morality, but the tree of life called righteousness. We can all come to that tree. If you would like to eat freely of the tree of life, read this next section. God bless you.

The word salvation comes from the Greek word sōtēria *(pronounced so-tay-ree'-ah)*[83] means to *rescue* or deliver to *safety* (physically or morally) or to give health. And the word salvation is used for saving, healing, preserving, and making one whole from death. The theological word soteriology, or the study of salvation, is derived from the Greek word sōzō *(pronounced sode'-zo)* means to save.[84]

The word is becoming in total wholeness of the spirit, soul, and body. Moreover, there are five steps of salvation, which the steps are to admit, repent, confess, be baptized, and obey. Let's go through them in the next paragraph.

So, my question to you is this. After reading this book. Do you still think you are right before God? Are you a good person? Do you think that because you go to church pay your tithes, you are the right person? If you were standing in front of God and he asked you why should let you into heaven? What would your answer be? If you don't know, read the next paragraph.

The word is becoming alive in your heart, total wholeness of the spirit, soul, and body. Moreover, there are five steps of salvation, which the steps are to admit, repent, confess, be baptized, and obey. Let's go through them in the next paragraph.

So, my question to you is this. After reading this book. Do you still think you are right before God? Are you a good person? Do you think that because you go to church pay your tithes, you are the right person? If you were standing in front of God and he

---

[83] (Strong, 1890 [Public Domain]) G4991
[84] (Strong, 1890 [Public Domain]) G4982

173

asked you why should let you into heaven? What would your answer be? If you don't know, read the next paragraph.

THE FIVE STEPS OF SALVATION:

1) **ADMIT:** that you are a sinner. Behold, I was shaped in iniquity, and in sin did my mother conceive me. (Psalms 51:5 KJV)

2) **REPENT:** from your sinful nature. From that time, Jesus began to preach, and to say, Repent: for the kingdom of heaven is at hand. (Matthew 4:17 KJV) [*To repent means to change your mind and direction from destruction, and to forgive all who offended you.*]

3) **CONFESS:** that Jesus Christ is Lord over your life. That if thou shalt confess with thy mouth the Lord Jesus, and shalt believe in thine heart that God hath raised him from the dead, thou shalt be saved. (Romans 10:9 KJV)

4) **BE BAPTIZED FIRST IN WATER AND THEN IN SPIRIT (HOLY GHOST):** I indeed baptize you with water unto repentance: but he that cometh after me is mightier than I, whose shoes I am not worthy to bear: he shall baptize you with the Holy Ghost, and *with* fire: (Matthew 3:11 KJV)
A) Jesus Christ was baptized by the prophet John Baptist (Matthew 3:13-15 KJV)
B) Jesus Christ promised to baptize all who asked the Father for the Holy Spirit. (Luke 11:13; John 16:7; Acts 11:16; Acts 19:2-6 KJV).
C) How to receive the Holy Ghost will be discussed later.

5) **OBEY:** the word of God and not the traditions and doctrines of man. For this is the love of God, that we keep his commandments: and his commandments are not grievous. (1 John 5:3 KJV)

Now have the people you are praying with pray a prayer from there heart using the five steps, which would sound something like this [REMEMBER DON'T HAVE THEM REPEAT THIS PRAYER. IF THEY CAN'T PRAY ANYTHING LAY YOUR HANDS ON THEIR HEAD AND BIND THE SPIRIT OF FEAR, THE SPIRIT OF THE ANTICHRIST, THE SPIRIT OF DIVINATION, OR A FAMILIAR SPIRIT.]:

"Father God in the name of Jesus. I admit that I am a sinner, and I repent of all my sins and forgive all who have sinned against me. I believe that Jesus Christ was raised from the dead by your power. I ask that you fill me with your Holy Spirit, and I will, from this day forward, obey your word in Jesus Christ name, amen."

THE SEVEN STEPS OF RECEIVING THE BAPTISM OF THE HOLY GHOST

1) Repent of all sins and forgive those who have sinned and offended you. (Matthew 6:15; Mark 11:26 KJV)
2) You must be born again by receiving Christ as savior. (John 3:3-8 KJV)
3) You will receive the baptism of the Holy Spirit by the laying on of hands. (John 1:26; Acts 19:6 [Matthew 3:11] KJV)
4) You must wait for the gift of the Holy Spirit. (Luke 24:49; Psalms 27:14 KJV)
5) You will speak in another language and prophesy (Isaiah 28:9-12; Acts 2:4; Acts 19:6; Revelation 19:10 KJV)
6) You will not receive another spirit! (1 Corinthians 12:3; 1 John 4:1 KJV)
7) Ask God the Father for the Holy Spirit. (Luke 11:9-13; Romans 8:15 KJV)

With the person being filled with the baptism of the Holy Spirit. Please have them pray again from the heart and ask God the Father to fill them with the Holy Spirit. These steps can and should be done by anyone who is a Spirit-filled believer. The prophet is the catalyst that brings comfort, exhortation, and encouragement to humanity and the Body of Christ. I hope my book has shed light on the ministry, mission, and office of the prophet. The proof of the New Testament prophet being relevant in the 21th Century has been defined.

Besides, the mission and ministries of the prophet, along with the Spiritual gift of prophecy, were also shown to operate today. Both the scripture in the Old and New Testament were defined, and evidence they are needed. Moreover, whether you will believe it is now up to you. And giving those who have the gift of prophesying a clearer purpose. Writing for the blog: "The Chronicle." This is Michael Tsaphah. God bless you.

The End

הסוף

If you are interested in further works of the author:

Go to his website at: http://www.chokepublicationandproductions.com and download all non-fictional material free of charge. These materials and other nonfictional books will be available for a limited time only. I copy of two thousand and eighteen copies will be given for each person.

<u>To get his novels:</u>

The Watchmen's Chronicle: The Tower of Babel is Rising
Go to Amazon, Barnes and Noble, iBook.

Coming soon to the world wide web: *these books and novels will be available.*

A Tree Called Morality (Revised)
The Incarnate Word: A Study of the Spiritual and Natural laws
The Darkside of Supremacy: A study of the spirit, soul, and the demonic realm
The Watchmen's Chronicle Part 2: The Line of Succession
The Flame
The Watchmen's Chronicle Part 3: The Hermon Conspiracy

BIBLIOGRAPHY

i   Encyclopedia.Wikipedia.org. (2018, December 6). *Catholic Apostolic Church*. Retrieved from Wikipedia, the free encyclopedia: https://en.wikipedia.org/wiki/Catholic_Apostolic_Church#Separation_of_the_apostles_and_their_"testimony"

ii   Aquinas, T. (1265–1274). *The Summa theologiae*. Paris: (Public Domain).

iii   Aurelius, M. (AD 364 (c.1558 [Public Diminion]). *Meditations*. Roman (Vatican Library): Wilhelm Xylander in 1558.

iv   Britton, B. (1959). *A Closer Look at the Rapture*. Springfield: The Church in Action.

v   Darby, J. (1882). *Synopsis of the Old and New Testament*. Philidephia : Yale Press.

vi   Descartes, R. 1. (1637). *Discours on Method*. Paris: Unknow French Publishing Company.

vii Draper, W. F. (1882). *The Book of Enoch*. Washington: Andover.

viii Green, Jay P. (1985). *Green's Literal Translation of the Holy Bible*. Louisville: Sovereign Grace Publishers.

ix   Henry, M. (1662-1714 [Public Domain]). *Old and New Testament Comentary of the Whole Bible*. London, United Kingdom: Zondervan.

x   Jefferson, T. (1776 [Public Domain], July 4). The Declaration of Independance. *The Declaration of Independence "The Want, Will, and Hopes of the People"*. Philadelphia, Pennsylvania, United States of America: The Continental Congress.

xi   John Bois and John Ward. (1611 (Public Dominion)). *The Authorized King James Version Bible*. London England: Cambridge University Press.

xii Kirby, J. (2020, May 10). *From Wikipedia, the free encyclopedia*. Retrieved from Chrysippus: https://en.wikipedia.org/wiki/Chrysippus#Fate

xiii Matty, J. 1. (Director). (2018). *Charismatic Pentecostal False Teaching "We Are God's"* [Motion Picture].

xiv Non-Profit from Wikipedia, the free encyclopedia. (2020, July 18). *Logos*. Retrieved July 20, 2020, from https://en.wikipedia.org/wiki/Logos#Heraclitus.

xv   Paine, T. (1776). *Common Sense*. Philadelphia : Pennsylvania Evening Post.

xvi Random House Publisher Group. (1833). *Noah Webster Composite Dictionary of American English*. New York: Random House Press.

xvii Sonnenfeld, B. (Director). (2002). *Men In Black* [Motion Picture].

xviii Strong, J. (1890 [Public Domain]). *Strong's Exhaustive Concordance*. New York: Zondevan Press.

xix The ISV Committee on Translation. (2011). *International Standard Version*. Wheaton,_Illinois: Crossway Books.

xx   Webster, N. (1833 [Public Domain]). *Webster King James Version*. New York City: Webster Press.

xxi Wikimedia Foundation, Inc. (2019, February 15). *Duns Scotus*. Retrieved from Wikipedia, the free encyclopedia: https://en.wikipedia.org/wiki/Duns_Scotus#Illuminationism

xxii Wikimedia Foundation, Inc. (2019, February 19). *Paul Tillich*. Retrieved from Wikipedia, the free encyclopedia.: https://en.wikipedia.org/wiki/Paul_Tillich

xxiii Wikipedia Foundation. (2018, May 23). *Roman Republic*. Retrieved from Wikipedia, the free encyclopedia: https://en.wikipedia.org/wiki/Roman_Republic

xxiv   Wikipedia Foundation. (2018, May 13). *Roman–Persian Wars.* Retrieved from Wikipedia, the free encyclopedia: https://en.wikipedia.org/wiki/Roman–Persian_Wars#Early_Roman–Sasanian_conflicts

xxv   Wikipedia Foundation. (2006, March 10). *Word of Faith.* Retrieved from From Wikipedia, the free encyclopedia: https://en.wikipedia.org/wiki/Word_of_Faith#'Little_gods'_controversy

xxvi   Wikipedia Foundation. (2018, May 22). *History of democracy.* Retrieved from From Wikipedia, the free encyclopedia: https://en.wikipedia.org/wiki/History_of_democracy

xxvii   Wikipedia Foundation. (2018, May 12). *OPEC.* Retrieved from Wikipedia, the free encyclopedia: https://en.wikipedia.org/wiki/OPEC

xxviii Wikipedia Foundation. (2018, May 10 May 2018). *Wikipedia, the free encyclopedia.* Retrieved from Carnal Knowledge: https://en.wikipedia.org/wiki/Carnal_knowledge

xxix   Wikipedia Foundation LLC. (2008, June 20). *Rapture.* Retrieved from From Wikipedia, the free encyclopedia: https://en.wikipedia.org/wiki/Rapture

xxx   Zondervan Press and the Lockman Foundation. (1965). *The Amplified Bible.* Grand Rapids: Zondervan Publishing House.

Printed in the United States
By Bookmasters